EDUCATION FOR THE CHILDREN WITH SPECIAL NEEDS

EDUCATION FOR THE CHILDREN WITH SPECIAL NEEDS

Meena Kumari
Lecturer, Deptt. of Education,
Nalanda Open University,
Nalanda

CENTRUM PRESS
NEW DELHI-110002 (INDIA)

CENTRUM PRESS
H.O.: 4360/4, Ansari Road, Daryaganj,
New Delhi-110 002 (India)
Ph.: 23278000, 23261597

B.O.: No. 1015, Ist Main Road, BSK IIIrd Stage
IIIrd Phase, IIIrd Block,
Bangalore - 560 085 (India)
Tel.: 080-41723429
Visit us at: www.centrumpress.com

Education for the Children with Special Needs

First Edition, 2009

PRINTED IN INDIA

Printed at Balaji Offset, Delhi

Contents

Preface

Special education is the education of students with special needs in a way that addresses the students' individual differences and needs. Ideally, this process involves the individually planned and systematically monitored arrangement of teaching procedures, adapted equipment and materials, accessible settings, and other interventions designed to help learners with special needs achieve a higher level of personal self-sufficiency and success in school and community than would be available if the student were only given access to a typical classroom education. Common special needs include learning differences, communication challenges, emotional and behavioral disorders, physical disabilities, and developmental disabilities. Students with these kinds of disabilities are likely to benefit from additional educational services or different approaches to teaching. Intellectual giftedness is a difference in learning and can also benefit from specialized teaching techniques or different educational programs, but the term "special education" is generally used to specifically indicate instruction of students whose special needs reduce their ability to learn independently or in a classroom, and gifted education is handled separately.

Special education programs need to be individualized so that they address the unique combination of needs in a given student. Students with special needs are assessed to determine their specific strengths and weaknesses. Placement, resources, and goals are determined on the basis of the student's needs. Modifications to the regular program may include changes in curriculum, supplementary aides or equipment, and the provision of specialized physical adaptations that allow students to participate in the educational environment to the fullest extent possible. It is now widely accepted that children with disabilities should be educated alongside their age peers and be treated as full members of the community. However, this ideal is still a long way from being realised in India.

The present book is a complete treatise on inclusive education with particular emphasis on children with special needs. It provides a comprehensive coverage of all the aspects needed to become an efficient teacher of such children. An attempt has been made to cover up most of the topics included in M.Ed. syllabus of the Indian universities.

— *Meena Kumari*

UNIT-I

Overview of Different Disabilities

Concept, Nature and Characteristics of Visual Impairment and Mental Retardation

Visual Impairment

Visual impairment or vision impairment is vision loss (of a person) having reduced vision as to constitute a handicap that constitutes a significant limitation of visual capability resulting from disease, trauma, or a congenital or degenerative condition that cannot be corrected by conventional means, including refractive correction, medication, or surgery. This functional loss of vision is typically defined to manifest with

1. best corrected visual acuity of less than 20/60, or significant central field defect,
2. significant peripheral field defect including homonymous or heteronymous bilateral visual, field defect or generalized contraction or constriction of field, or
3. reduced peak contrast sensitivity either of the above conditions.

In the U.S., the terms partially sighted, low vision, legally blind, and totally blind are used in the educational context to describe students with visual impairments. They are defined as follows:

1. *Partially sighted* indicates some type of visual problem, with a need of person to receive special education in some cases;

2. *Low vision* generally refers to a severe visual impairment, not necessarily limited to distance vision. Low vision applies to all individuals with sight who are unable to read the newspaper at a normal viewing distance, even with the aid of eyeglasses or contact lenses. They use a combination of vision and other senses to learn, although they may require adaptations in lighting or the size of print, and, sometimes, braille;
   1. *Myopic*-unable to see distant objects clearly, commonly called near-sighted or short-sighted
   2. *Hyperopic*-unable to see close objects clearly, commonly called far-sighted or long-sighted
   3. *Legally blind* indicates that a person has less than 20/200 vision in the better eye after best correction (contact lenses or glasses), or a field of vision of less than 20 degrees in the better eye; and
   4. *Totally blind* students learn via braille or other non-visual media.

Visual impairment is the consequence of a functional loss of vision, rather than the eye disorder itself. Eye disorders which can lead to visual impairments can include retinal degeneration, albinism, cataracts, glaucoma, muscular problems that result in visual disturbances, corneal disorders, diabetic retinopathy, congenital disorders, and infection." Visual impairment can also be caused by brain and nerve disorders, in which case it is usually termed cortical visual impairment (CVI).

The American Medical Association's *Guides to the Evaluation of Permanent Impairment* attempts to provide "a standardized, objective approach to evaluating medical impairments." The Visual System book "provides criteria for evaluating permanent impairment of the visual system as it affects an individual's ability to perform activities of daily living." The *Guide* has estimated that the loss of one eye equals 25% impairment of the visual system and 24% impairment of the whole person; total loss of vision in both eyes is considered to be 100% visual impairment and 85% impairment of the whole person.

Visual impairments have considerable economic impact on even developed countries.

Visual impairment is one of the potential dangers of ultraviolet germicidal irradiation.

Self-Concept and Visual Impairment

Although the importance of having a positive, well-adjusted self-concept is clear, we must accept that anyone may find this difficult, regardless of whether they have a disability or not. We also accept that a visual impairment may, in itself, affect the formation of someone's personality. With this in mind, we would like to establish the basic framework for an integral, individualized intervention programme.

From the knowledge we have acquired on the development of visually-impaired children, a series of general *tendencies* can be mentioned that affect these children's development (Warren, 1994; Ammerman, Van Hasselt, Hersen, 1986; Frailberg, 1977; Ochaíta, 1993; Leonhardt, 1992, Díaz-Aguado, 1995):

- A difficulty in making generalizations.
- The major role that adults play.
- The social significance of blindness.
- The perspective of development.

Research into questions of self-concept and visual impairment has centred mainly on comparative studies between people with or without a visual impairment. Of these, we should highlight:

- Research that finds lower levels of self-concept in people with a visual impairment (Meighan, 1971; Beaty, 1991).
- Research that finds lower levels for specific areas related to the visual impairment (Obiakor & Style, 1989, 1990; Díaz-Aguado et al. 1995).
- Research that finds a tendency for people with visual impairments to present extreme opinions and attitudes about themselves, both positively and negatively (Jervis, 1959; Zunich & Ledwith, 1965).
- Research using schools as the context for the study, leading to diverse results (Schindele, 1974; Bauman,

1964; Coker, 1979; Head, 1979; Díaz-Aguado et al. 1995; Alexander, 1996).

- Research that finds levels similar to sighted people (Obiakor & Stile, 1989, 1990; Martínez & Sewell, 1996).

How can the results of studies and research carried out to date be incorporated into educational practice in a way that is clear and effective? We believe that this type of action cannot be focused on a specific area or contained within a specific programme, but must instead be based on a number of different, interrelated focal points.

Self-Concept

Self-concept can be defined as "the perception one has of oneself with regards to different facets of that perception (i.e. cognitive and emotional) that vary in importance during the person's life (the evolutional and temporal facet), influenced by social interaction which, in turn, is conditioned by the fact that the person belongs to certain social groups (the importance of the social structure)" (Rodríguez Cao, 1993, as quoted in Rodríguez et al, 1995, page 67). According to Burns (1990), a number of basic factors can be emphasized that contribute towards the formation of a person's self-concept:

- Body image
- Language
- The acquisition of a sexual identity and the role of gender
- The interpretation of information received from the surrounding environment: how others see me.
- Educational practice.

A person's self-concept will gradually be reformulated during different stages of development, increasing in its degree of organization, complexity, consistence and stability. We can observe an evolution that ranges from a self-concept based on physical appearance, to a whole system of beliefs that appear in adolescence and a single sense of self-discovery. This process continues developing during the person's entire life. (L'Ecuyer, 1985).

Self-Concept and Visual Impairment: Basic Aspects

The development of a child's self-concept, when they have a visual impairment, follows similar steps to that of a sighted child, although the visual defect will influence this process. However, we have no evidence that the lack of vision has a general effect on visually-impaired children. Warren (1994) highlights the major roles that body image and language play in the case of these children.

Clock-Clampert (1981, 233) underlines the importance of a blind child's self-concept: "The most fundamental aspect of the blind child is his self-concept. The manner in which the child learns to view himself has a tremendous impact on his future ambitions, accomplishments and personal happiness".

The author emphasizes that, among the background work that has been used to contribute towards current studies, we should also bear in mind the descriptive research carried out, which has offered practical information to both parents and professionals:

- Parents' reactions to blindness.
- Lack of eye contact.
- Person and object permanence.
- Body image.
- Overprotection.
- Self-acceptance.
- Imitation of the sighted.

Brazelton (1993) considers parental attitudes to be fundamental in the early years of a child's life, as it represents one of the aspects that most influences the development and consolidation of the child's self-confidence and positive self-concept.

Following the stages in the development of a sense of self-awareness proposed by Stern (1985), Inghsholt (1990) describes what difficulties a blind child can encounter in the development of his or her identity: fewer reciprocal and also shorter relationships with which to organize his or her world; difficulty in benefiting from the necessary amount of experiences involving a high degree of regulated excitement and difficulties when intentional communication is attempted, all of which would lead to problems in the development of a progressive understanding of intersubjectivity. From all this, we can see how necessary it is to stimulate the child by offering him or her a large variety of different experiences with which to create his or her own personal sense of identity.

During the phase of developing a verbal sense of identity, language will provide the blind child with new forms of contact with others and will be the key to the world.

The person's image of their body, orientation and mobility, specific aspects of language, the acquisition of a sexual identity, the role of gender, play, interaction with their peers and an acceptance of the impairment can, among other things, be areas of special difficulty for children who are visually impaired. This is why early action is needed.

Uttermohlen (1997) speaks of the risks that the adolescent stage of life can represent for young people who are visually impaired and he reminds us that, throughout their entire lives, people with a visual impairment have to deal with the challenge of how to reach a balance between the need for help and the need to regard themselves as competent, independent people and for others also to see them as such.

During the adult stage of life, the process of integration into the labour market and the emotional facet of a person's life can be a determining factor in what they make of their lives.

Case Histories

"Personal identity is the result of presenting each of the events in one's life as parts of a meaningful whole and, in consequence, of presenting oneself to others as the protagonist of a unique story" (Widdwershoven, 1994, as quoted by Perinat, 1998).

A substantial amount of the research carried out into self-concept makes use of instruments like: the question "who am I?", life stories or personal autobiographies based on the stories recounted by the subjects involved.

Using L'Ecuyer's "who are you?" method, the study on self-concept by Ruíz and Esteban (1996) highlights the fact that, in general, the description blind people make of themselves is very much an inner one, i.e. it is focused on themselves, on their qualities and defects, their aspirations, feelings, interests and abilities, with less emphasis on externally-related assessments, i.e. the things that surround them and that they possess, their relationships with others and their ability to adapt to their surroundings.

The Nature and Degree of Visual Impairment

You will be better able to help your student's learning process if you understand the nature and degree of the vision loss and what the educational implications may be for your work together in the classroom.

Visual impairment refers to a significant loss of vision in both eyes which cannot be corrected with glasses. The degree of loss may vary significantly, which means that each student with low vision or blindness needs individual adjustments to learn most effectively.

There are two main categories of visual impairment: Low Vision and Blind. Most British Columbia students with visual impairments have low vision, which means they are print users but require special equipment and materials. They should be encouraged to use their residual vision in their educational programmes as much as possible. Students who are described as "legally blind" usually have some usable vision. The term "legally blind" is used to indicate entitlement to important government and private agency services.

Visual impairments are also classified as congenital (vision loss which is present at birth) or adventitious (vision loss later in life as a result of illness or accident). The age of onset and level of development before sight loss occurs are critical factors in the student's ability to acquire skills and concepts.

It is important for you to be aware that although two children with visual impairment may be assessed as having the same visual acuity, they may each learn and function in very different ways. Vision may actually fluctuate or may be temporarily influenced by such factors as fatigue, light glare, or inappropriate lighting. An understanding of the type of visual impairment is certainly important, but generalizations about the student's visual functioning cannot be made solely on the basis of the diagnosed eye condition.

Characteristics of Cortical Visual Impairment Checklist

Children with other types of visual impairments may exhibit some of these characteristics.

CHILD'S NAME____________ AGE_______ DATE______

RESPONDENT'S NAME & RELATION TO CHILD______

A child may be suspected of having a cortical visual loss when the extent of visual loss is unexplained by ocular abnormalities. Etiologies may include cerebral palsy, asphyxia, intracerebral hemorrhage, and meningitis.

Please check any areas below that pertain to the child.

Appearance:

- Does not look blind
- Blank facial expression
- Lack of visual communication skills
- Eye movements smooth, but aimless
- Nystagmus (rapid eye movement) rarely seen

Vision Function:

- Visual function varies from day to day or hour to hour
- Limited visual attention and lacks visual curiosity
- Aware of distant objects, but not able to identify
- Spontaneous visual activity has short duration
- Visual learning tiring
- Closes eyes while listening
- Balance improved with eyes closed
- Look away from people and objects
- Consistently look to either side when visual looking
- When visually reaching looks with a slight downward gaze

- Turns head to side when reaching, as if using peripheral fields
- Uses touch to identify objects

Mobility Skills:

- Occasionally "sees" better traveling in a car
- Difficulties with depth perception, inaccurate reach
- Unable to estimate distances
- Difficulties with spatial interpretation
- Avoids obstacles, but unable to use vision for close work

Improved Visual Performance:

- When in familiar environments and when using familiar objects
- When told "what" to look for and "where" to look
- When objects are held close to eyes when viewing
- When objects are widely spaced
- When looking at one object verses a group of objects
- When colour is used to assist in identification of objects or shapes
- When objects are against a plain background and paired with movement and sound

Nature of Mental Retardation

Mental Retardation is a diagnostic classification denoting significantly low intellectual functioning or other brain functioning problems. It is not a disease in of itself.

Classification of mental retardation indicates that developmental immaturities are present in the form of intellectual deficits, and often emotional deficits as well. This immaturity interferes with an individual's ability to function at age-appropriate levels and makes independent living a challenging proposition. A mentally retarded individual's cognitive abilities are impaired. This means that they acquire new information slowly and have difficulty understanding complex concepts.

Cognitive Functioning

Mental retardation is defined by sub-average intellectual ability. General intelligence quotient (IQ) scores for mentally retarded individuals are, by definition, seventy (70) or below. By definition, this score is set two standard deviations below the average IQ of 100, and only occurs about 2.5 percent of the time when considered against the entire distribution of IQ scores in the population. Because of these intellectual deficits, mentally retarded individuals' ability to learn is impaired. Language processing and logical thinking deficits are often present, as are impairments in reasoning and problem-solving abilities. Mental retardation interferes with language processing and impairs judgment and analytical skills.

Although the disorder affects an individual's capacity for learning, mental retardation is not a learning disorder in the academic sense. Mental retardation is distinguished from learning disabilities that are specific to academic learning such as dyslexia (a reading and writing disorder) and dyscalculia (a math disorder) in that it is more general in nature. In mental retardation, learning abilities are impaired generally, rather than in specific areas. Learning disabilities relate to specific deficits in the ability to acquire academic skills like reading and math, while mental retardation relates to basic and broad impairments in cognitive functioning that affect the individual's ability to process and retain information across the board.

Emotional Functioning

Mental retardation often affects people emotionally as well as intellectually. Many mentally retarded people function on an emotional and social level that is below what is appropriate for their age. This emotional immaturity is often considered an endearing aspect of mentally retarded individuals' personalities, however. Mentally retarded individuals are commonly thought of as being friendly, lovable, and possessing a child like quality in their overall personality.

The emotional maturity of individuals who are diagnosed with mental retardation is generally a function of how severely impaired they are. Severely mentally retarded individuals are generally more emotionally immature than are individuals with mild mental retardation.

Mental Retardation: Typical Characteristics

Individuals with mild mental retardation (formerly referred to as "educable"):

- are likely to need only intermittent to limited support;
- typically do not "look" different from their non-disabled peers;
- often have only mild or moderate developmental delays, except in academics, which is often the major area of deficit;
- therefore, they are often not identified until they enter the school setting, where their cognitive disability is most apparent;
- in Minnesota, students with mild MR spend most of the school day in the regular classroom;
- they typically attain 3rd-to 6th-grade academic achievement levels by the time they finish high school;
- as adults, many, though not all, with mild MR will be able to obtain independent employment;
- many will marry, have children, and blend rather indistinguishably into the community; for those who achieve total independence, the label of mental retardation is no longer appropriate.

Individuals with moderate to severe mental retardation (formerly called "trainable"):

- will probably need limited to extensive supports;
- they are more likely to have a recognizable syndrome (such as Down Syndrome);
- therefore, may "look" different than their non-disabled peers;.
- their development is often significantly delayed;
- they are typically identified as infants or toddlers;.
- most begin receiving special education during the preschool years;

- they may be included in the regular classroom part of the school day (particularly here in Minnesota);
- but often spend much of the school day in a separate classroom where they learn adaptive living skills;
- as adults, most individuals with moderate to severe MR will not achieve total independence;
- rather, they are likely to continue to need limited to extensive support such as that provided in group homes or semi-independent living situations (SILs); some may continue to live with their parents;
- some individuals with moderate to severe MR may be able to succeed in modified competitive employment situations;
- however, many will work in supported, non-competitive settings such as sheltered workshops.

Individuals with profound mental retardation:

- will generally need services at the pervasive level, typically throughout their life;
- they are likely to have multiple disabilities, particularly in the areas of mobility and communication;.
- therefore, many use wheelchairs and alternate forms of communication;
- their communication deficits make it difficult to accurately assess their intellectual functioning;
- in educational settings, they may be placed along with students with moderate to severe MR or in their own classroom;
- some adults with this level of retardation remain in institutional settings, but most currently live in group homes.

Concept, Nature and Characteristics of Hearing, Speech and Language Impairments

The Precise Nature of Hearing

The ear is one of the most elaborate and extraordinary structures in the body. Sound waves from our surroundings pass through a series of delicately balanced bones and exotic fluids before arriving at a set of exquisitely sensitive hair cells, aligned in precise rows along the organ of Corti. These hair cells perform a remarkable task: they transform a mechanical impulse into an electrical signal that, carried to the brain, is interpreted as sound. In the language of science, they are "a mechanotransduction apparatus."

Xiaowei Lu, assistant professor of cell biology, has been drawn to these cells—not specifically to tease out the process of mechanotransduction—but to address the fundamental mystery of their development. She is using mouse genetics to determine how these cells manage to organize themselves exactly so that their hair bundles, the part of the cell that senses motion, all face in the same direction. This tight formation is absolutely essential for hearing. If the cells are not aligned uniformly, the signal from the organ of Corti will be helplessly confused; a person with this condition would have impaired hearing.

The uniform alignment of hair cells is an example of planar cell polarity (PCP). Typical AAA batteries have positive and negative poles at their ends. In order for a digital camera to work, for example, all the batteries have to be inserted with the positive poles touching the positive contacts. By analogy, auditory hair cells would have 'positive' and 'negative' sides. PCP is a fundamental biological phenomenon, found in plants and animals at all levels of complexity. Understanding the underlying mechanism that drives this process can shed light on how multicellular organisms develop.

Thanks to a Fund for Excellence in Science and Technology (FEST) grant from U.Va., Lu has been able to combine a number of approaches to uncover the components of PCP and to find out how they work together. She uses gene trapping, a method of inducing mutations at precise locations in the genome, and she analyzes the proteins these genes produce. "If the protein looks interesting, I produce a knockout mouse in which the gene is inactive and see how the mouse is different," Lu says.

Lu can also grow the mouse auditory epithelium in a laboratory dish, producing an organ that is virtually identical to one developed in a living mouse. This explant system creates a host of opportunities for Lu. "We can mark the different molecules involved in the process with fluorescent tags and use live imaging to see how proteins move through hair cells to produce asymmetry," she says. "We can also insert genes of interest and see how they affect molecular dynamics and hair bundle orientation."

Lu has found that the hair cells in knockout mice that lack the ability to produce protein tyrosine kinase 7 (PTK7) don't face in the same direction. "Our current focus," Lu says, "is to figure out more about how PTK7 regulates PCP and guides the development of tissues and organs."

In her work, Lu is able to take advantage of the world-class expertise at U.Va. about inner ear development and developmental biology in general. "This department fits me like a glove," she comments. "I've greatly benefited from the suggestions and support of my colleagues."

Characteristics of Hearing-Impaired Students

Students with hearing impairments may have partial or full hearing loss in one or both ears. The characteristics exhibited by the student depend primarily on the degree of hearing loss and the onset of that loss. With proper support, most hearing-impaired children can and do succeed in school.

Language: Hearing-impaired children who have been deaf or have experienced impaired hearing since birth, or sometime before the acquisition of language, face more communications difficulties than those who became impaired after they learned the basics of a language.

Lip Reading: Children who suffer hearing loss due to illness or accident often are able to continue to communicate verbally. They can become skilled lip readers. According to Ball State University, however, even the most skilled lip readers are only able to decipher 20 to 30 percent of spoken English. Lip readers may appear to understand everything that happens in the classroom, but may misinterpret information or miss the verbal interaction of their peers, causing them to fall behind in academic tasks.

American Sign Language: Depending on the severity of the hearing loss and the philosophical beliefs of the parents and community, many hearing-impaired students learn to use American Sign Language as their primary means of communication.

A child may require an interpreter to communicate effectively with others and begin to become dependent on the interpreter. This may interfere with the hearing-impaired child's ability to acquire age-appropriate social and negotiation skills with his peers.

Isolation: Hearing-impaired students may become isolated from their peers and feel helpless to rectify the situation. This may result in behavioral difficulties or aggressive behavior if interventions are not put in place.

Grammar and Syntax: American Sign Language does not translate every word spoken in the English language, but instead functions much as a form of shorthand. As such, the hearing-impaired child may not learn the subtle nuances of a language and may struggle with grammar and syntax.

Expressing Ideas: A student with partial hearing loss may appear to understand what is happening in the classroom, but he may miss background conversations or comments. Articulation may be affected, but it is more likely his use of the English language will be affected, resulting in difficulty in expressing ideas or answering questions.

Definition

Speech and language disorders refer to problems in communication and related areas such as oral-motor function—sucking, swallowing, drinking, eating. These delays and disorders range from simple sound substitutions to the inability to understand or use language or use the oral-motor mechanism for functional speech and feeding. Some causes of speech and language disorders include hearing loss, neurological disorders, brain injury, intellectual disability, drug abuse, physical impairments such as cleft lip or palate, and vocal abuse or misuse. Frequently, however, the cause is unknown.

Incidence

More than 1.4 million students served in the public schools' special education programmes in the 2002-2003 school year were categorized as having a speech or language impairment (*Twenty-sixth Annual Report to Congress*, U.S. Department of Education, 2006). This estimate does not include children who have speech/language problems secondary to other conditions such as deafness. Language disorders may be related to other disabilities such as intellectual disability, learning disability, autism, or cerebral palsy. It is estimated that communication disorders (including speech, language, and hearing disorders) affect one of every 10 people in the United States.

Characteristics

A child's communication is considered delayed when the child is noticeably behind his or her peers in the acquisition of speech and/or language skills. Sometimes a child will have greater receptive (understanding) than expressive (speaking) language skills, but this is not always the case.

Speech disorders refer to difficulties producing speech sounds or problems with voice quality. They might be characterized by an interruption in the flow or rhythm of speech, such as stuttering, which is called dysfluency. Speech disorders may be problems with the way sounds are formed, called articulation or phonological disorders, or they may be difficulties with the pitch, volume or quality of the voice. There may be a combination of several problems. People with speech disorders have trouble using some speech sounds, which can also be a symptom of a delay. They may say "see" when they mean "ski" or they may have trouble using other sounds like "l" or "r." Listeners may have trouble understanding what someone with a speech disorder is trying to say. People with voice disorders may have trouble with the way their voices sound.

A language disorder is an impairment in the ability to understand and/or use words in context, both verbally and nonverbally. Some characteristics of language disorders include improper use of words and their meanings, inability to express ideas, inappropriate grammatical patterns, reduced vocabulary and inability to follow directions. One or a combination of these characteristics may occur in children who are affected by language learning disabilities or developmental language delay. Children may hear or see a word but not be able to understand its meaning. They may have trouble getting others to understand what they are trying to communicate.

Educational Implications

Because all communication disorders carry the potential to isolate individuals from their social and educational surroundings, it is essential to find appropriate timely intervention. While many speech and language patterns can be called "baby talk" and are part of a young child's normal development, they can become problems if they are not outgrown as expected. In this way an initial delay in speech and language or an initial speech pattern can become a disorder which can cause difficulties in learning. Because of the way the brain develops, it is easier to learn language and communication skills before the age of 5. When children have muscular disorders, hearing problems or developmental delays, their acquisition of speech, language and related skills is often affected.

Speech-language pathologists assist children who have communication disorders in various ways. They provide individual therapy for the child; consult with the child's teacher about the most effective ways to facilitate the child's communication in the class setting; and work closely with the family to develop goals and techniques for effective therapy in class and at home. The speech-language pathologist may assist vocational teachers and counselors in establishing communication goals related to the work experiences of students and suggest strategies that are effective for the important transition from school to employment and adult life.

Technology can help children whose physical conditions make communication difficult. The use of electronic communication systems allow nonspeaking people and people with severe physical disabilities to engage in the give and take of shared thought.

Vocabulary and concept growth continues during the years children are in school. Reading and writing are taught and, as students get older, the understanding and use of language becomes more complex. Communication skills are at the heart of the education experience. Speech and/or language therapy may continue throughout a student's school years either in the form of direct therapy or on a consultant basis.

Speech/Language Disorders

Speech and language disorders refer to problems in communication and related areas. They can range from simple sound substitutions to the inability to understand or use language. Some causes would be hearing loss, neurological disorders, brain injury, mental retardation, drug abuse, cleft lip or palate, and vocal abuse or misuse. Frequently, the cause is unknown. It is estimated that one of every ten persons in the United States is affected by a communication disorder.

Characteristics

Speech disorders refer to difficulties in producing speech sounds or problems with voice quality. Disorders would include

- Stuttering (dysfluency) — an interruption in the flow or rhythm of speech.
- Articulation or phonological — problems with the way sounds are formed.
- Other — difficulties with pitch, volume, or quality of voice.

People with speech disorders have trouble using some speech sounds. They may say "see" when they mean "ski" or have trouble with sounds like "I" or "R."

A language disorder is an impairment in the ability to understand and/or use words in context. Characteristics include the improper use of words and their meanings, the inability to express ideas, inappropriate grammatical patterns, reduced vocabulary, and the inability to follow directions.

Some youth with speech and language disorders isolate themselves from social interaction and have a problem forming interpersonal relationships.

Concept, Nature and Characteristics of

(i) Learning Disabilities

The Causes of Learning Disabilities

Successful intervention is dependent on finding the cause or causes of a problem. Most problems can only be solved if one knows their causes. A disease such as scurvy claimed the lives of thousands of seamen during their long sea voyages. The disease was cured fairly quickly once the cause was discovered, viz. a Vitamin C deficiency. A viable point of departure would therefore be to ask the question, *"What causes learning disabilities?"*

In the literature on learning disabilities, it is generally assumed that learning disabilities are caused by a neurological dysfunction. This theory has so far, however, been unable to produce any tangible practical results.

Another popular theory is that learning disabilities are genetically transmitted. According to an American study the risk that a child will have a reading problem is increased from four to thirteen times if one of the parents has a similar problem. This tendency for learning disabilities to "run in families" has been confirmed by numerous studies.

The tendency for learning disabilities to "run in families" does not necessarily prove, however, that a learning disability is genetically determined. The ability to speak English also runs in families, yet nobody would attribute this to genetics. We all know that a child learns to speak the language that he hears on a daily basis.

A straight line is the shortest distance between two points. However, the seemingly shortest route from one conclusion to the next is not necessarily the best—or the correct—one. It sometimes turns out that a problem may have an explanation and a solution that may seem so obvious and so simple that people tend to overlook it.

The theory below is of this nature. For its understanding one requires no specialist knowledge of the intricacies of the human brain. Decades of experience has shown that for the successful application of this theory one does not even need to have the vaguest inkling of what genetics is about.

In this theory it is not denied that the brains of learning-disabled people might be different from the non-learning disabled. In fact, it is conceded that they probably are. The "chicken-and-egg" problem should, however, not be overlooked: are the brain differences the cause of the learning disabilities, or is it the other way round? Furthermore, in this theory it is conceded that genes may well play a role in the origin of learning disabilities. However, I hold the optimistic view that neurological differences and negative genetics merely increase the educational responsibility of parents and teachers. A learning disability is therefore not a permanent condition. By following the correct method of instruction and with sustained practice according to this method, any person can overcome a learning disability.

The Causes of Learning Disabilities: An Alternative Theory

To understand this theory on the causes of learning disabilities it is important to take note of the fact that there is *nothing that any human being knows, or can do, that he has not learned.* If you dump a little puppy into water, it will swim. Do the same with a human child, and it will drown. The child must *learn* to swim.

There is yet another, equally important fact, which is also a *sine qua non* towards the understanding of learning disabilities, and which has also so far been overlooked, viz. that *learning is a stratified process.* This is a self-evident fact, yet its significance in the situation of the learning-disabled child has apparently never been fully comprehended. Throughout the world in all educational systems it is commonly accepted that a child must start at the lower levels of education and then gradually progress to the higher levels. If human learning had not been a stratified process, if it had taken place on a single level, this would have been unnecessary. It would then not have been important to start a child in first grade. It would have been possible for the child to enter school at any level and to complete the school years in any order.

Even more astounding is that this very important principle of learning is hardly noted in any of the present-day theories on learning. In fact, when this principle of learning is mentioned, it often happens by way of an *en passant* reference to discarded notions from the past:

> *Baldwin (1896) introduced the concept of a hierarchy of senses and proposed that sense perception ability varied from person to person. As we ascend Baldwin's pyramidal scale we find that each capability rests on, and is chronologically and psychologically dependent on, all the capabilities below it (for example imagination, which could not act but for its predecessors perception and memory). This notion of training competencies hierarchically was the premise on which perceptual training and perceptual motor training were based.*

When this principle *is* noticed, then its significance is often distorted by reductionist thinking such as, "Cognitive abilities develop in a sequential fashion that cannot be altered," or, "Another prerequisite for reading includes a certain level of physiological development of the brain."

The stratified nature of learning is an age-old—but ageless—principle. This principle was already pointed out by Herbart (1776-1841), and it is based on the further principle that: One never...apprehends anything in isolation, but always in terms of one's background of previous experience and learning. *So the first consideration in properly organized learning would be to make sure that the learner had the right background* (my italics).

A simpler example, which explains the stratified nature of learning, is the fact that one has to learn to count before it becomes possible to learn to add and subtract. Suppose one tried to teach a child, who had not yet learned to count, to add and subtract. This would be quite impossible and no amount of effort would ever succeed in teaching the child these skills. The child must learn to count *first*, *before* it becomes possible for him to learn to add and subtract. In the same way, there are things that a child must learn *first*, *before* it becomes possible for him to learn to read, spell, write, et cetera. Bartoli, who says that it is "the actual practice with the real task of reading that leads to more skilful reading," is only partially correct. "Of course," she adds, "any soccer, tennis, or basketball coach will tell you the same thing: If you want to get better, you have to play the game — not just practice skill drills." Now, I know very little about tennis and basketball, but I do happen to know about soccer. The game of soccer consists of many fragmented elements or skills — passing, control, shooting, dribbling, goal keeping and heading. Before any child is expected to play in a full-game situation, he should first be trained to pass, head, control, dribble and shoot the ball. In fact, until these skills have been *automatized*, the child will have two left feet on the soccer field.

The reading "game," just like the game of soccer, rests upon certain skills and until these skills have become automatized, the child will have "two left eyes" in the reading situation.

Characteristics of Adults with Specific Learning Disabilities

How to Think about Characteristics?

A number of considerations should be kept in mind when considering the characteristics of adults with learning disabilities (LD). First, there is a great diversity within the population (Gerber & Reiff, 1991). This diversity exists because learning disabilities are not a unitary construct. An individual can have one specific problem or a constellation of problems. Moreover, learning disabilities do not manifest themselves in individuals in exactly the same way. Some learning disabilities can be mild, while others can be quite severe. Those who have severe learning disabilities obviously are those who are most challenged (Dowdy & Smith, 1994; Gerber & Reiff, 1991).

Second, it is important to note that, by definition, an adult who has learning disabilities is of average or above average intelligence. This wide span of ability means that it is possible for IQs to be low average to high or even gifted. What is noteworthy about those who have learning disabilities is that ability does not match achievement — whether in academic areas, in functional behaviors, or in employment outcomes. There seems to be a significant gap between what would be expected, given the individual's ability, and what is actually accomplished (Reiff, Gerber, & Ginsberg, 1993).

Last, we know that learning disabilities are a persisting problem, a life-long condition that evolves throughout the developmental continuum (Gerber & Reiff, 1994). For example, what is problematic in a grade-school student can be very different from what is manifested in an adolescent with a learning disability. Similarly, learning disabilities in adulthood present some different themes, challenges, and issues. Therefore, it is important to acknowledge that the experience of being learning disabled varies as an individual progresses through the various levels of development — childhood, adolescence, and adulthood. Even in adulthood, a stage of human development that can be as long as 70 years (early adulthood to senior citizen), there are a multitude of issues to address. In the field of learning disabilities, it is not prudent or wise to approach an understanding of the characteristics of learning disabilities simply by taking a generic approach—that a learning disability is a learning disability no matter what age, stage, or phase of development (Gerber, 1992).

Critical Characteristics

Adults with LD show a wide array of critical characteristics that are problematic for them in their daily lives (Gerber & Reiff, 1990; Gerber & Reiff, 1994; Johnson & Blablock, 1990). First, academic skills that were not mastered during the school-age years remain difficult. Problems arise in such areas as reading, math, spelling, and writing. In each case, there can be a wide variety of reasons for lack of attainment of academic skills. In reading, for example, the reason might be poor comprehension enhancement strategies. Related to mathematics, problems evidence themselves in using math concepts and thinking in mathematical ways (either for daily use or for more sophisticated applications). Finally, in writing, whether the problem is spelling, handwriting, or written expression, there can be many reasons for apparent difficulties.

In each case, there is a high probability that the source of the problem(s) is the underlying dynamics of the learning disability: the psychological processes that have a bearing on the presenting problem. These psychological processes include cognition, perception, language, attention, motoric abilities, and social skills. These processes, individually or collectively, have a bearing on academic skills, but they have equal impact on all areas of adult functioning — whether at home, at work, or in the community.

Secondary Characteristics

There also are numerous secondary characteristics relevant to the adult learning disabled experience. These characteristics can be viewed as the "next layer" of manifestations of learning disabilities, which emerge as a collection of coping mechanisms or a set of thoughts and feelings evidenced in either positive or negative ways. Because of the complex nature of learning disabilities in adulthood, generalization about secondary characteristics must be viewed with a "discriminating eye"; that is, the characteristics discussed below may present themselves in various forms and exist around a multitude of themes. An understanding of the secondary characteristics of adults with LD, therefore, must be based on the perspectives of the individual as an adult, the learning disability, and the context of lifespan issues.

Social and emotional characteristics are most notable in adults with LD. An overall feeling of lack of self-worth, low self-esteem, and a poor self-concept can be pervasive (Barton & Fuhrmann, 1994). A number of writers in the area of adults with LD have commented that this area typically is where this otherwise heterogeneous population shares a great deal of similarity. Many adults with LD have had particularly painful experiences during their school-age years, both in and out of the classroom. And it seems that they carry their pain each day of their lives, whether they are successful or unsuccessful in their adult lives. Consequently, it is not uncommon for them to feel dumb, stupid, and incompetent (Gerber, Ginsberg, & Reiff, 1992).

Many have carried self-attributions into adulthood, stemming from the notion, "I am a person who cannot," as opposed to "I am a person who can," and they often take on the attitudes and behaviors of learned helplessness (Groteluschen, Barkowski, & Hale, 1990). As a result, many adults with LD see themselves as incapable or as losers. In essence, they feel that if they get something right, they are lucky, and if they get it wrong, then they are dumb! Even adults who have experienced mostly successful lives have reported that they sometimes feel as if they are "impostors." Their impostor syndrome (Clance, 1985) always make them feel that, despite past accomplishments, they still are not worthy of achievement, and that someone "will find out" that they are not qualified or capable.

For these reasons, it is understandable that adults with LD often experience a sense of frustration and exasperation. The cost is a set of "emotional baggage" that is carried into most social and learning experiences and daily living tasks (Barton & Fuhrmann, 1994). Confronted with myriad challenging tasks every day combined with a history of self-doubt lays the seeds of emotional liability (Gerber & Reiff, 1991). Moreover, stress and anxiety become part of the mix, often leading to an uncontrollable feeling of being overwhelmed by what has to be accomplished. When, in some cases, everything becomes too overwhelming, more intense and protracted emotional reactions become likely, leading to a wide array of mental health problems, including depression.

Within the social and emotional realm, it is particularly difficult to generalize about positive or negative motivation, which in so many cases is situation-specific. For example, some describe adults with LD as having little motivation because of the accumulation of failure experiences over the span of their lives. Unfortunately, this often can be the case. Others are highly motivated at times during their adult years for a variety of reasons. Motivation can be heightened, for instance, when a parent wants to learn to read so he/she can read bedtime stories to his/her children, or when he/she wants to learn a new skill for job advancement or for retraining purposes. In addition, when adults with LD want to take control of their lives, motivation that fuels initial success, and that begets further success, can create an awesome set of dynamics and become a source of lasting intrinsic motivation.

Certain secondary characteristics have been found to be effective for taking control of one's life, which, in turn leads to greater possibilities of successful adaptation to adult life. One characteristic is the capacity of some adults with LD to be resilient despite past failure. In many cases, the lives of individuals with LD are punctuated with successes and failures. Those who been able to move forward undeterred by failure (and sometimes strengthened by it) have a greater sense of inner strength and self-confidence. In essence, in tough times, they know that there are good times ahead, if they are able to stick with it (Gerber, et al., 1994).

Resilience is a set of dynamics that affects different segments of the population of adults with LD in different ways. Whereas all individuals with LD have the capacity to be resilient in some cases (e.g., those who typically attend literacy centers), resilience may be more of an exception than a rule.

Another positive characteristic is the unconventional way in which some adults with LD devise learning strategies or adaptive methods to master a task or learn a new routine. They have unique ways in which they approach tasks, and, when given the time and opportunity, they are able to problem solve in their own style. This process has been termed "learned creativity" and is credited with adaptive techniques used in employment, daily living tasks, and social situations (Gerber, et al., 1992; Reiff, et al., 1997).

What are the Myths?

The myths regarding adults with LD begin long before adulthood. In fact, one major myth has been debunked as a result of studying highly successful adults with LD. Oftentimes, students with learning disabilities are "written off" as individuals who have limited potential, leaving a guarded prognosis for adjustment to adulthood. But a seven-year-old student with learning disabilities can become a hard-working

17-year-old high school student, a focused 27-year-old parent and employee, and a successful family member and contributor to his/her work group. In essence, there are many possibilities and opportunities for adults with LD to be successful in myriad ways, despite a past spotted with failure and dire prediction of future problems (Gerber, 1992).

Another myth stems from the general notion about employment outcomes for adults with LD. Learning disabilities do not preclude individuals from becoming successful, from being leaders in their organizations or, even better, in their fields. There are countless examples of adults with LD across the country who have ìmade itì in the professions, in business and industry, in politics and the arts, and some who have become well-known entrepreneurs (Gerber, et al., 1992; Reiff, et al., 1997).

Nevertheless, it should be remember that there are low-income and poor adults with LD. Learning disabilities are not a middle-class phenomenon, as once believed. There are numerous adults with LD who are underserved and, if identified through social service safety nets, have potential to learn to read, find suitable employment, and participate more fully in their communities (Young, Gerber, Reder, & Cooper, 1996).

The penultimate myth acknowledges an aspect of adult development not written or spoken about in the adult learning disabled literature. Not only are adults with LD different because of the heterogeneity of learning disabilities, but adults with LD are different depending on the phase of adulthood that they are in. There are distinct differences in physical, mental, and psychosocial traits depending on early, middle, or late adulthood. Research even has shown deterioration in cognitive and other abilities as individuals with LD age (Gerber, Schneiders, et al., 1990). Thus, adulthood is not a constant, and adults with LD are not the same-and should not necessarily be approached in the same manner.

Last, adults with LD have a great deal in common with non-disabled adults. To stress differences without recognizing similarities is to miss the big picture. All adults have strong qualities and human frailties. They yearn for independence, love, and acknowledgement. They are mothers, fathers, aunts, and uncles. They are line-workers, supervisors, and leaders in their professions. They have an agenda that is incomplete in terms of making their adult experiences full. But they are adults first, and their learning disabilities define only part of what they are all about!

(ii) Behavioral and Emotional Disorders

Assessment and classification of school-aged children with emotional and behavioral disorders (EBD) have proven to be difficult for school personnel and educators alike (Gresham, 1985; Smith, Wood, & Grimes, 1988). Current epidemiological research indicates that at least 7% of children under age 18 may have emotional disorders, yet fewer than 1% of school-aged children are served as seriously emotionally disturbed (SED) (U. S. Department of Education, 1991). In California, prevalence rates of SED are even lower than the national rate, illustrating the extent of underidentification. Quite often students are not identified as emotionally/behaviorally disturbed (EBD), until the concluding elementary years. This has grave implications for the efficacy of intervention (Walker, Colvin, & Ramsey, 1995). More typically, students who exhibit externalizing problem behaviors are classified and placed under the learning disability (LD) category (Duncan, Forness, & Hartsough, 1995, Gresham, 1985, MacMillan, Gresham, & Bocian, in press). School or Student Study Teams seem to underidentify and have difficulty in assessing SED for a variety of reasons including:

- the ambiguity of the state definitions
- school psychologists' lack of training in conducting SED assessments
- financial limitations of school districts, and
- hesitation to use labels such as BD/EBD/SED.

Despite evidence to the contrary (MacMillan, Jones, & Aloia, 1974), the pervasive notion that the act of labeling exacerbates the condition influences individual decisions in classification, and school personnel choose to use a more socially desirable label such as LD (Gresham, 1985). Therefore, despite meeting several eligibility criteria, it seems that EBD students are not classified correctly, which lessens their chance to receive the treatment that best serves their needs.

The current definition of SED (Federal Register, 42, 474, 1977) as proposed under provisions of the Individuals with Disabilities Education Act (IDEA), lists five areas or behavioral characteristics that define SED, as follows:

A condition exhibiting one or more of the following characteristics over a long period of time and to a marked degree which adversely affects school performance:

(a) An inability to learn which cannot be explained by intellectual, sensory, or health factors.

(b) An inability to build or maintain satisfactory relationships with peers and teachers.

(c) Inappropriate types of behavior under normal circumstances.

(d) General pervasive mood of unhappiness or depression.

(e) A tendency to develop physical symptoms or fears associated with personal/school problems.

The current definition of SED excludes children who are socially maladjusted, yet it provides no direction or specific criteria that should be used to exclude. Further confusion and lack of precision result when schools equate conduct disorder, externalizing behaviors, and juvenile delinquency with the social maladjustment clause, as this successfully excludes many of the children who otherwise might be identified correctly (Slenkovich, 1992). In addition, identifying a child as SED precludes the possibility of expulsion for the very behaviors that are problematic for the school.

The behavioral correlates associated with emotional and behavioral disorders include maladaptive patterns of responding that are commonly designated as externalizing or internalizing in nature. Externalizin,%or undercontrolled behavior problems are characterized by a host of defiant, aggressive, disruptive, and noncompliant responses. Conduct disorder, oppositional defiant disorder, and attention deficit disorder are but a few examples of externalizing behavior. Externalizing behavior problems in children and adolescents represent a widespread and troublesome obstacle for parents, teachers, schools, society, and the individual child who engages in it (Walker et al., 1995, Webster-Stratton, 1993). These behaviors typically are seen in all children at one time or another. For the emotionally or behaviorally disordered child, however, these same behaviors often escalate and magnify into patterns that persist throughout a child's life. Ultimately, this response pattern evolves into psychiatric problems, social maladjustment, and criminal acts (Kazdin, 1987).

In the context of the classroom, externalizing behaviors seem to be more intolerable to teachers than other undesirable behaviors because they directly challenge the teacher's authority, interfere with the delivery of instruction, disrupt classroom routines, and affect classmates adversely (McConaughy & Skiba, 1993; Safran & Safran, 1987). Relentless disruptive and noncompliant behavior requires training for effective management, and, according to Kaufman and Wong (1991), many general education teachers do not have sufficient behavior management training to control such aversive behavior. Thus, teacher tolerance for externalizing-type behavior is low and, in turn, referral for externalizing behavior far exceeds that of internalizing-type referrals (Walker & Fabre, 1987).

Internalizing behavior patterns can include, but are not limited to, withdrawal, shyness, depression, dysthymia, emotional and personality disorders. In general, internalizing or overcontrolled behaviors are more inner-directed and covert in nature. These behavior patterns also are predictive of social adjustment difficulties and psychopathology in later life (Achenbach,1985). Because of their internal or private nature, however, they do not readily come to the attention of teachers or authorities. Quite often such behaviors are not seen as difficulties and, therefore, are overlooked in assessment and not subject to direct interventions within the school systems. In recent literature the comorbidity of externalizing and internalizing behavior patterns has been suggested by Loney (1987) and by McConaughy & Skiba, (1993). Often, conductdisordered and antisocial youth also present with low self-esteem, low self-concept, and depression (Walker et al., 1995). Characteristic behaviors that comorbid children exhibit are highly correlated with hyperactivity (ADHD), explosiveness, impulsivity, academic failure, and poor social skills (Campbell, Gonzalez, & Silva, 1992). This comorbid diagnosis, which seriously hinders the development and functioning of many children, is increasingly prevalent (Loney, 1987, McConaughy & Skiba, 1993). These students are at higher risk for high school dropout, gang affiliation, juvenile offenses, substance abuse, and teen pregnancy (Walker et al.,1995). Their complex problems warrant more intensive intervention efforts.

Although SED children currently are underidentified and frequently are not served as such until the later educational years, the evidence indicates that intervention efforts are more likely to enjoy success when applied during earlier ages. According to Walker et al. (1995), maladaptive behavior patterns that remain untreated by the third grade should be considered a chronic disorder that has no cure and at best can be managed given appropriate strategies. Early identification, prevention, and screening procedures may well aid in eliminating behavior patterns before they can progress into conduct disorder, depression, and the like. A more preventive, rather than reactive, approach is necessary (Walker et al., 1995).

Valid and reliable assessment of SED necessitates multimethod assessment practices and early identification. Duncan et al. (1995) reported a considerable lag time between initial SED symptoms/behavior and referral for services, classification/diagnosis, intervention efforts, and educational placement. In addition, discrepancies are present between clinical diagnosis (e.g., employing DSM-IV) and school classification (IDEA) systems, which pose further obstacles for prevention and early identification of SED. The need for appropriate placement, is crucial, wherein the student can receive intensive intervention to remediate and redirect challenging behaviors. Research has indicated that a process of least to most restrictive placements (i.e., regular Ed->RSP-SDC) is most often adopted (Duncan et al., 1995). The underlying premise of LRE was to mandate appropriate placement, not sequential movement on a continuum from regular education to special day classes. While current trends in litigation are supporting education within the regular education classroom (full inclusion), this practice may not always serve the best interest of the child with emotional and behavioral disorders (MacMillan, Gresham, & Forness, 1996).

The use of empirically-based assessment methods is paramount in the identification and classification of students with EBD. Empirically based assessments are procedures based upon direct observations and experience (Achenbach, 1985) which have several benefits over clinical methods for assessing children's emotional and behavioral functioning (Edelbrock, 1983). These advantages include: (a) quantitative scores from rating scales which provide more reliable measures of functioning than do subjective judgments, (b) comparison to normative samples which corroborate and enhance judgments of deviance in reported behavior, (c) multiple items, which can be incorporated to represent a diverse range of problems, and (d) minimal time qnd training to administer, which make rating scales an efficient and economical method of assessment. Empirically based multi-informant assessment provide a more comprehensive basis for making these categorical decisions such as special education eligibility.

Walker and Severson (1990) developed a multiple gating procedure, the Systematic Screening for Behavior Disorders (SSBD), which employs a progression of screening and assessment stages, beginning with general screening tools, and advancing to more precise and stringent evaluations. Stage 1 requires the teachers to rank order their students on externalizing and internalizing behavior patterns.

In Stage 2 the teacher completes a behavior checklist; the Critical Events Index (CEI). This tool is a 33-item teacher checklist of behavioral events having high intensity and salience but relatively low frequency (e.g., fire-setting, physical assault of another, self-abuse). Past research has demonstrated that the CEI separates the more severe cases of EBD even within a restricted sample of youth in residential care (Duncan,

Forness, & Hartsough, 1995). In school settings the CEI identified students had lower social skills and higher externalizing problem behaviors within a sample of at-risk children (Gresham, MacMillan & Bocian, 1996). Further examination of the CEI as a screening component in the assessment of EBD is warranted. In the present article we attempt_to identify the earliest, most efficient, and accurate predictors of EBD. To examine the correlates of EBD, a group of third-grade students was classified as being at high-risk for emotional and behavioral disorders, based on a criterion-level CEI score. These "high risk" (HR) students were drawn from a larger sample of third graders that included students at risk for academic failure (AR) and students achieving at grade level, the control group (CC).

Mean differences were examined between these three groups on a host of variables including teacher ratings of academic competence and interpersonal social skills, student selfconcept ratings, and peer sociometric status ratings. In addition, these dependent variables were-considered for their utility as significant predictors of group membership, or their ability to classify children effectively into HR, AR, or CC groups. These data also will illustrate that, although the HR or EBD groups evidence nearly all of the eligibility criteria of the current SED definition, they are not being served as such under IDEA. Finally, our efforts to characterize children at risk for EBD (HR) as a homogeneous group, will be tempered by an examination of the behavior profiles of three HR students. These profiles illustrate the variability of comorbidity-morbidity and intervention needs of students who meet the SED criteria.

Emotional and behavioural disorders (EBD) is a broad category which is used commonly in educational settings, to group a range of more specific perceived difficulties of children and adolescents. Both general definitions as well as concrete diagnosis of EBD may be controversial as the observed behaviour may depend on many factors.

Strategies for Students Classified with EBD

1. *Routine:* Provide a structured routine with visual time clock. Auditory sound cues may be helpful in addition

to visual cues to help students manage their time efficiently. Post schedule and refer to schedule on regular basis. Routines may take 6-8 weeks to establish or even more for this population of students.

2. *Changes in Routine:* Convey any changes of routine to students as soon as available. The sooner students are aware of changes the more time students have to adjust to the new routine.
3. *Classroom Jobs Chart / Classroom Order Chart:* Classroom jobs offer an opportunity for student to show responsibility. In order to ensure success, make sure students have an opportunity to experience every job. One suggestion is having a chart with each students name and according job. Every week rotate the jobs. The list can double as the order in which students line up or choose preferred activities. Students with EBD classification tend to be competitive and need specific procedures informing the order students line up and choose activities.
4. *Logical Consequences:* Students must fix what they break. If a student pushes over a desk, he or she must pick it up. If a student runs in the hall, she must practice walking the correct way. If the student talks during the lesson, student must make up the work on his time. Be consistent with consequences so students know what is expected of them.
5. *Target Behaviors:* After taking data on students observable behavior, determine which behavior or behaviors to direct attention. Work with student to develop a plan to replace undesirable behavior with a more suitable behavior. If student throws desks and pencils when angry, have student work on communicating anger to an adult or trusted peer and how to be assertive without being aggressive.
6. *Small Flexible Grouping:* Students with EBD may have difficulty establishing relationships with peers. Abusive language and other behaviors may interfere with learning. Smaller groups decrease distractions and

student-to-teacher ratio. Differentiation of instruction is more manageable with smaller groups.

7. *Audience:* During a serious behavior episode, the most effective strategy may be to remove the audience. The audience typically is other peers but may be other adults. The audience can be removed by moving the student if he or she is willing. However, moving the audience may be necessary in some cases. Develop a procedure with your class which will function as an "everybody out" drill. Behaviors amplified with an audience may be reduced or complete stopped when an audience is removed.
8. *Calm spot: Have a designated area of the classroom for students to calm down.* This spot can be used pro actively to prevent behaviors. Alternatively, the spot may be used after a behavior occurs to give the student a chance to refocus.
9. *Choices:* Students may frustrate easily when doing work. Giving students an option of when to complete the work is a powerful tool. For example, a teacher may say, "You need to get this done today. Would you rather do it now or during your free time?"

(iii) Intellectual Impairment

Promoting and Facilitating Development

What is Intellectual Impairment?

Intellectual impairment is a term used to describe a set of conditions involving deficits in abilities of cognitive functioning and adaptive skills. In other words, intellectual impairment can affect a person's ability to reason and understand, to acquire skills and master developmental milestones within "typical" age ranges, to problem-solve and adapt to new situations, and to learn and remember as easily as others.

Many terms have been applied to this set of conditions. Derogatory terms such as "feeble minded" or "retard" are no longer acceptable. In America the term "mental retardation" is still widely used however, in Australia "intellectual impairment" or "intellectual disability" are the preferred terms as demonstrated by their use on official government and education policy documents.

The acceptable term to describe a child with this impairment is as "a child with an intellectual impairment". Similarly, a child with Down Syndrome should not be referred to as "our Down Syndrome" or "our Downies" as the child is not their disability. He or she is a child first and foremost, and any disability they may have is of secondary importance to that.

Incidence

The World Health Organisation estimates that between 1 and 3% of the world's population have an intellectual impairment. In Australia estimates are at around 2% of the population.

Diagnosis of Intellectual Impairment

The diagnosis of an intellectual impairment involves two indicators:

1. Intellectual functioning which is significantly below average for age.
2. Marked impairment in ability to adapt to cultural demands of society, i.e. evidence of deficits in adaptive behaviours.

Evidence of both indices must be provided before a diagnosis of intellectual impairment can be made. A third requirement is that it manifests before the age of 18 years (during the developmental years).

What is Intellectual Functioning?

Intellectual functioning involves finding, processing, and organising information and then using that information appropriately. Kozma and Stock (1993) relate that intellectual functioning is :

"...the ability to gather and make sense of the information that surrounds a person in the world, to act on it, and then to use it in other situations to make sense of new experiences. In order to function in the world, people

must be able to put many different intellectual skills together. We must be able to pay attention *to the world around us,* remember *what we have experienced before,* abstract *or pull out the important information, use it to* problem solve, *and then* generalize *or apply what we have learned to new situations".*

What is Adaptive Behaviour?

Adaptive functioning refers to a person's ability to function socially and independently compared to other people of the same age and culture. Gething (1992) defines adaptive behaviours within the following three areas:-

1. Ability to accomplish tasks demanded by society;
2. Personal responsibility and willingness to undertake such tasks; and
3. Social responsibility and the ability to behave appropriately in terms of cultural expectations.

More simply, adaptive behaviours include all the abilities to interact socially, communicate and take care of personal needs. Abilities include activities of daily living (dressing, eating, bathing, toiletting); communication skills (both understanding and expression of language); and socialization (relating to other people).

Adaptive functioning is gauged against age and cultural norms, by comparing a child's abilities against those of other children of the same chronological age and cultural group.

Assessment of adaptive functioning also needs to take into account any sensory or motor difficulties which may be interfering with the child's adaptive behaviour. For instance, problems with motor skills of a child with cerebral palsy may delay the child's potty training rather than deficits of adaptive functioning.

Ways of Classifying Intellectual Impairment

Classifications of mild, moderate, severe or profound are used in reference to people with an intellectual disability. In the past, determination of these categories was based primarily on IQ (Intelligence Quotient) Tests. Over the last 25 years there has been growing dissatisfaction with the concept of IQ tests and their validity when used alone to assess capabilities and potentials of people with intellectual impairment (Gething, 1992).

Criticisms relate to the fact that on determination of an IQ score there is a tendency to stereotype the person to our perception of that level/ classification and to then ignore the individual's pattern of strengths and weaknesses. Also such labeling encourages a static view of a person which does not allow for development and change or for the effects of environment on the person's performance.

> *"Functional age" has also been an approach used to describe the level of ability of children. Determination of "functional age" is based on how a child performs against checklists or testing of skills compared to the expected average ability per chronological age. This method also draws criticism as being prescriptive and misleading. For a start, development is variable-that's why we have age ranges for achieving skills as part of normal development-the idea of functional age ignores these normal developmental variables. In addition, "functional age" can only be true in the most general way. For instance, you might hear that a child at the chronological age of five is said to function at the level of a three year old. It could be true that the child only has an attention span typical of a three year old, but it might not be true of their problem solving or language skills. "Functional age" can also ignore the child's individual pattern of strengths and weaknesses.*

More recently, there is a shift towards a system of classification based on individualised assessment of a person's strengths, weaknesses, and support needs. This system acknowledges the individuality of each person and provides more useful information. It does not define a person by deficits in abilities but rather seeks to give an indication of the level of support the person is likely to require to get along in a given environment. In line with this shift we now use terms like "additional needs" and "high support needs".

Causes of Intellectual Impairment

The underlying cause of intellectual impairment is often unknown. Known causes of intellectual impairment can be categorised under these groupings-prenatal, perinatal and postnatal.

Prenatal Causes

Intellectual impairment can sometimes be traced to a genetic difference. That is, at some time during the prenatal period something has altered the child's chromosomes or genes.

Some genetic problems that cause intellectual impairment are inherited. In other words, the background for these conditions was present in one of the parent's genetic make-up even before conception. The parent may pass on a chromosome with an abnormal gene, or pass on too many or too few chromosomes. Some inherited causes of intellectual impairment include tuberous sclerosis, Fragile X syndrome, Hurler Syndrome, Tay-Sachs disease and phenylketonuria (PKU).

Noninherited genetic causes of intellectual impairment involve changes that occur to the genes or chromosomes after conception and during early development. In these instances, the genetic material supplied by the each parent is normal, but then-during the early stages of cell division of the morula or embryo-an error in separation, recombination, or distribution of chromosomes occur. Chromosomal problems during early cell division are very common, however the majority of chromosomal problems are not compatible with life. That is, most of the time that this type of chromosomal abnormality occurs the fetus does not live long enough to be born. Chromosomal abnormalities that are compatible with life and are known to cause intellectual impairment include Down Syndrome, Trisomy 13, Trisomy 18, and Cri du Chat Syndrome.

Early alteration of embryonic development or congenital malformation is also linked with intellectual impairment. A congenital malformation is an abnormality in function or structure of any organ that appears during fetal development. Children with birth defects or congenital anomalies (differences), commonly have physical symptoms or characteristics that indicate that there may be an underlying problem with brain development. Generally there are no tests available to determine the cause of congenital anomalies. Diagnosis is often based on comparison of the child's physical and mental traits to previously identified syndromes. Such syndromes would include Williams syndrome, Cornelia de Lange syndrome and Sturge-Weber Syndrome. Other congenital anomalies which may be associated with intellectual impairment are hydrocephalus and microcephaly.

Maternal health factors which may affect a developing fetus include maternal age, maternal nutrition, substance use during pregnancy and maternal illness. Women over 35 years and teenagers are more likely, for various reasons, to have high risk pregnancies (Umansky, Hooper, 1998). Poor maternal nutrition will affect the child by not sufficiently meeting the nutritional requirements of the developing fetus and by weakening the mother and, consequently, the intrauterine environment. Substance use during pregnancy is also of serious concern. Generally, the specific effects of a drug on the developing fetus are uncertain though they will be determined by the type of drug, the dosage level, and the stage of pregnancy during which the drug was taken. Effects of substance use are often notable at birth, however sometimes the problems aren't apparent until later in early childhood. Drugs which are known to affect the developing fetus include thalidomide, anti-convulsants, anticancer drugs, sex hormones, acne medications, antibiotics, alcohol, drugs of abuse, and tobacco (Batshaw, Perret, 1992). Alcohol abuse is one of the leading known causes for intellectual impairment in America.

Maternal infections can have adverse affects on the developing fetus. Ironically, the pregnant woman may have few if any signs of the infection however, depending on the stage of development of the fetus the infection can be disruptive enough to cause intellectual impairment or other problems such as hearing or visual impairments. On the other hand, an infection may cause little, if any, harm to the child at all. Maternal infections which are known to increase the risk of intellectual impairment to the developing child include cytomegalovirus (CVM), rubella, measles, chicken pox, syphilis, toxoplasmosis, hepatitis B, coxsackie virus group and acquired auto immune deficiency syndrome (AIDS).

Other maternal factors that are potentially harmful to the developing fetus include:

- chronic illness, such as diabetes, thyroid disease
- obstetrical complications, such as uterine fibroids
- toxemia, a possible complication of pregnancy
- RH incompatibility (if not detected and treated).

Perinatal Causes

Sometimes the brain develops normally, but is injured or damaged during birth. Usually, this kind of damage occurs as a result of poor oxygen supply to the brain (hypoxia) or no oxygen (anoxia). Problems involving the placenta or the umbilical cord, or difficulties during labour and delivery can all cause disruption to the fetal blood circulation and oxygen supply. Whether intellectual impairment results depends upon the location and size of the area deprived of oxygen, the length of time it is affected, the resulting cell death from the lack of oxygen, the unavailability of glucose, the buildup of toxins, and the age, weight and health of the child. Cerebral palsy is another condition that may result from episodes of hypoxia or anoxia. Prematurity, or birth at or before the 36th week of gestation, also puts the infant at risk of developing intellectual impairment or cerebral palsy. This is because premature babies still have a fragile network of blood vessels that supply their brain. This leaves them vulnerable to hemorrhaging or bleeding into the brain tissue and if the bleeding is severe damage can result. Lung immaturity, common in premature babies, may result in the disruption of the oxygen supply throughout the body and cause damage to the brain. Improved medical technology has however, increased the survival rates of infants born prematurely.

Postnatal Causes

Intellectual impairment may begin anytime before the child reaches 18 years of age. Therefore a child can be born with normal intellectual functioning but then suffer damage which results in intellectual impairment. It is important to know that not all brain damage causes intellectual impairment. Some children who receive brain damage recover completely. Others may have pervasive effects but not have intellectual functioning impaired. For instance a child may have long term speech and language problems as a result of damage to the brain but may regain skills in other areas. A child is only considered to have intellectual impairment rather than brain damage when "he has lower than average skills in all areas of development as a result of the injury" (Smith,1993).

Infections can affect young infants and if severe cause brain damage and intellectual impairment as a result. Such infections include viral meningitis and encephalitis.

Serious head injuries or severe blood lose that leaves the brain starved for oxygen can result in intellectual impairment. Car accidents and falls are the most common causes for these type of injuries, however physical abuse (eg. "shaken baby" syndrome) can also cause brain damage.

Tumors are relatively rare in children, however if a tumor can put enough pressure on surrounding tissue it can cause damage. If enough area is thus damaged then intellectual impairment can result.

Intellectual impairment can also develop gradually from lead poisoning. For more information about the affects and treatment of lead poisoning ring the Poisons Info Line on 13 11 26 or The NSW Lead Advisory Service 02 9550 0095.

How does Intellectual Impairment affect a Child?

There are more differences between people with intellectual disabilities than there are similarities. Each person is a unique individual. The only common attribute is a slower rate of learning than average for age.

Umansky and Hooper (1998) suggest that problems in memory and attention are responsible for the difficulties in learning or functioning experienced by people with an intellectual impairment. This is a generalisation and doesn't hold true for all people with an intellectual impairment.

Kozma and Stock (1993) state that intellectual impairment may affect attention, memory, abstract thinking, problems solving and generalisation skills. According to these authors, abstract thinking-the ability to grasp concepts, or processes that cannot be directly experienced through the senses-and generalisation-the ability to apply what has been learned to new situations-are typically among the weakest areas for children with intellectual impairment.

Besides intellectual impairment, a number of other factors will affect the potential growth and development. These include:-

- the inborn characteristics of the child-both physical and personal traits, such as temperament, motivation
- the co-existence of an additional disability, such as cerebral palsy or epilepsy for instance
- any medical problems of the child-cardiac problems, for instance, can cause fatigue and slow gross motor development. Similarly ear problems, such as middle ear infections, can affect balance (and cause difficulties if the child is at the stage of learning to sit, stand or walk) or hearing (and delay speech and language development).
- the process of maturation-the central nervous system, for example, continues to develop and mature for some years after birth with the process of myelination of nerve cells continuing on into early adulthood.
- the environment-the stimulation provided by the things and the people that surround a child. Parents and other carers can make a significant impact on the rate and quality of a child's development.

With the interplay of all these variables affecting development it is impossible to predict precisely a child's eventual potential, particularly while a child is still only young.

What are the Developmental Needs of Children with an Intellectual Impairment?

Every child is unique. Even among children with the same condition or disability, there can be vast differences in their specific support needs. Whilst saying this it should be remembered that children with an intellectual impairment are still children and everything we know about children's developmental needs is still applicable. In planning developmentally appropriate programmes and activities for children with intellectual impairments caregivers need to apply their knowledge of children's general needs and their understanding of child development. Programs also need to allow children to gain from experiences at all stages of the learning cycle.

All children, whether they have a disability or not, have a number of physical and psychological needs that must be meet if they are to survive, thrive and develop to their optimum potential. Children's general needs are defined by Allen and Marotz (1994) as:-

Basic Physical Needs

- shelter, protection from harm.
- nourishment, an appropriate diet
- warmth, adequate clothing
- preventative health and dental care
- cleanliness
- rest and activity in balance

Psychological Needs

- affection and consistency-nurturing parents and caregivers who can be depended upon to be there for the child
- security and trust-familiar surroundings with parents and caregivers who respond reliably and appropriately to the child's needs
- appropriate adult expectations as to what the child can and can not do at each level of development *(as Miller reminds us we should be looking at stages not ages)*

The Need to Learn

- freedom to explore and experiment with necessary limits clearly and consistently maintained

- access to developmentally appropriate experiences and play materials
- an appropriate match between a child's skills levels and the materials and experiences available to the child-just enough for newness to challenge, but not so much that the child feels overwhelmed, incapable or excessively frustrated.
- errors, mistakes and failures treated as important steps in the learning process, never as reasons for ridiculing or giving up on a child
- adults who demonstrate in everyday life the appropriate behaviours expected of the child, be it attitudes, behaviours or skills. Remember children model their behaviour from the adults around them and caregivers can do a great deal to accelerate children through the learning process

The Need for Respect

- a respectful and helpful environment in which the child's efforts are encouraged, approved and aided: "You packed up the blocks. Good job. Shall I put them in the cupboard for you?"
- respect for accomplishments whether large or small, for errors as well as successes: "Well look at you. You put on you cardigan all by yourself." (No mention of the button holes that were missed.)
- recognition that accomplishment, the "I can do it" attitude, is the major and most essential component of a child's self-esteem: " You're really getting good at building block towers."
- sincere attention to what the child is doing well; using descriptive praise to help children learn to recognise and respect their accomplishments; "You got your shoes on the right feet all be yourself."
- awareness of the tremendous amount of effort and concentration that goes into acquiring developmental skill; positive responses to each small step along the way as a child works towards mastery of a complex

skill such as self-feeding from a spoon. "Right! Just a little yoghurt on the spoon so it stays on."

Feelings of frustration, failure or rejection can limit motivation. As children with an intellectual impairment can take longer to respond or to do things, they are at risk of developing such negative feelings. It is therefore very important that caregivers acknowledge, encourage and praise a child's efforts.

As well as having the same general needs, children with an intellectual impairment also go through the same process of development as other children. That is, they go through the same general sequence of development and their progress is dotted with stops and starts.

Development occurs in stages. It usually takes place in an orderly, sequential fashion with later developing skills building upon earlier skills. For example, children most often learn to babble first and then speak single words before learning to speak in sentences. Difficulties with motor skills however can disrupt this process. Low muscle tone, for instance, can make it very difficult for a child to crawl so the child may go from sitting to standing and walking before developing the strength and co-ordination to crawl. Even so the child's development has progressed from simpler skills to more complex or advanced skills.

Child development usually proceeds as a series of stops and starts. The "stops" are periods when children do not appear to be achieving new skills. These lulls in development are very necessary for children. During such phases they consolidate what they have already learned by practising the skills they already have. In addition, although it may not be apparent to the observer, they are beginning to develop components of future skills. Take for example a child who pulls himself up to standing but does not seem to progress to taking that first step. If watched carefully, you will probably find that while the child is simply repeating the same action he is getting more muscular control and co-ordination of the movement and increasing in confidence. This may be necessary for the child to feel ready to go on and extend from that skill.

Preoccupation with one area of development can also result in slower progression in other developmental areas. While a child is intent on practising or extending gross motor skills, for example, she may be less interested in fine motor or language skills and this would still be considered a normal part of development.

Similarly, a child with intellectual impairment will go through the same cycle of learning as all children do. The cycle of learning involves awareness, exploration, inquiry and utilisation (Carata, Workshop notes, 1999).

- Awareness-physical awareness comes from sensory experience, things we see, hear, smell, taste, touch and feel. That may elicit emotional awareness-curiosity, motivation, pleasure, discomfort, fear, security, etc.
- Exploration-manipulation of information or sensory experience to try to determine what possibilities it has.
- Inquiry-the process to understand the classes of information, to generalise or utilise previous information for comparison
- Utilisation-trying out what has been learnt. Applying it to different situations.

This cycle of learning occurs over and over again and it is important to recognise where the child is in that cycle when they are learning a new skill or knowledge. Programs need to be designed to allow children to gain experiences at all stages of the learning cycle.

For a variety of reasons, children with intellectual impairment might not get as much out of an experience as their peers and may need encouragement and time to experience and explore before being expected to participate in higher skills levels.

Promoting and Facilitating Development

To promote a child's development it can be useful to incorporate the following:-

Bear in mind that the child is part of a family. More will be achieved for a child if caregivers work collaboratively with parents to determine needs and to set learning goals. Begin by showing your respect for their role as parents. Take time over the enrolment interview. Ask them what their goals are for the child and how they hope their child will benefit by being in child care. Communicate the message that this is a team effort, that as a caregiver you know about child development but they are the experts on their child.

Try not to be judgmental. Parents have other responsibilities and concerns in addition to the needs of their child. Their energy levels will fluctuate. Focus on the mutual concern for the child.

Get to know the child well. Get information on the child from parents. Observe the child carefully to find out what they can do, what they enjoy, and what they are interested in.

Gather information about the child from as many sources as possible. Parents know their child best but, for a variety of reasons, may feel reluctant to share their knowledge with caregivers. Ask parent permission to contact professionals working with the child. Older children often understand their problems well and may be prepared to discuss their needs directly with caregivers.

Develop roles for yourself. Thinking of yourself as a coach for example, can bring forth some new qualities and free you up to interact with a child in a different way.

Focus on the child, not their condition/ disability. Focussing on the problems may not be the best way to help a child and it may even disadvantage the child by making more of their "differences". That is not to say that we should not learn about how the condition effects the child, but caregivers need to keep the focus on the child, the whole child.

Focus on strengths and accept individual differences. Focussing on what the child can do rather than what a child can't do, will go a long way towards building a child's confidence and motivation to take on new learning. Also your acceptance and respect for differences between children may affect other children's attitude to the child.

Try to ensure that you connect with the child. The best way to let a child know that you care about them is to give them your full attention. Making eye contact reassures a child that you know they are there. In addition, making eye contact before you start to speak can help a child to tune in and realise that you are talking to them. Provide time to allow the child to respond and acknowledge any efforts by the child to communicate to you.

See every child's potential. If you sincerely believe that a child can succeed, regardless of any challenges they may face, you can be of great service to them in their development. If your words, tone of voice, facial expression and posture all consistently reflect this belief, the child will believe you mean it. This will help him/ her to believe in themselves.

Offer a variety of experiences. Like all children, children with an intellectual experience need caregivers who make sure that they have interesting things to look at, touch, smell, and taste. Even if a child does not show much interest in the world around them, keep offering a variety of experiences. Try pointing out things in the environment and talk about them, even though the child might not understand right now. Progress might be slow, but it is important for the child's development. For a child who has limited mobility, trying changing their position so they can see around the room from different perspectives.

Boredom and Curiosity

There is a delicate interplay between boredom and curiosity which governs what infants pay attention to and hence, what they learn about and what further cognitive abilities they develop.

Each stage has its attention getting stimuli. Typically a six month old will be eager to attend to a lively conversation or a smiling face, a mechanical rabbit can hold the attention of a toddler, as can a computer game for a school aged child. In short attention preferences change with age or maturity.

One theory suggests that a factor underlying developmental changes in attention preferences is "optimal schema discrepency". By attending to something repeatedly, the individual develops a mental image or "schema" of it. Once a schema has been built up, attention to the object is no longer necessary and boredom sets in. But if some minor change in the object arises, curiosity is piqued again and attention is mobilised until these new features become incorporated into the old schema.

Major changes sometimes capture attention too, but if they are too drastic they may be ignored, either because fear is evoked instead or because there is a lack of a schema to relate the changes to (Peterson, 1989).

Use visual materials and real objects as often as possible. Children with intellectual impairment typically think in very concrete terms-it is easier to think about something they have actually seen, felt or touched than it is for them to think about something they don't have any concept of. Using real objects, physically doing something, will promote faster learning then simply talking about it.

Give the child opportunities to make choices and develop their self esteem. Over-protection can prevent a child from finding out what they can do and may affect their self-perception. In our rush to save time, we sometimes do things for a child so we can move on to do the next thing. Long term goals are best served if we allow the time and encourage independence, self-care, responsibility and autonomy.

Plan beforehand how you might modify an activity for a child.

Keep instructions simple. Give instructions in short simple sentences. Add gestures to give more visual clues if it will help the child understand. Caregivers may need to be prepared to repeat instructions, give instructions one step at a time, show the child what to do and physically guide a child through activities if necessary. Allowing a child to watch and follow peers can also be a useful strategy.

Set achievable tasks. Activities should allow for each child to have success. If catching a ball is too hard at first try using small bean bags or let the child sit with legs outstretched and roll the ball. Build up success.

Break down a skill or activity into small steps. Allow a child to learn parts of a task or activity until they are ready to try more. Show them what you expect and let them gain confidence in their skill. Encourage any attempts made by the child to increase their independence in task.

Provide children with appropriate challenges. Children need challenges in order to realise their potential. Create environments and activities in which each child has the opportunity to face appropriate challenges. If the challenge is too low, a child may quickly become bored and lose their motivation to try. If it's too high, a child may get discouraged and give up trying.

Give honest and realistic encouragement. This is a natural and powerful way to communicate to a child that we believe in him or her. Frequent and sincere encouragement can make an enormous difference to a child's development. It can inspire a child to jump in and try their best. Providing a child with some direct attention can encourage a child who is hesitant or holding back. Encouragement is also important for a child who is having difficulties with something they are learning and feeling discouraged.

Reinforce learning. Use different methods, materials and situations to reinforce learning rather than just talking about things. Teaching a child to count, for example, could involve singing the numbers, counting off blocks (or anything else that is handy) and counting paving steps. Each approach reinforcing the others.

Children with an intellectual impairment can have trouble generalising their learning. A child might know how to turn off and on a light switch but not readily understand that it is the same principle when turning off and on an electronic toy. By using different modes to reinforce learning you will also be teaching how something that applies in one situation may be applicable in another.

Give specific feedback. If a child is having difficulty learning something, observe what they are doing and let them know what they can do to be more successful. Perhaps even demonstrate the action, or physically guide them through the part they are having trouble with. Use a positive tone and offer encouragement. Your goal is to reassure the child that they can do it and to give them a better understanding of what is required.

Allow plenty of opportunity for practice. A child with intellectual impairment may need more opportunities to practice before they learn a new skill. If a child shows interest it could be a good time to repeat an activity.

Include activities that promote listening and attending skills as these are important for children to learn.

Use play to encourage all areas of development. Do not focus all your attention on areas that cause a child problems.

Use age appropriate toys to give developmentally appropriate experiences. You can generally find age appropriate substitutes for a toy a child likes to play with. For instance, a 3 year old who likes a crib-side activity board could be offered a box of items that do the same sorts of things-bells, dials, etc.

Vary active and quiet activities. Some children have short attention spans, so for them you may need to plan brief activities and plan to switch between active and quiet ones. Also remember to plan "wind-down activities before rest time.

Be sensitive to the needs of other children. Answer their questions openly and honestly. Help children to understand and respect differences in appearance, behaviour and ability.

Have fun. Don't get so serious that you forget to share happy times. Have fun with children.

A Differentiated Model of Giftedness and Talent

Gagné's Differentiated Model of Giftedness and Talent (DMGT) proposes a clear distinction between the two basic concepts of giftedness and talent:

Giftedness designates the possession and use of untrained and spontaneously expressed natural abilities (called aptitudes or gifts), in at least one ability domain, to a degree that places an individual at least among the top 10% of age peers.

Talent designates the superior mastery of systematically developed abilities (or skills) and knowledge in at least one field of human activity to a degree that places an individual within at least the top 10% of age-peers who are or have been active in that field or fields.

(iv) Giftedness and Talent

Gifts

The DMGT proposes five aptitude domains intellectual, creative, socioaffective, perceptual/motor, and "others." These natural abilities, whose development and level of expression is partially controlled by the individual's genetic endowment, can be observed in every task children are confronted with in the course of their schooling; for instance, the intellectual abilities needed to learn to read, speak a foreign language or understand new mathematical concepts, the creative abilities needed to solve many different kinds of problems and produce original work in science, literature and art, the physical abilities involved in sport, music or woodwork, or the social abilities which children use daily in interactions with classmates, teachers, and parents.

High aptitudes or gifts can be observed more easily and directly in young children because environmental influences and systematic learning have exerted their moderating influence in a limited way only. However, they still show themselves in older children and even in adults through the facility and speed with which individuals acquire new skills in any given field of human activity. The easier or faster the learning process, the higher the natural abilities. It is these high natural abilities that many laypersons call "talent" or "natural talent".

Talents

As defined in the DMGT, talents progressively emerge from the transformation of these high aptitudes into the well-trained and systematically developed skills characteristic of a particular field of human activity or performance. These fields can be extremely diverse. Some of the many talent fields relevant to school-aged youth. A given natural ability can express itself in many different ways, depending on the field of activity adopted by the individual. For example, dexterity as a natural physical ability can be modelled into the particular manual skills of a pianist, a painter or a video game player.

Similarly, intelligence as a natural ability can be modelled into the scientific reasoning of a chemist, the game analysis of chess player or the strategic planning of an athlete.

Talent Development

In the DMGT, high natural abilities or aptitudes act as the "raw material" or the constituent elements of talents. It follows from this relationshipthat talent necessarily implies the presence of high natural abilities; one cannot be talented without first being gifted. The reverse is not true, however. It is possible for high natural abilities to remain simply as gifts and not be translated into talents, as witnessed by the well-known phenomenon of academic underachievement among intellectually gifted children. The process of talent development manifests itself when the child or adolescent engages in systematic learning, training and practising; the higher the level of talent sought, the more intensive these three activities will be.

Intrapersonal Catalysts

The developmental process is facilited (or hindered) by the action of two types of catalysts: intrapersonal and environmental. The intrapersonal catalysts are subdivided into physical and psychological factors, all of them under the partial influence of the genetic endowment. Among the psychological catalysts, motivation and volition play a crucial role in initiating the process of talent development, guiding it, and sustaining it through obstacles, boredom and occasional failure. Hereditary predispositions to behave in certain ways (temperament), as well as acquired styles of behaviour (e.g., traits and disorder), also contribute significantly to support and stimulate, or slow down and even block, talent development.

Environmental Catalysts

The environment manifests its significant impact in many different ways. The surroundings exert their influence both at a macroscopic level (e.g.geographic, demographic, sociological) and in a more microscopic framework (size of family, socioeconomic status, etc). Many different persons, not only parents and teachers but also siblings and peers, may exert positive or negative influences on the process of talent development. Gifted education programmes within or outside the school belong to the category of undertakings; they are a more systematic form of intervention to foster or hinder talent development. Finally, significant events (the death of a parent, winning a prize or award, suffering a major accident) can influence markedly the course of talent development.

Chance

Chance could be added as a fifth causal factor associated with the environment; but, strictly speaking, it is more exactly a characteristic of some of the elements placed in any of the other four categories (e.g., the "chance" of being born in a particular family; the "chance" of the school in which the child is enrolled deciding to develop a programme for gifted and talented students). Chance is also a major causal factor in the determination of the genetic endowment.

Prevalence

Any definition of normative concepts must specify how subjects differ from the norm, and what it means in terms of the prevalence of the population subsumed under the label. In the DMGT, the threshold for both the giftedness and talent concepts is placed at around the 90th percentile (approximately 1.3 standard deviations above the mean); in other words, those who belong to approximately the top 10% of the relevant reference group in terms of ability (for giftedness) or achievement (for talent) may receive the relevant label.

Levels

It must be clearly noted, however, that this generous choice of threshold is counterbalanced by a recognition of levels or degrees of giftedness or talent. Within the 10% population of "basically" gifted or talented persons, the DMGT recognizes four progressively more selective subgroups. They are labelled "moderately" (top 1%), "highly" (top 1 in a thousand), "exceptionally "(top 1:10 000) and 'extremely" (top 1: 100 000) respectively. In the cognitive domain, the five groups correspond to approximate 1Qs of 120, 135, 145, 155, and 165.

As in other fields of special education, the nature of the intervention programme which a school develops for gifted or talented students should be influenced by the level of the students' giftedness or talent as well as the domain(s) or field(s) in which it is sited.

Giftedness Characteristics

The attributes and issues of the gifted do not disappear in adulthood. However, indicators of giftedness are frequently less obvious than in childhood, often hidden within a matrix of defensive cover-ups developed over the years to offset the powerful expectations of the norm group.

Many gifted adults do not live and work in an atmosphere of understanding and support that allows them to feel valued and to make full use of their talents.

Characteristics often experienced by gifted individuals:

Are you a good problem solver? Can you concentrate for long periods of time?

Are you perfectionistic?

Do you persevere with your interests?

Are you an avid reader?

Do you have a vivid imagination?

Do you enjoy doing jigsaw puzzles?

Often connect seemingly unrelated ideas?

Do you enjoy paradoxes?

Do you set high standards for yourself?

Do you have a good long-term memory? Are you deeply compassionate?

Do you have persistent curiosity?

Do you have an excellent sense of humor?

Are you a keen observer?

Do you have a love of mathematics?

Do you need periods of contemplation?

Do you search for meaning in your life?

Are you aware of things that others are not?

Are you fascinated by words?

Are you highly sensitive?

Do you have strong moral convictions?

Do you often feel out-of-sync with others?

Are you perceptive or insightful?

Do you often question rules or authority?

Do you have organized collections?

Do you thrive on challenge?

Do you have extraordinary abilities and deficits?

Do you learn new things rapidly?

Feel overwhelmed by many interests/abilities? Do you have a great deal of energy?

Often take a stand against injustice?

Do you feel driven by your creativity?

Love ideas and ardent discussion?

Were you advanced developmentally in childhood?

Have unusual ideas or perceptions?

Are you a complex person?

"If 75% of these characteristics fit you, you are probably a gifted adult.

"Giftedness was not commonly identified in children until recently, so many adults are unaware that they were gifted as children. But even those who were identified tend to believe their giftedness disappeared before adulthood."

Definitions of Gifted

Defining the term *gifted* is no easy task. Numerous definitions have been suggested, but no single definition of giftedness is accepted by everyone or even by a majority of people. Because so many definitions exist, people often get confused over just what it means to be gifted. Not only that, parents and teachers sometimes find it difficult to communicate because what they say is based on different definitions! To help eliminate the confusion, it's a good idea to understand where the term came from and the different perspectives that led to the many definitions that exist today.

Origin of the Term Gifted

The term *gifted children* was first used in 1869 by Francis Galton. He referred to adults who demonstrated exceptional talent in some area as gifted, for example, a gifted chemist. Children could inherit the potential to become a gifted adult, and Galton referred to these children as gifted children. Lewis Terman expanded Galton's view of gifted children to include high IQ. In the early 1900s, he began his a long-term study of gifted children, whom he defined as children with IQs of 140 or more. His study found that IQ alone could not predict success in adulthood. Leta Hollingworth, too, believed that the potential to be gifted was inherited. However, she felt that providing a nurturing home and school environment were also important in the development of that potential. In 1926, she published her book, *Gifted Children, Their Nature and Nurture*, and the term *gifted* has been used ever since to refer to children of high potential.

Different Definitions of Gifted

The early uses of the term *gifted* have led to different uses of the word and different ways of defining giftedness. Galton's view left us with the idea that a gifted person is one with a gift, a special talent demonstrated in adulthood. People today may use *gifted child* the way Galton used the term *gifted adult*. In other words, to be a gifted child is to demonstrate an exceptional talent in a particular area. Terman's view led to definitions of gifted, which not only included high IQ, but also the notion that giftedness should be a predictor of adult achievement. Hollingworth's view, however, led to definitions of gifted as childhood potential that must be nurtured in order for it to be developed in adulthood.

- *Giftedness as Predictor of Adult Achievement:* Definitions of *gifted* that consider adult achievement add factors such as task commitment or motivation. Those who define gifted this way begin by looking at adults who have demonstrated exceptional achievement in their chosen field, like Einstein, and work backward to see what traits other than high IQ that adult had in childhood. A child without that trait, regardless of IQ, is not gifted according to these definitions. Renzulli's Three-Ring Conception of Giftedness is an example.
- *Giftedness as Potential That Must be Nurtured:* Definitions that consider giftedness as potential to be developed make a distinction between what a child is capable of achieving and what the child will achieve. The fact that a child has exceptional potential is part of what makes him or her gifted. The child's environment determines whether potential leads to achievement, so people who define gifted this way stress the importance of providing an appropriate environment. Gagne's Differentiated Model of Giftedness and Talent is an example.
- *Giftedness as Asynchronous Development:* Linda Silverman added a new dimension to definitions of *gifted* when she included the uneven development of gifted children, which she called asynchronous development. Definitions of gifted that include asynchronous development consider not only IQ and talent, but also emotional traits of gifted children, such as heightened sensitivity. The definition developed by the Columbus Group is an example of this type of definition.
- *Columbus Group Definition:* "Giftedness is 'asynchronous development' in which advanced cognitive abilities and heightened intensity combine to create inner experiences and awareness that are qualitatively different from the norm. This asynchrony increases with higher intellectual capacity. The uniqueness of the gifted renders them particularly vulnerable and

requires modifications in parenting, teaching and counseling in order for them to develop optimally." (Columbus Group, 1991)

- *School-Based Definitions:* Schools may use a definition of *gifted* based on relative ability. Students are identified by how well they perform compared to other students in the school. Students in the top 5 or 10 (or some other number) percent are those singled out as needing a curriculum more challenging than the regular curriculum. *Gifted* in this definition is relative because a student who is identified as gifted in one school may not be identified as gifted in another school, leaving parents confused.

Knowing which definition of *gifted* a teacher or principal is using can help make communication less frustrating and more productive.

(v) Autism B

Autism is a brain development disorder characterized by impaired social interaction and communication, and by restricted and repetitive behavior. These signs all begin before a child is three years old. Autism affects many parts of the brain; how this occurs is not understood. The autism spectrum disorders (ASD) also include the related conditions Asperger syndrome and PDD-NOS, which have fewer signs and symptoms.

Autism has a strong genetic basis, although the genetics of autism are complex and it is unclear whether ASD is explained more by rare mutations, or by rare combinations of common genetic variants. In rare cases, autism is strongly associated with agents that cause birth defects. Controversies surround other proposed environmental causes, such as heavy metals, pesticides or childhood vaccines; the vaccine hypotheses are biologically implausible and lack convincing scientific evidence. The prevalence of ASD is about 6 per 1,000 people, with about four times as many males as females. The number of people known to have autism has increased dramatically since the 1980s, partly due to changes in diagnostic practice; the question of whether actual prevalence has increased is unresolved.

Parents usually notice signs in the first two years of their child's life. Although early behavioral or cognitive intervention can help children gain self-care, social, and communication skills, there is no known cure. Not many children with autism live independently after reaching adulthood, though some become successful. An autistic culture has developed, with some individuals seeking a cure and others believing autism should be tolerated as a difference and not treated as a disorder.

Characteristics

Autism is a highly variable brain development disorder that first appears during infancy or childhood, and generally follows a steady course without remission. Symptoms tend to continue through adulthood, although often in more muted form. It is distinguished not by a single symptom, but by a characteristic triad of symptoms: impairments in social interaction; impairments in communication; and restricted interests and repetitive behavior. Other aspects, such as atypical eating, are also common but are not essential for diagnosis. Autism's individual symptoms occur in the general population and appear not to associate highly, without a sharp line separating pathologically severe from common traits.

Social Development

Social deficits distinguish autism and the related autism spectrum disorders (ASD; see *Classification*) from other developmental disorders. People with autism have social impairments and often lack the intuition about others that many people take for granted. Noted autistic Temple Grandin described her inability to understand the social communication of neurotypicals, or people with normal neural development, as leaving her feeling "like an anthropologist on Mars".

Unusual social development becomes apparent early in childhood. Autistic infants show less attention to social stimuli, smile and look at others less often, and respond less to their own name. Autistic toddlers differ more strikingly from social norms; for example, they have less eye contact and turn taking, and are more likely to communicate by manipulating another person's hand. Three-to five-year-old autistic children are less likely to exhibit social understanding, approach others spontaneously, imitate and respond to emotions, communicate nonverbally, and take turns with others. However, they do form attachments to their primary caregivers. They display moderately less attachment security than usual, although this feature disappears in children with higher mental development or less severe ASD. Older children and adults with ASD perform worse on tests of face and emotion recognition.

Contrary to common beliefs, autistic children do not prefer being alone. Making and maintaining friendships often proves to be difficult for those with autism. For them, the quality of friendships, not the number of friends, predicts how lonely they feel. Functional friendships, such as those resulting in invitations to parties, may affect their quality of life more deeply.

There are many anecdotal reports, but few systematic studies, of aggression and violence in individuals with ASD. The limited data suggest that, in children with mental retardation, autism is associated with aggression, destruction of property, and tantrums. A 2007 study interviewed parents of 67 children with ASD and reported that about two-thirds of the children had periods of severe tantrums and about one-third had a history of aggression, with tantrums significantly more common than in children with a history of language impairment. A 2008 Swedish study found that, of individuals aged 15 or older discharged from hospital with a diagnosis of ASD, those who committed violent crimes were significantly more likely to have other psychopathological conditions such as psychosis.

Communication

About a third to a half of individuals with autism do not develop enough natural speech to meet their daily communication needs. Differences in communication may be present from the first year of life, and may include delayed onset of babbling, unusual gestures, diminished responsiveness, and vocal patterns that are not synchronized with the caregiver. In the second and third years, autistic children have less frequent and less diverse babbling, consonants, words, and word combinations; their gestures are less often integrated with words. Autistic children are less likely to make requests or share experiences, and are more likely to simply repeat others' words (echolalia) or reverse pronouns. Joint attention seems to be necessary for functional speech, and deficits in joint attention seem to distinguish infants with ASD: for example, they may look at a pointing hand instead of the pointed-at object, and they consistently fail to point at objects in order to comment on or share an experience. Autistic children may have difficulty with imaginative play and with developing symbols into language.

In a pair of studies, high-functioning autistic children aged 8–15 performed equally well, and adults better than individually matched controls at basic language tasks involving vocabulary and spelling. Both autistic groups performed worse than controls at complex language tasks such as figurative language, comprehension and inference. As people are often sized up initially from their basic language skills, these studies suggest that people speaking to autistic individuals are more likely to overestimate what their audience comprehends.

Repetitive Behavior

Autistic individuals display many forms of repetitive or restricted behavior, which the Repetitive Behavior Scale-Revised (RBS-R) categorizes as follows.

- Stereotypy is repetitive movement, such as hand flapping, making sounds, head rolling, or body rocking.
- Compulsive behavior is intended and appears to follow rules, such as arranging objects in a certain way.
- Sameness is resistance to change; for example, insisting that the furniture not be moved or refusing to be interrupted.
- Ritualistic behavior involves the performance of daily activities the same way each time, such as an unvarying menu or dressing ritual. This is closely associated with sameness and an independent validation has suggested combining the two factors.

- Restricted behavior is limited in focus, interest, or activity, such as preoccupation with a single television programme or toy.
- Self-injury includes movements that injure or can injure the person, such as eye poking, skin picking, hand biting, and head banging. A 2007 study reported that self-injury at some point affected about 30% of children with ASD.

No single repetitive behavior seems to be specific to autism, but only autism appears to have an elevated pattern of occurrence and severity of these behaviors.

Other Symptoms

Autistic individuals may have symptoms that are independent of the diagnosis, but that can affect the individual or the family. An estimated 0.5% to 10% of individuals with ASD show unusual abilities, ranging from splinter skills such as the memorization of trivia to the extraordinarily rare talents of prodigious autistic savants. Many individuals with ASD show superior skills in perception and attention, relative to the general population. Unusual responses to sensory stimuli are more common and prominent in autistic children, although there is no good evidence that sensory symptoms differentiate autism from other developmental disorders. Differences are greater for under-responsivity (for example, walking into things) than for over-responsivity (for example, distress from loud noises) or for sensation seeking (for example, rhythmic movements). Several studies have reported associated motor problems that include poor muscle tone, poor motor planning, and toe walking; ASD is not associated with severe motor disturbances.

Unusual eating behavior occurs in about three-quarters of children with ASD, to the extent that it was formerly a diagnostic indicator. Selectivity is the most common problem, although eating rituals and food refusal also occur; this does not appear to result in malnutrition. Although some children with autism also have gastrointestinal (GI) symptoms, there is a lack of published rigorous data to support the theory that autistic children have more or different GI symptoms than usual; studies report conflicting results, and the relationship between GI problems and ASD is unclear. At some point in childhood, about two-thirds of individuals with ASD are affected by sleep problems; these most commonly include symptoms of insomnia such as difficulty in falling asleep, frequent nocturnal awakenings, and early morning awakenings. Sleep problems are associated with difficult behaviors and family stress, and are often a focus of clinical attention over and above the primary ASD diagnosis.

Parents of children with ASD have higher levels of stress. Siblings of children with ASD report greater admiration of and less conflict with the affected sibling than siblings of unaffected children or those with Down syndrome; siblings of individuals with ASD have greater risk of negative well-being and poorer sibling relationships as adults.

Classification

Autism is one of the five pervasive developmental disorders (PDD), which are characterized by widespread abnormalities of social interactions and communication, and severely restricted interests and highly repetitive behavior. These symptoms do not imply sickness, fragility, or emotional disturbance.

Of the five PDD forms, Asperger syndrome is closest to autism in signs and likely causes; Rett syndrome and childhood disintegrative disorder share several signs with autism, but may have unrelated causes; PDD not otherwise specified (PDD-NOS; also called *atypical autism*) is diagnosed when the criteria are not met for a more specific disorder. Unlike autism, Asperger's has no substantial delay in language development. The terminology of autism can be bewildering, with autism, Asperger's and PDD-NOS often called the *autism spectrum disorders* (ASD) or sometimes the *autistic disorders*, whereas autism itself is often called *autistic disorder*, *childhood autism*, or *infantile autism*. In this article, *autism* refers to the classic autistic disorder; in clinical practice, though, *autism*, *ASD*, and *PDD* are often used interchangeably. ASD, in turn, is a subset of the broader autism phenotype (BAP), which describes individuals who may not have ASD but do have autistic-like traits, such as avoiding eye contact. The manifestations of autism cover a wide spectrum, ranging from individuals with severe impairments—who may be silent, mentally disabled, and locked into hand flapping and rocking—to high functioning individuals who may have active but distinctly odd social approaches, narrowly focused interests, and verbose, pedantic communication. Sometimes the syndrome is divided into low-, medium-or high-functioning autism (LFA, MFA, and HFA), based on IQ thresholds, or on how much support the individual requires in daily life; these subdivisions are not standardized and are controversial. Autism can also be divided into syndromal and non-syndromal autism; the syndromal autism is associated with severe or profound mental retardation or a congenital syndrome with physical symptoms, such as tuberous sclerosis. Although individuals with Asperger's tend to perform better cognitively than those with autism, the extent of the overlap between Asperger's, HFA, and non-syndromal autism is unclear.

Some studies have reported diagnoses of autism in children due to a loss of language or social skills, as opposed to a failure to make progress, typically from 15 to 30 months of age. The validity of this distinction remains controversial; it is possible that regressive autism is a specific subtype, or that there is a continuum of behaviors between autism with and without regression. Research into causes has been hampered by the inability to identify biologically meaningful subpopulations and by the traditional boundaries between the disciplines of psychiatry, psychology, neurology and pediatrics. Newer technologies such as fMRI can help identify biologically-relevant phenotypes (observable traits) that can be viewed on brain scans, to help further neurogenetic studies of autism. It has been proposed to classify autism using genetics as well as behavior, with the name *Type 1 autism* denoting rare autism cases that test positive for a mutation in the CNTNAP2 gene.

Causes

It has long been presumed that there is a common cause at the genetic, cognitive, and neural levels for autism's characteristic triad of symptoms. However, there is increasing suspicion that autism is instead a complex disorder whose core aspects have distinct causes that often co-occur. Autism has a strong genetic basis, although the genetics of autism are complex and it is unclear whether ASD is explained more by rare mutations with major effects, or by rare multigene interactions of common genetic variants. Complexity arises due to interactions among multiple genes, the environment, and epigenetic factors which do not change DNA but are heritable and influence gene expression. Early studies of twins estimated heritability explains more than 90% of the risk of autism, assuming a shared environment and no other genetic or medical syndromes. However, most of the mutations that increase autism risk have not been identified.

Typically, autism cannot be traced to a Mendelian (single-gene) mutation or to a single chromosome abnormality like Angelman syndrome or fragile X syndrome, and none of the genetic syndromes associated with ASDs has been shown to selectively cause ASD. Numerous candidate genes have been located, with only small effects attributable to any particular gene. The large number of autistic individuals with unaffected family members may result from copy number variations—spontaneous deletions or duplications in genetic material during meiosis. Hence, a substantial fraction of autism cases may be traceable to genetic causes that are highly heritable but not inherited: that is, the mutation that causes the autism is not present in the parental genome.

Autism caused by some rare mutations may disrupt some synaptic pathways, such as those involved with cell adhesion. Gene replacement studies in mice suggest that autistic symptoms are closely related to later developmental steps that depend on activity in synapses and on activity-dependent changes. All known teratogens (agents that cause birth defects) related to the risk of autism appear to act during the first eight weeks from conception, and though this does not exclude the possibility that autism can be initiated or affected later, it is strong evidence that autism arises very early in development. Although evidence for other environmental causes is anecdotal and has not been confirmed by reliable studies, extensive searches are underway. Environmental factors that have been claimed to contribute to or exacerbate autism, or may be important in future research, include certain foods, infectious disease, heavy metals, solvents, diesel exhaust, PCBs, phthalates and phenols used in plastic products, pesticides, brominated flame retardants, alcohol, smoking, illicit drugs, vaccines, and prenatal stress. Parents may first become aware of autistic symptoms in their child around the time of a routine vaccination, and this has given rise to theories that vaccines or their preservatives cause autism. Although these theories lack convincing scientific evidence and are biologically implausible, parental concern about autism has led to lower rates of childhood immunizations and higher likelihood of measles outbreaks.

The Nature of Autism and Autistic Spectrum Disorder

These notes were prepared to provide a brief introduction to the characteristics of Autism and ASD and their management for inclusion in the LEA Handbook on Special Educational Needs.

Nature

The current definition of Autism refers to a pervasive disorder involving severe impairment in the areas of social interaction and communication, stereotyped behaviours, and a preference for sameness. Autism was first described in the 1940s and three particular disabilities have been defined as core and characteristic (the "triad") .....

- *Rigidity of thought and behaviour*, together with limited imagination and imaginative play.
- *Limited verbal and nonverbal communication* with a lack of true two-way interchange, and a weakness in recognising the feelings or perspectives of others.
- *Fragile or absent social relationships* with an appearance of aloofness or indifference.

The concept of "spectrum" indicates the wide range of levels of difficulty or of permutations of symptoms that may apply to all children diagnosed with autism, but these core characteristics will be observable to some degree in all cases. At the level of marked or severe difficulties, the children are likely to need specialist educational provision, but children towards the higher end of the spectrum will probably benefit from mainstream provision.

Asperger Syndrome, also first described in the 1940s, may be differentiable from high functioning autism in some specific ways, but is usually perceived as a less severe form of the condition whose characteristic signs include marked and sustained impairment in social interaction or play, restricted and repetitive behaviours and activities, particular interests to the exclusion of all others, and a strong dislike of changes to routine. Motor delays or clumsiness are commonly associated with this syndrome.

However, children with Asperger Syndrome have adequate vocabulary and expressive language, may have cognitive scores in the average range or above, and do not commonly experience additional learning difficulties. Consequently, diagnosis may be delayed until the difficulties with social interaction become evident, and the children are at increased risk for emotional or stress-related disorders as a result of the "invisibility" of the condition and the inappropriate expectations that may be applied.

Approximately 4 times more boys than girls are affected by autistic spectrum disorders.

Key Issues

Many of the (social) anomalies characteristic of autism may reflect a deficit in *Theory of Mind* in that the individual cannot readily appreciate the feelings, beliefs, or knowledge held by other people (and perhaps cannot fully recognise or interpret his or her own thought processes). Therefore, there will be stilted communication, a lack of self consciousness, and weakness in understanding or entering social situations.

Stimulus Over-Selectivity refers to the trend to respond only to part of a stimulus rather than the whole object or to the whole social setting. This may explain why some individuals with ASD are not confused by optical illusions or why they may be unusually proficient at tasks like copying patterns since they are able to examine the stimulus in small bits at a time. Along the same lines, there may be a limit in *Central Coherence* which implies an inability to use context to make full sense of what is presented (eg words with similar appearance but different meanings and pronunciations like " There is a *tear* in my shirt /There is a *tear* in my eye " may present problems because of the lack of rapid scanning of the whole phrase or sentence to identify how to deal with the given word).

Executive Functioning, ie the ability to plan ahead, or to bring together bits of information from different sources, and to generalise or learn for experience, may be limited.

ASD is noted for idiosyncrasies in *Attention.* In very young children, the lack of capacity with regard to gaze monitoring and, therefore, to *sharing* attention may explain some of the social interactional problems. The absence of shared attention by around 18 months of age is a diagnostic pointer. Further, the individual with ASD may be able to focus well upon certain activities, especially those that he or she has chosen, but will probably have problems in *shifting* attention from one task to the next, especially if the type of attention required is also changing. For example, to move from some individually-pursued and quiet task to a whole class activity involving verbal interchange will be challenging.

Literalness or *Concreteness* in receptive language implies that nothing can be taken for granted in the individual's understanding of instructions that are not specific, and humour or figurative speech will be very confusing. A request such as " Would you like to finish that writing now? " may only evoke the answer "No" .... (and this might be wrongly interpreted by the teacher as provocative when this was not intended).

Further, this style might underlie the weaknesses in imaginative play so that, eg, a cardboard tube is a cardboard tube and not a telescope ; and there is a common need to see some direct purpose in activities so that certain games, such as football involving rushing to one end of the playground only to rush back again, would be seen as pointless by many ASD children.

Intervention and Management

A common theme still concerns the need for early diagnosis and for equally early intervention, and a range of approaches is available to use with young children with ASD. Significant components in such programmes include the understanding of, and involvement of the parents or carers in, the goals and strategies, consistency of application, and the capacity to generalise the skills learnt to different settings and occasions.

Early provision and structured support may not lead to a cure for autism, but they can enhance progress, reduce pressure and stress upon the child, and limit the incidence of maladaptive behaviours. Mainstream inclusion is a viable prospect for those children with higher functioning autism or Asperger Syndrome, but flexibility of approaches and raised awareness of autistic "style" among staff (and, perhaps, peers as well) is required.

The major issue is concerned with reducing any stress in the children which might otherwise stem from some uncertainty over what is expected or from communication breakdown, and which might be reflected in what appears to be non-compliant or challenging behaviour. The programme for any given child will be based upon individual observations and assessments, but *basic* strategies could well include some or many of the following :

- Providing a clear structure and set daily routines
- Visual timetables and picture boards to provide checks on tasks to be covered
- Providing warnings of impending changes of activity or interruption to routine
- Use of clear and unambiguous language
- Addressing requests or directions directly to the child, and not assuming that s(he) will adhere to group directions or that any incidental learning will occur
- Teaching what "finished" means
- Repeating instructions and checking understanding
- Using a range of means of presenting ideas .... visual, peer-modelling, etc.

- Specific teaching and practising of social skills like turn-taking, and of theory of mind skills
- Minimising of distractors
- Exploring the use of computer-based learning and word-processing
- Not insisting on those activities which the child particularly dislikes, such as games.

Conclusion

A child with ASD can be successfully included within mainstream classes but this will depend on the willingness to adopt a whole-school approach whereby all staff are aware of the child's needs and style, and can pursue shared targets and approaches. The child is not going to be made ordinary so that it may be necessary long term to individualise the programme for social and scholastic progress ... ie seek to modify the environment rather than the child.

Concept, Nature and Characteristics of Multiple Disabilities

Persons with *severe disabilities* are: "individuals of all ages who require extensive ongoing support in more than one major life activity in order to participate in integrated community settings and to enjoy a quality of life that is available to citizens with fewer or no disabilities" (TASH). Mental retardation is regarded as a characteristic common to those with severe disabilities. Most severely disabled individuals are limited in their ability to communicate, though these skills can become functional with appropriate intervention. In addition, these individuals often have medical conditions or physical limitations that affect their movement, vision, or hearing.

Persons with *multiple disabilities* have a combination of two or more serious disabilities (e.g., cognitive, movement, sensory), such as mental retardation with cerebral palsy. The U.S. federal government definition includes those who have more than one impairment, "the combination of which causes such severe educational needs that they cannot be accommodated in special education programmes solely for one of the impairments" (Code of Federal Regulations, 1999, Vol. 34 Sec. 300.7). (Dual sensory impairment, or deaf-blindness, is defined as a separate disability group.) Multiple disabilities have interactional, rather than additive, effects, making instruction and learning complex.

In 1996 Fred Orelove and Dick Sobsey defined this group as individuals with mental retardation who require extensive or pervasive supports and who also possess one or more significant motor or sensory impairments and/or special health care needs. These physical and medical problems result in the presence of two or more of the following characteristics: restriction of movement, skeletal deformities, sensory disorders, seizure disorders, lung and breathing control, or other medical problems related to these characteristics, such as skin breakdown or bladder infections.

The two groups overlap somewhat in definition. *Multiple disabilities,* depending upon the definition used, may or may not include mental retardation as one disability, while *severe disabilities* requires mental retardation but does not require an additional disability. Some movement disabilities are associated with mental retardation; for example, 60 to 70 percent of those with cerebral palsy have some degree of mental retardation. However, a child with cerebral palsy who does not meet the cognitive requirements of mental retardation might fit the federal definition of multiple disabilities, due to having movement and communication disabilities, but not the definition of severe disabilities. Most individuals who have multiple disabilities also fit the criteria for severe disabilities, while not all with severe disabilities have multiple disabilities.

The primary measures used to diagnose these individuals are individual intelligence tests and tests of adaptive behavior. Early assessment of movement limitations, muscle tone and flexibility, seizure activity, breathing control, sucking and swallowing, vision and hearing, and genetic makeup are also, and prenatal assessment of genetic material or physical identification of deformities via sonograms may be conducted. Accurate psychological testing of these individuals is challenging due to their frequent limitations in controlled movement, vision, hearing, communication, or cooperative behavior. Thus, interviews with family members and educators regarding the person's adaptive behavior skills (i.e., communication, self-care, home living, social skills, community use, self-direction, health and safely, functional academics, leisure, and work) may be more informative and reliable than a norm-based IQ or achievement score.

Definitions of this highly variable group with both severe and multiple disabilities are less precise than some other disability groups, making an estimate of their prevalence difficult. Prevalence ranges from less than .25 percent to .50 percent of the population; and is considered relatively uniform across socioeconomic classes.

Persons with severe and multiple disabilities may carry a variety of diagnostic labels, including:(1) severe or profound levels of mental retardation (IQ scores below 40); (2) mental retardation that requires extensive or pervasive supports for an extended time; (3) autism, childhood disintegrative disorder, or Rett syndrome (several types of autism spectrum disorders); and (4) various genetic disorders accompanied by extensive mental retardation (e.g., Tay-Sachs disease, untreated phenylketonuria, tuberous sclerosis, Lesch-Nyhan syndrome). Individuals with several autism spectrum disorders, by definition, have significant developmental delays in communication and social interaction, and may exhibit extensive limitations in many adaptive skills. Thus, their disability may be extensive enough to fit the definition for mental retardation and severe disabilities, though this is not true for all persons identified with autism (e.g., Asperger's syndrome).

A Brief History of Education of People with Disabilities

In the United States individuals with severe and multiple disabilities are legally entitled to education and other support services; however, these groups do not have the same rights in much of the world. Those with severe and multiple disabilities are identified early in life by their noticeable delays in development or by their physical abnormalities. Many require medical interventions not available until recently; thus, earlier in history (and still today in less-developed countries), many with severe disabilities did not live long. Historically, in many cultures, the presence of severe physical abnormalities at birth has been associated with stigma and shame. Current technology has enabled interventions that extend both the length and quality of life of these persons.

Historical reports of individuals with severe and multiple disabilities who survived indicate that they were subjected to the same poor treatment experienced by persons with milder forms of mental retardation. They suffered greatly prior to the 1700s; but from 1700 to the late 1800s there was an optimistic period, due to education methods that were "discovered" by Jean-Marc-Gaspard Itard (1775-1838) and Edouard Seguin (1812-1880) in France and spread to other Western countries. This period was followed by disillusionment with the nonuniform results of these education practices. From the late 1800s through the 1960s there was widespread building of institutions to house these individuals, and then, starting in the 1970s, the institutional population in the United States was gradually reduced, due primarily to a reduction in admissions. Many former residents were relocated to smaller community-based settings, while others remained in their own homes with services and supports provided to their families. Of those now remaining in state institutions, persons over forty who have profound mental retardation and multiple disabilities dominate the population.

Implications of Educational Legislation

Legislation in the early 1970s addressed the right to education and other habilitation services for all individuals with disabilities. In 1975 the Education for All Handicapped Children Act (known since 1990 as the Individuals with Disabilities Education Act, or IDEA) formed the legal basis for public education for all children, including those with severe and multiple disabilities. IDEA added requirements that are especially valuable for these individuals, including:(1) early intervention starting at birth or whenever a disability is suspected; (2) related services such as physical, occupation, and speech and language therapy, including augmentative and alternative communication (AAC) methods; (3) the requirement for a plan and services to facilitate transition to work and adulthood; and (4) a value placed on inclusion in general education with nondisabled peers. Most states provide services to these students until age twenty-two or beyond, focusing upon functional skill development.

Prior to the 1975 law mandating public education for all children, students with severe and multiple disabilities, if educated, received services in institutions or settings operated by parent groups or state mental health departments. When laws enacted in the mid-1970s required publicly funded special education, most schools established programmes for these students but continued to isolate them from their nondisabled peers in separate buildings or self-contained classrooms in elementary schools. Currently in many states, the "least restrictive environment" for most of these students is the age-appropriate school setting alongside nondisabled peers, though not necessarily in the general education classroom. Currently, a majority of these students are served in separate classrooms for most of the school day.

Since 1975 U.S. courts have defined specific portions of special education law. For those with severe and multiple disabilities, several legal battles have resulted in: (1) summer educational programmes being required in many states to lessen or prevent skill regression; (2) interventions that enable students to stay at school (e.g., providing catheterization for those unable to urinate voluntarily); (3) related services and technology to assist with movement, positioning, speech, and alternate forms of communication; (4) the mandate to educate all students with disabilities, and not limit services based on an assessment of educational potential; and (5) the provision of regular opportunities for interaction with nondisabled peers and inclusion in general education classrooms-or justification for not providing these opportunities. While all states are required to provide a free and appropriate education for these students, there are many differences in how localities implement the law and thus in the actual quality of educational services for these students.

Educating Students with Severe and Multiple Disabilities

When compared to their peers, most students with severe and multiple disabilities learn more slowly, forget more readily, and experience problems generalizing skills from situation to situation. These characteristics are best addressed when educators follow accepted practices. First, the public education of these students must start early and continue at some level throughout life. Second, all students typically need speech and language intervention, while many others will need physical and occupational therapy. Students with sensory impairments may need interpreters and mobility trainers, while some with medical needs may require nursing services or supervision. Third, because the educational teams of students are often large, close collaboration between members is essential if their expertise is to result in improved student functioning. The benefits of integrating therapy into natural activities is widely accepted over the traditional practice of isolated, or pull-out, therapy.

Fourth, curriculum for these students tends to be functional in nature, reflecting skills needed in everyday life across domestic, leisure, school, community, and vocational domains. Students are taught to make choices, communicate in functional ways (which may include AAC methods such as signing, use of pictures, etc.), develop useful skills that reduce their dependence on others, and learn social skills suited to their chronological age. Fifth, when skills are taught in multiple, normalized settings, generalization problems are lessened. Thus, communication and social skills are most effectively taught in the context of interactions with typical classmates, while job and community skills are best taught during community-based instruction.

Trends and Controversies

Several important trends, some considered controversial because they advocate the inclusion of these students in general education with the necessary supports, reflect improvements in the lives of these students. First, through advancements in medicine and technology these individuals not only experience longer lives, but also have better options in mobility, communication, sensory augmentation, and other areas. Second, starting in the 1960s, there has been gradual improvement in societal attitudes toward people with significant disabilities. This has led to legal protections, special education, community living alternatives, supported employment, and an increase in relevant supports. Third, with the Timothy W. decision (*Timothy W. v. Rochester, New Hampshire, School District,* 1989), "free and appropriate education for all" was reaffirmed, schools were required to keep current with best practices for educating those with significant disabilities, and the procedure of selecting who can and cannot learn was declared illegal.

The current trend to include individuals with severe or multiple disabilities in classrooms and community activities with their nondisabled peers has been particularly controversial. Special education placement data show gradual growth of students with disabilities who are placed in a general education setting, but much slower growth for students with severe and multiple disabilities. Schools have complained that they are not able to include these students or provide the necessary supports and services to achieve a meaningful education for all involved. Some general education teachers have communicated an unwillingness to have these students in their classrooms, even with support, and they also may lack the required skills necessary to teach these children in a general education classroom. However, there are numerous examples of schools meaningfully including these students in ways that promote social and educational participation, as well as evidence to support the benefits of inclusion for both students with severe disabilities and typical classmates. More research, the dissemination of information on inclusion, and improvements in teacher training are needed.

Characteristics and Background Information for Students with Multiple Disabilities: Children with multiple disabilities will have a combination of various disabilities that may include: speech, physical mobility, learning, mental retardation, visual, hearing, brain injury and possibly others. Along with multiple disabilities, they can also exhibit sensory losses and behavior and or social problems. Children with multiple disabilities-also referred to as multiple exceptionalities will vary in severity and characteristics. These students may exhibit weakness in auditory processing and have speech limitations. Physical mobility will often be an area of need. These students may have difficulty attaining and remembering skills and or transferring these skills from one situation to another. Support is usually needed beyond the confines of the classroom. There are often medical implications with some of the more severe multiple disabilities which could include students with cerebral palsy and severe autism and brain injuries. There are many educational implications for these students.

Strategies and Modifications

What can you do?

- Early intervention is necessary-as soon as the child begins school
- Involvement of the appropriate professionals, i.e., occupational therapists, speech/language therapists, physio therapists, etc.
- A team approach at the school level involving external agency/community liaison who meet on a regular basis is essential
- The physical arrangement of the classroom will need to best accommodate this child. Consideration of special equipment and assistive technology is essential.
- Integration among their peers is important to assist these students with social development. It's important to integrate multiply disabled children as much as is possible. Research does indicate that when these students attend their community school and participate in the same activities as their peers is social skills develop and are enhanced. (Sometimes these students are place full time in a regular classroom with support, however, in the majority of cases, these students are place in a developmental skills type of classroom with some integration.

- Ensuring that all students demonstrates respect for the multiply disabled student becomes a teacher responsibility and needs to be taken seriously with ongoing activities that develop respect from the other students in the class.
- An Individual Education Plan will need to be carefully planned out and adjusted on a regular basis and will need to be aligned to the child.
- Remember, these children are often completely dependent upon others for most/all of their daily needs.
- Assistive technologies may assist this child and the support team will need to decide which assistive technologies will be most appropriate. (In the IDEA act: ASSISTIVE TECHNOLOGY. Consider whether the child requires assistive technology devices and services. (See §300.346(a)(2)(v).)
- A safety plan will need to be developed and is often included in the IEP.
- Care needs to be given in your expectations of this student to ensure the child doesn't not become frustrated.

Most importantly, these idenditifed children are to be given the same rights as non-identified school age children including screening, evaluation and an appropriate programme and services.

UNIT-II

Educational Psychology and Human Development

Applications of Educational Psychology in the Field of Disabled

Application of scientific method to the study of the behavior of people in instructional settings. Although the behavior of teachers and students is of greatest interest, educational psychologists also study the behavior of other groups, such as teacher aides, infants, migrants, and the aged. The areas covered by educational psychologists inevitably overlap with other areas of psychology, including child and adolescent development, social psychology, psychological testing, and educational counseling.

Development of the Field

The philosophic, rather than the scientific, method was the main mode for inquiry about learning and the mind until 1879, when the German psychologist Wilhelm Wundt founded a laboratory in Leipzig devoted to the scientific study of psychology. Another German psychologist of the time, Hermann Ebbinghaus, developed techniques for the experimental study of memory and forgetting. Before Ebbinghaus, these higher mental processes had never been scientifically studied; the importance of this work for the practical world of schooling was immediately recognized.

At the same time, the American philosopher and psychologist William James started a laboratory at Harvard

University for experimental psychology. James, influenced by Charles Darwin, was interested in how behavior adapted in different environments. This functional approach to behavioral research led James to study practical areas of human endeavor, such as education. In 1899 he published *Talks to Teachers,* in which he discussed the relation between psychology and teaching.

James's student Edward Lee Thorndike is usually considered the first educational psychologist. In his book *Educational Psychology* (1903), Thorndike claimed to report only scientific and quantifiable research. In 1913–14 he published three volumes of material containing reports of virtually all the scientific study in psychology that had relevance to education. Thorndike made major contributions to the study of intelligence and ability testing, mathematics and reading instruction, and the way learning transfers from one situation to another. In addition, he developed an important theory of learning that describes how stimuli and responses are connected.

The field of educational psychology flourished within the progressive movement in education that had begun in the early 20th century. The Great Depression, however, led psychologists to adopt a more modest position about their potential for improving education. From the early 1930s until the mid-1940s, empirical research in educational psychology was conducted by only a few people. Four things changed the outlook of the field again: World War II, the postwar baby boom, the curricula reform movement, and the growing concern for disadvantaged children.

During World War II, psychologists in the armed forces were required to solve practical educational problems. They learned to predict, for instance, who would make a good pilot or radio repairman; they learned to teach skills such as aircraft gunnery and cooking quickly. When the war ended, many of these psychologists turned their attention to testing and instruction in education. Concurrently, as schools were filled by the postwar baby boom, educational psychologists were needed to design and evaluate instructional materials, training programmes, and tests. By the late 1950s, when the U.S. was carrying on a technological race with the Soviet Union, efforts to update the American school curriculum were increased. Educational psychologists worked with leaders in science and mathematics to develop new curricula and new teacher-education programmes. Later, millions of dollars of federal money were allocated to improve the academic performance of disadvantaged students. Educational psychologists were deeply involved in the design and evaluation of programmes to accomplish this goal.

These societal forces led to rapid growth in the field after 1960. Today, more than 3000 educational psychologists belong to the American Psychological Association, and almost 5500 members of the American Educational Research Association are concerned with issues in the field. Most universities now require preservice teachers to take at least one course in educational psychology. Empirical research is constantly conducted at the university level and reported in dozens of journals.

Theories in Educational Psychology

Because of the wide diversity in human beings, instructional settings, and fields of study, no general theory has been formulated that is applicable to all educational psychology. Instead, psychologists work on developing theories about particular phenomena in learning, motivation, development, teaching, and instruction.

Learning Theory

Different theories of learning help educational psychologists understand, predict, and control human behavior. For example, educational psychologists have worked out mathematical models of learning that predict the probability of a person's making a correct response; these mathematical theories are used to design computerized instruction in reading, mathematics, and second-language learning. To understand a child's emotional aversion to school, the respondent (or classical) conditioning theory originated by the Russian physiologist Ivan Pavlov may be used. Pavlov's theory describes how stimuli that occur together may come to evoke similar responses. To inquire about the origins of a child's disruptive classroom behavior, the operant (or instrumental) conditioning theory of Thorndike and the American psychologist B. F. Skinner may be applicable. This theory describes how rewards shape and maintain behavior. School violence and vandalism may be partially understood through the social-learning theory of the Canadian-American psychologist Albert Bandura (1925–), which describes the conditions under which people learn to imitate models. Information-processing theory is used to understand how people solve problems by analogy and metaphor.

Motivation

Attribution theory describes the role of motivation in a person's success or failure in school situations. Success on a test, for instance, could be attributed to luck or hard work; the theory predicts the behavior of students depending on their responses.

Development

The theory of the Swiss psychologist Jean Piaget that intellectual ability is qualitatively different at different ages and that children need interaction with the environment to gain intellectual competency has influenced all of education and psychology. This new concept of intelligence affected the design of learning environments for young children and the development of mathematics and science programmes.

Theory in Teaching

The scientific study of teaching is a relatively new development; until the 1950s, little systematic observation and experimentation took place. The research on teaching has been consistent in its implications for academic achievement. The variables that educational psychologists have found to be important in classroom teaching include the time teachers allocate to instruction, the amount of content they cover, the percent of time that students are engaged in learning, the congruence between what is taught and what is tested, and the ability of the teacher to give clear directions, provide feedback, hold students accountable for their behavior, and create a warm, democratic atmosphere for learning.

Instructional Theory

The American educator Robert Gagné (1916–) developed a hierarchical theory that some types of learning are prerequisites to other kinds of learning. His research has been fruitfully used in determining the sequence of instruction.

Applications

In schools, educational psychology has been applied recently to creating a system of instruction known as mastery learning, which is based on the belief that most students can achieve high grades if certain procedures are followed: (1) The curriculum is broken down into logically sequenced units of about two weeks' duration; (2) the students pass a test at the end of each unit of learning before proceeding to the next unit; (3) alternate forms of instruction and tests are available so that students can do remedial work if they fail the first time; and (4) students determine for themselves the amount of time they need to complete a unit. This form of instruction is usually successful in courses that stress acquisition of knowledge.

Educational psychologists frequently engage in curriculum research and development. Instructional plans and test items are designed to match specified objectives. The plans then are tested and, if necessary, redesigned on the basis of empirical findings. This method has also been used to design instructional television programmes and a wide range of ancillary curriculum materials.

Techniques of educational psychology are used in teacher-training programmes. Principles of BEHAVIOR MODIFICATION, (q.v.) are applied to a wide set of teaching problems such as reducing the noise level of disorderly classrooms or increasing the study time of students who daydream.

Educational psychologists have devised in-service teacher-training programmes to improve reading and mathematics instruction in accord with the findings of recent empirical research. These studies demonstrate that research on teaching can be used to train teachers in ways that will increase student achievement, even in low-achieving classrooms.

Psychological Implications of Yoga in the Teaching of Disabled

The philosophy of Yoga and the psychology behind its practice—the two are bound up together in such a way that any consideration of the one inevitably has to simultaneously take into account the other, because the practice of Yoga is laid upon the basis of a psycho-philosophical background. The philosophy of Yoga and the psychology of Yoga are present not only as a background to this science of Yoga, but also as the basis for the practice of the Yogic processes. It is upon this basis that the different practices have been formulated and presented and this point should be borne in mind always, not only when we make a study of Yoga, but also when we actually practise the different Angas of Yoga. Only then will the practice become more meaningful to us and only then can the practice itself be done in a right way and in a rational way. If this Yoga practice is to be effective, you must know why you are engaging in this practice, what this practice is supposed to achieve for you, what you are expected to gain out of this practice, and what the effect of this practice is supposed to be upon your own nature, upon your own spiritual state. Otherwise, there would be no terms of reference by which you can ascertain whether the practice is actually proceeding in the right direction or not, whether it is bearing fruits step by step or not. Upon what hypothesis, upon what thesis will you judge whether your Yoga practice is progressive or stagnant, whether it is fruitful or sterile? How can you make out? It is only when you have a certain frame of reference with which you can tally your practice from time to time that you will be in a position to engage in your practice meaningfully, in an effective and satisfactory manner. And that is why it is necessary to bear in mind the psycho-philosophical basis of these Yoga practices even while you are engaged in them.

Warding off Painful Experiences—The Main Motivation Behind all Human Activity

In the book we saw a broad outline of the philosophy behind Patanjali's Yoga Darshana. An analysis of the present condition of the individual shows that he is subject to many afflictions and painful experiences, many limitations and imperfections, upon the physical level and upon the psychological level—hunger and thirst, pleasure and pain, elation and depression, what they call Harsha-Soka, Sukha-Duhkha. So, bodily and mentally, the pattern of experience of the common individual does not seem to be very, very satisfactory, very desirable even, not at all beautiful. Most human beings are constantly engaged in an endless struggle of warding off painful experiences, of keeping at bay experiences that are distressing, that cause great discomfort and inconvenience.

If you analyse human activity, you find that it is inextricably interconnected and interwoven with human experiences; and most of the activities are a reaction called up or thrown forth to counter these experiences, to try to change them, to try to overcome them, to try to nullify them, to try to eliminate them. So, we cannot say that human activity is in a large measure anything creative, anything gainful. It is all negative. Nothing comes out of it, except that you try to escape from bad experiences and manage to get rid of something here and something there which you do not want. It is not that you have brought forth something wonderful. So, it is neither constructive nor creative, neither gainful nor really meaningful. But, it is seen to be petty, Alpa. The Upanishad calls it Alpa. Constantly, a vast aggregate of the human race on this earth is engaged in a never-ending process of trying to ward off painful experiences, try to get rid of suffering and pain, that which it does not want. *Duhkham Ma Bhuyat:* Let no sorrow befall. That is the motivation. That is the idea behind most human activity. "I do not wish sorrow; I do not wish pain; I do not wish discomfort; I do not wish to have inconvenience and suffering." So, it is not a gainful process. It is not a creative or a constructive process. Life goes on like this in this struggle.

When you consider this aspect of human activity and endeavour, you find that it is not so much an original activity, due to human will or human initiative, but something forced upon the human individual. Willy-nilly he is compelled to engage in these activities, not out of his own volition, but due to the force of circumstances or outer conditions. In the light of this situation, the ancient seers tried to find out what was the cause of this. They asked themselves: "Why has this situation arisen? How has this situation come about?". And as a result of their intuitive discoveries, they came out with this knowledge that these experiences stem from an unfortunate involvement of a being who really is not subject to these experiences, who is in a pristine state, who is in his own independent native state, who is always in a state of perfect bliss, freedom and joy.

So, this is an unnatural condition, an abnormal condition, resulting from an involvement in a factor which Yoga Shastras call the phenomenal nature or Prakriti. And, due to involvement in this Prakriti, the Purusha, who is a perfect being, independent, free from all afflictions, weeps and wails. So they said: "We shall try to formulate a method by which there may be brought about once again the isolation of the Purusha from this involvement, by which there may be brought about once again a separation of these two factors—Purusha and Prakriti—the coming together of which has resulted in all sorts of suffering".

The Nature of Purusha's Involvement in Prakriti—The Interplay of the Three Gunas

What is the form of this involvement of the Purusha in Prakriti? In what way is Purusha involved in Prakriti? What is Prakriti? In what way is it present? Advaita Vedanta uses the term Maya also with reference to this phenomenal nature and the Gita gives a certain extent of information, a certain hint that this Prakriti is made out of three Gunas—they call it qualities for want of a better term—or three states of being, namely, Sattva, Rajas and Tamas. This divine cosmic illusory power called Prakriti comprises three Gunas. And Prakriti herself is present in the form of the gross physical body, the vital power that manifests as the living breath, the senses that are situated in the physical body with their natural urges towards their respective sense-objects, and the inner man, the inner being, in the form of thinking and feeling, in the form of remembering and recollecting, in the form of reasoning and willing. It is due to your involvement in this Prakriti that you are experiencing this present state of a mixture of joy and sorrow, a constantly fluctuating mixed state, like a person tasting in the mouth an equal mixture of sand and sugar. One moment you feel the sweetness; another moment the teeth grind upon the sand particles and you feel very bad about it. When it is said that the Purusha is involved in Prakriti in its variegated modes as the gross physical body, the senses, the inner Prana, mind, intellect, memory and ego, all these go to make up the sum-totality of your individual human personality. All these represent the Prakriti in its various aspects. And the involvement of the Purusha in these aspects of Prakriti necessarily affects their manifestation or expression.

It affects the way in which your mind expresses itself, your feelings express themselves, your thoughts express themselves. It affects the way in which your senses manifest their nature and your body displays its dynamics in its various movements in the form of restlessness, in the form of wanting to be active, in the form of hunger, in the form of various desires to eat, drink and rest, to sleep and to move about. These manifestations constantly keep you in a state of restlessness and agitation, and also drag you out of your innermost centre and forcibly bring you out into contact with the external universe of names and forms, of temporary things. And Prakriti being a composition of the three Gunas, the manifestations and movements of these various aspects of Prakriti—inner and outer, psychological and physical—also tend to fall under one or the other of these Guna categories.

All this came in for the study of the ancient seers. They observed the human individual, observed his nature, in just the same way as a modern scientist would observe an ants' colony in a glass case, day after day, keeping the ants some food and observing them by day and by night, how they go after food, what their activities are, what their nature is, what code of conduct they have got, what their laws of behaviour are and so on. In a like manner, the ancient seers, the great scientists of the inner man, observed the human individual, his nature, his behaviour and his experience. And they studied the various manifestations of the different modes of Prakriti in the human individual within the area of framework of his nature. They made a study of how Sattva manifested in man, how Rajas manifested and how Tamas manifested.

An urge to activity, a constant restlessness, a tendency to movement, was the effect of the Rajas in Prakriti. Everything ugly, negative, anti-social and destructive was the result of the manifestation of the Tamas in Prakriti. Everything beautiful, sublime, elevating, refined and subtle was seen to be the effect of the manifestation of the Sattva in Prakriti. When we say "Prakriti", you should not have in your mind the picture of some goddess or some lady creating a lot of trouble. It is not like that. Prakriti is only a word to indicate a cosmic principle which is in the form of a force. It is not so much a power as a force. Power is exercised or wielded, whereas force just manifests itself, carries everything before it.

Prakriti is therefore a cosmic force, a cosmic principle which is in the form of a force, manifesting upon different levels. When this force manifests upon one level, it is said to be Tamasic. When this force manifests upon another level, it is said to be Rajasic. And when this force manifests upon yet another level, a third level, it is said to be Sattvic. And, on all these three levels, it keeps on manifesting. How this goes on has been hinted at in the famous Bhagavad Gita which is both a Brahma Vidya and a Yoga Shastra. They have hinted at a cyclic manifestation of this Prakriti wherein sometimes Sattva predominates overriding Rajas and Tamas, sometimes Rajas predominates overriding Sattva and Tamas, and sometimes Tamas predominates overriding Sattva and Rajas.

Svabhava—The Individual's Pre-acquired Pattern of Samskaras and Vasanas

Quite apart from this aspect of the movement of the three Gunas of Prakriti, there is another even more important aspect of the presence of these three Gunas of Prakriti in human nature, and that more important aspect is also to be grasped only upon the basis of philosophy. Philosophy behind and beyond Yoga has expounded the presence of recurring embodiments for the Purusha as long as the Purusha has not succeeded in dissociating himself from Prakriti and regaining his splendid isolation, his pristine independent condition. As long as that is not achieved, there is ever-recurring embodiment for the Purusha, and in each new embodiment the Purusha comes with a pre-acquired background condition. What is this pre-acquired background condition? When you have completed one page in an accounts book and you have to start upon a fresh page, you bring forward to the beginning of the fresh page the last entry that is at the end of the previous page. That will be the basis of commencement of fresh entries upon the new page. Thus, the fresh page is not a blank page. It already commences with a starting background condition.

It is already there. Whether it is a credit or a debit or whatever it is, it is there. In a similar manner, at the time of each embodiment, you come into this world with a certain pre-acquired pattern of Samskaras and Vasanas, of impressions and innate tendencies, latent tendencies, which already have set the pattern of your nature in this fresh embodiment. So, this condition in which you start your life, commence your career, human career, with a certain set pattern, with an intermixture of Rajas, Tamas and Sattva in a certain ratio, is the state of Prakriti in you, is your inborn Prakriti, your built-in Prakriti state. And this is an even more important aspect of the presence of Prakriti in you than the cyclic manifestation of the three Gunas in Prakriti continuing in a sort of an ever-recurring movement within you. This condition in which you come into the world with a certain set pattern of the Prakriti with its three Gunas is indeed a very vital factor, because this decides the exact form in which the cyclic manifestation of the three Gunas will take place in you.

Will Prakriti keep on manifesting in you as the truthfulness of Harischandra or Yudhishthira or George Washington who, as the story goes, cut down an apple tree in the garden and confessed it to his father? Or, will the three Gunas manifest in you as a compromising attitude—an attitude where if it is not too inconvenient, you will stick to truth, but if it is likely to bring suffering to you, you will not mind uttering a falsehood? Or, will Rajas and Tamas manifest in you as a downright lying habit, so much as to say that you are born with a tendency to speak only false, never to utter truth? What decides the nature of manifestation of the three Gunas of Prakriti in you? The deciding factor is the background nature which you have already acquired and brought along with you when you have come into this present embodiment, into this fresh page of your account book. It is your background nature that decides the exact form, the exact Rupa-Rekha, the exact blueprint, of the dynamics of the recurring manifestation of the three Gunas in you—the precise form in which Prakriti will manifest in your particular character, in your particular individuality. And this background nature brought forward from previous births will differ from person to person. In a family there may be seven children, say, two daughters and five sons.

In each one, the cyclical manifestation of the three Gunas will be there, the ever-changing pattern of their manifestation will be there. But the exact form in which this changing pattern will express itself in actuality may be completely different in each one of the children, though they are born of the same parents, brought up in the same home and environment, fed with the same food. It will be completely different, because of this other aspect of each one's involvement in Prakriti, namely, the ratio in which the three Gunas of Prakriti happen to be present in the background nature, in the foundation, in the pre-acquired built-in born nature. We call this foundation nature by the name "Svabhava". Svabhava will never change. The foundation will never change. One can go on altering the building, the superstructure, demolishing and remodelling and all that, but the foundation is unalterably there, and upon that foundation only all the remodelling will have to be done. So, the foundational aspect of your involvement in Prakriti is a very important factor.

Development Delays and Disorders Associated with Disabilities

Parents are often have concerns about their children's development, especially when they see other children of the same age who have already attained a milestone that their child still hasn't met, causing them to think that their child is 'slow' or 'seems behind.' It is important to keep in mind that for each milestone, there is a range of ages during which a child will normally meet it. For example, some children may walk as early as 11 months, while others may not walk until they are 15 months old, and it is still concerned normal.

Developmental milestones are determined by the average age at which children attain each skill, therefore, statistically, about 3% of children will not meet them on time, but only about 15-20% of these children will actually have abnormal development. The rest will eventually develop normally over time, although a little later than expected.

Be sure to bring up any concerns that you have about your child's development with your Pediatrician, especially if he seems to be losing milestones, or not doing things that he was able to previously do. A developmental delay occurs when your child has the delayed achievement of one or more of his milestones. This may affect your child's speech and language, his fine and gross motor skills, and/or his personal and social skills.

Your Pediatrician should screen for delays at your child's well child visits. This may consist of simple questions to see what your child is able to do at different ages, or it may include a formal screening test, such as the Denver II Developmental Screening Test. The Denver test can look for delays in your child's social and personal skills, fine and gross motor skills and language. Developmental delays, especially if they involve a language delay which may be secondary to a hearing loss, should be identified as early as possible.

A child with a global delay will have delays in all areas of development. It is usually caused by a static (does not worsen with time) encephalopathy caused by a disorder before or near the time or birth. Causes of global delays include prematurity, cerebral malformations, chromosomal disorders, infections, and progressive (may worsen with time) encephalopathies (metabolic diseases, hypothyroidism, neurocutaneous syndromes (neurofibromatosis, tuberous sclerosis), Rett syndrome, and hydrocephalus). Testing to look for the cause of a global developmental delay may include a head MRI.

Some signs that your infant may not be meeting his normal motor milestones include not being able to bring his hands together by 4 months, not rolling over by 6 months, having head lag when pulled to a sitting position after 6 months, not sitting by himself without support by 8 months, not crawling by 12 months, and not walking by 15 months. Remember that mild delays in motor development can be normal, and there is a range during which these milestones are usually met, so your child may not meet each one at the same time as other children. Delayed motor development, with normal language skills, can be caused by a neuromuscular disorder or mild cerebral palsy.

A delay in fine motor skills in older children may be manifested by not being able to use a spoon or fork, tie his shoes, button his clothes, write his name, draw shapes, colour inside the lines, or hold a pencil correctly at the age appropriate time, or by having poor handwriting. A delay in gross motor skills in older children may include not being able to ride a tricycle or bicycle, being clumsy, or not walking correctly.

The early speech and language milestones which are listed below include the upper limit of when 75% of infants meet this milestone, so your child may still be developing normally if he has not mastered a milestone by the age indicated. These milestones should be used as a general guideline to help identify infants that are at risk for having speech and language problems so that their development can be watched closely. Among the screening tests available that your Pediatrician may perform are the Early Language Milestone (ELM) Scale-2 and the Clinical Linguistic and Auditory Milestone Scale (CLAMS). Delayed speech and language development can be caused by a developmental language disorders (DLD), hearing loss, mental retardation and autism.

Early Speech and Language Milestones:

- Newborns can localize a sound to their right or left side shortly after being born and will turn their head or look in the direction of a sound. This works best with loud noises when your baby is awake and alert, but they should also be able to hear soft sounds. They can also begin to smile spontaneously and in response to someone by 1 month. Infants learn to recognize their parents by 1-2 1/2 months.

- Infants can imitate speech sounds by 3-6 months.
- Monosyllabic babbling, or making isolated sounds with vowels and consonants (ba, da, ga, goo, etc) usually begins by 4-8 months.
- Polysyllabic babbling, or repeating vowels and consonants (babababa, lalalalala, etc) usually begins by 5-9 months.
- Comprehending individual words (mommy, daddy, no) usually occurs by 6-10 months.
- By 5-10 months, most infants can say mama/dada nonspecifically, using the words as more than just a label for his parents.
- Many infants can follow a one step command with a gesture (for example, asking for an object and holding your hand out) by 6-9 months. He should be able to follow a one step command without a gesture by 7-11 months.
- The correct use of mama/dada as a label for a parent usually occurs by 7-12 months.
- The first word (other than mama/dada) is usually spoken by 9-14 months.
- By 10-15 months, he should be able to point to an object that he wants.
- Your child will be able to say 4-6 words (other than mama/dada and names of family members or pets) by 11-20 months.
- He should be able to follow a two step command without a gesture by 14-21 months.
- Two word combinations or sentences are used by 18-22 months and can include phrases like 'Want milk', 'More juice', etc.
- A vocabulary spurt leading to a 50+ word vocabulary occurs by 16-24 months.

Parents are usually the first ones to think that there is a problem with their child's motor, social, and/or speech and language development, and this parental concern should be enough to initiate furthur evaluation. In addition to a formal hearing test (for children with speech delays), neurological exam (which will look at your child's muscle tone, strenght, reflexes, coordination, etc), and developmental assessment by their Pediatrician, children with developmental delays should be referred to an early childhood intervention programme (for children under 3), so that an evaluation can be initiated and a treatment plan developed, including physical therapy, occupational therapy and possible speech therapy. He may also need a referal to a Pediatric Neurologist and/or a Developmental Pediatrician for furthur evaluation and treatment.

In addition to the screening tests described above, your Pediatrician may be able to calculate your child's motor quotient (MQ), which is his motor age (his age as calculated by what milestones he has met) divided by his chronological age and multiplied by 100. A motor quotient above 70 is considered normal, and between 50-70 is suspicious and requires furthur evaluation, although it is probably normal, and below 50 is considered abnormal. For example, if your child is 12 months old and has just begun to pull to a stand (motor age of 9 months, the age when most children are pulling to a stand), his MQ would be (9/12)*100 or 75, which is probably normal. On the other hand, if he has just begun to roll over (motor age of 5 months), then his MQ is (5/12)*100 or 42 and this is probably abnormal.

Developmental Disability

Developmental disability is a term used to describe life-long, disabilities attributable to mental and/or physical or combination of mental and physical impairments, manifested prior to age 18. The term is used most commonly in the United States to refer to disabilities affecting daily functioning in three or more of the following areas:

- capacity for independent living
- economic self-sufficiency

- learning
- mobility
- receptive and expressive language
- self-care
- self-direction.

The term first appeared in U.S. law in 1970, when Congress used the term to describe the population of individuals who had historically been placed in state institutions, in its effort to improve conditions in these dehumanizing facilities (P.L. 91-517, "The Developmental Disabilities Services and Facilities Construction Act of 1970"). The law has since been amended many times, and now calls for the full community inclusion and self-determination of people with developmental disabilities (P.L. 106-402).

Frequently, people with mental retardation, cerebral palsy, autism spectrum disorder, various genetic and chromosomal disorders such as Down syndrome and Fragile X syndrome, and Fetal Alcohol Spectrum Disorder are described as having developmental disabilities. This use of the term is synonymous with the use of the term learning disability in the United Kingdom, and intellectual disability in Australia, Europe, Canada and elsewhere. Cognitive disability is also used synonymously in some jurisdictions. Developmental disabilities are usually classified as severe, profound, moderate or mild, as assessed by the individual's need for supports, which may be lifelong.

Causes of Developmental Disabilities

There are many social, environmental and physical causes of developmental disabilities, although for some a definitive cause may never be determined. Common factors causing developmental disabilities include:

- Brain injury or infection before, during or after birth
- Growth or nutrition problems
- Abnormalities of chromosomes and genes
- Babies born long before the expected birth date-also called extreme prematurity

- Poor diet and health care
- Drug misuse during pregnancy, including alcohol intake and smoking.
- Child abuse can also have a severe effect on the development of a child, specifically the socio-emotional development.
- Diagnosis of an autism spectrum disorder.

Developmental disabilities affect between 1 and 2% of the population in most western countries, although many government sources acknowledge that statistics are flawed in this area.

The worldwide proportion of people with developmental disabilities is believed to be approximately 1.4%. It is twice as common in males as in females, and some researchers have found that the prevalence of mild developmental disabilities is likely to be higher in areas of poverty and deprivation, and among people of certain ethnicities.

Associated Issues

Physical Health Issues: There are many physical health factors associated with developmental disabilities. For some specific syndromes and diagnoses, these are inherent (such as poor heart function in people with Down's syndrome); however lack of access to health services and lack of understanding by medical professionals is also a major contributing factor. People with severe communication difficulties find it difficult to articulate their health needs, and without adequate support and education might not recognise ill health.

Epilepsy, sensory problems (such as poor vision and hearing), obesity and poor dental health are over-represented in this population. Life expectancy among people with developmental disabilities as a group is estimated at 20 years below average, although this is increasing with advancements in adaptive and medical technologies, and as people are leading healthier, more fulfilling lives, and some specific diagnoses (such as Freeman-Sheldon syndrome) do not impact on life expectancy.

Mental Health Issues (Dual Diagnoses)

Mental health issues, and psychiatric illnesses, are more likely to occur in people with developmental disabilities than in the general population. A number of factors are attributed to the high incidence rate of dual diagnoses:

- the high likelihood of encountering traumatic events throughout their lifetime (such as abandonment by loved ones, abuse, bullying and harassment)
- the social restrictions placed upon people with developmental disabilities (such as lack of education, poverty, limited employment opportunities, limited opportunities for fulfilling relationships, boredom)
- biological factors (such as brain injury, epilepsy, illicit and prescribed drug and alcohol misuse)
- developmental factors (such as lack of understanding of social norms and appropriate behaviour, inability of those around to allow/ understand expressions of grief and other human emotions)
- *External Monitoring Factor:* all people with developmental disabilities that are in a Federal or State funded residence require the residence to have some form of behavioral monitoring for each person with developmental disability at the residence. With this information psychological diagnosis are more easily given than with the general population that has less consistent monitoring.
- *Access to Healthcare Providers:* all people with developmental disabilities that are in a Federal or State funded residence require the residence to have annual visits to various health care providers (nurse, physician, psychologist, psychiatrist, etc.) With consistent visits to health care providers more people with developmental disabilities are likely to receive appropriate treatment than the general population that is not required to visit various health care providers.

These problems are exacerbated by difficulties in diagnosis of mental health issues, and in appropriate treatment and medication, as for physical health issues..

Abuse and Vulnerability

Abuse is a significant issue for people with developmental disabilities, and as a group they are regarded as vulnerable people in most jurisdictions. Common types of abuse include:

- Physical abuse (withholding food, hitting, punching, pushing, etc.)
- Neglect (withholding help when required, e.g., assistance with personal hygiene)
- Sexual abuse
- Psychological or emotional abuse (verbal abuse, shaming and belittling)
- Constraint and restrictive practices (turning off an electric wheelchair so a person cannot move)
- Financial abuse (charging unnecessary fees, holding onto pensions, wages, etc.)
- Legal or civil abuse (restricted access to services)
- Systemic abuse (denied access to an appropriate service due to perceived support needs)
- Passive neglect (a caregiver's failure to provide adequate food, shelter).

Lack of education, lack of self-esteem and self-advocacy skills, lack of understanding of social norms and appropriate behaviour and communication difficulties are strong contributing factors to the high incidence of abuse among this population.

In addition to abuse from people in positions of power, peer abuse is recognised as a significant, if misunderstood, problem. Rates of criminal offending among people with developmental disabilities are also disproportionately high, and it is widely acknowledged that criminal justice systems throughout the world are ill-equipped for the needs of people with developmental disabilities (as both perpetrators and victims of crime).

Challenging Behaviour

Some people with developmental disabilities exhibit challenging behaviour, defined as "culturally abnormal behaviour(s) of such intensity, frequency or duration that the physical safety of the person or others is placed in serious jeopardy, or behaviour which is likely to seriously limit or deny access to the use of ordinary community facilities". Common types of challenging behaviour include self-injurious behaviour (such as hitting, headbutting, biting), aggressive behaviour (such as hitting others, screaming, spitting, kicking), inappropriate sexualised behaviour (such as public masturbation or groping), behaviour directed at property (such as throwing objects and stealing) and stereotyped behaviours (such as repetitive rocking, echolalia or elective incontinence).

Challenging behaviour in people with developmental disabilities may be caused by a number of factors, including biological (pain, medication, the need for sensory stimulation), social (boredom, seeking social interaction, the need for an element of control, lack of knowledge of community norms, insensitivity of staff and services to the person's wishes and needs), environmental (physical aspects such as noise and lighting, or gaining access to preferred objects or activities), psychological (feeling excluded, lonely, devalued, labelled, disempowered, living up to people's negative expectations) or simply a means of communication. A lot of the time, challenging behaviour is learned and brings rewards and it is very often possible to teach people new behaviours to achieve the same aims.

Experience and research suggests that what professionals call 'challenging behaviour' is often a reaction to the challenging environments that those providing services create around people with developmental disabilities. 'Challenging behaviour' in this context is a method of communicating dissatisfaction with the failure of those providing services to focus on what kind of life makes most sense to the person, and is often the only recourse a developmentally disabled person has against unsatisfactory services or treatment and the lack of opportunities made available to the person. This is especially the case where the services deliver lifestyles and ways of working that are centred on what suits the service provider and its staff, rather than what best suits the person.

Societal Attitudes Towards Developmental Disabilities

Throughout history, people with developmental disabilities have been viewed as incapable and incompetent in their capacity for decision-making and development. Until the Enlightenment in Europe, care and asylum was provided by families and the church (in monasteries and other religious communities), focusing on the provision of basic physical needs such as food, shelter and clothing. Stereotypes such as the dimwitted yokel, and potentially harmful characterisations (such as demonic possession for people with epilepsy) were prominent in social attitudes of the time.

The movement towards individualism in the 18th and 19th centuries, and the opportunities afforded by the Industrial Revolution, led to housing and care using the asylum model. People were placed by, or removed from, their families (usually in infancy) and housed in large institutions (of up to 3,000 people, although some institutions were home to many more, such as the Philadelphia State Hospital in Pennsylvania which housed 7,000 people through the 1960s), many of which were self-sufficient through the labour of the residents. Some of these institutions provided a very basic level of education (such as differentiation between colours and basic word recognition and numeracy), but most continued to focus solely on the provision of basic needs. Conditions in such institutions varied widely, but the support provided was generally non-individualised, with aberrant behaviour and low levels of economic productivity regarded as a burden to society. Heavy tranquilisation and assembly line methods of support (such as 'birdfeeding' and cattle herding) were the norm, and the medical model of disability prevailed. Services were provided based on the relative ease to the provider, not based on the human needs of the individual.

Ignoring the prevailing attitude, Civitans adopted service to the developmentally disabled as a major organizational emphasis in 1952. Their earliest efforts included workshops for special education teachers and daycamps for disabled children, all at a time when such training and programmes were almost nonexistent. The segregation of people with developmental disabilities wasn't widely questioned by academics or policy-makers until the 1969 publication of Wolf Wolfensberger's seminal work "The Origin and Nature of Our Institutional Models", drawing on some of the ideas proposed by SG Howe a hundred years earlier. This book posited that society characterises people with disabilities as deviant, sub-human and burdens of charity, resulting in the adoption of that 'deviant' role. Wolfensberger argued that this dehumanisation, and the segregated institutions that result from it, ignored the potential productive contributions that all people can make to society. He pushed for a shift in policy and practice that recognised the human needs of "retardates" and provided the same basic human rights as for the rest of the population.

The publication of this book may be regarded as the first move towards the widespread adoption of the social model of disability in regard to these types of disabilities, and was the impetus for the development of government strategies for desegregation. Successful lawsuits against governments and an increasing awareness of human rights and self-advocacy also contributed to this process, resulting in the passing in the US of the *Civil Rights of Institutionalized Persons Act* in 1980.

From the 1960s to the present, most states have moved towards the elimination of segregated institutions. Along with the work Wolfensberger and others including Gunnar and Rosemary Dybwad, a number of scandalous revelations around the horrific conditions within state institutions created public outrage led to change to a more community-based method of providing services. By the mid-1970s, most governments had committed to de-institutionalisation, and had started preparing for the wholesale movement of people into the general community, in line with the principles of normalization. In most countries, this was essentially complete by the late 1990s, although the debate over whether or not to close institutions persists in some states, including Massachusetts.

It could be argued that we still have a very long way to go before people with such disabilities are seen as full citizens of society. Person Centred Planning and Person Centred Approaches are seen as methods of addressing the continued labelling and exclusion of socially devalued people, such as people with a developmental disability label, encouraging a focus on the person as someone with capacities and gifts, as well as support needs.

Services and Support

Today, support services are provided by government agencies, non-governmental organizations and by private sector providers. Support services address most aspects of life for people with developmental disabilities, and are usually theoretically based in community inclusion, using concepts such as social role valorization and increased self-determination (using models such as Person Centred Planning). Support services are funded through government block funding (paid directly to service providers by the government), through individualised funding packages (paid directly to the individual by the government, specifically for the purchase of services) or privately by the individual (although they may receive certain subsidies or discounts, paid by the government).

Individual Differences in Cognition and Information Processing Abilities of Disabled

Education and training opportunities for people with developmental disabilities have expanded greatly in recent times, with many governments mandating universal access to educational facilities, and more students moving out of special schools and into mainstream classrooms with support.

Post-secondary education and vocational training is also increasing for people with these types of disabilities, although many programmes offer only segregated "access" courses in areas such as literacy, numeracy and other basic skills. Legislation (such as the UK's Disability Discrimination Act 1995) requires educational institutions and training providers to make 'reasonable adjustments' to curriculum and teaching methods in order to accommodate the learning needs of students with disabilities, wherever possible. There are also some vocational training centers that cater specifically to people with disabilities, providing the skills necessary to work in integrated settings, one of the largest being Dale Rogers Training Center in Oklahoma City. See also Intensive interaction.

At-home and Community Support

Many people with developmental disabilities live in the general community, either with family members, or in their own homes (that they rent or own, living alone or with flatmates). At-home and community supports range from one-to-one assistance from a support worker with identified aspects of daily living (such as budgeting, shopping or paying bills) to full 24-hour support (including assistance with household tasks, such as cooking and cleaning, and personal care such as showering, dressing and the administration of medication). The need for full 24-hour support is usually associated with difficulties recognising safety issues (such as responding to a fire or using a telephone) or for people with potentially dangerous medical conditions (such as asthma or diabetes) who are unable to manage their conditions without assistance.

In the United States a support worker is known as a Direct Support Professional (DSP). The DSP works in assisting the individual with their ADLs and also acts as an advocate for the individual with a developmental disability, in communicating their needs, self expression and goals.

Supports of this type also include assistance to identify and undertake new hobbies or to access community services (such as education), learning appropriate behaviour or recognition of community norms, or with relationships and expanding circles of friends. Most programmes offering at-home and community support are designed with the goal of increasing the individual's independence, although it is recognised that people with more severe disabilities may never be able to achieve full independence in some areas of daily life.

Residential Accommodation

Some people with developmental disabilities live in residential accommodation (also known as group homes) with other people with similar assessed needs. These homes are usually staffed around the clock, and usually house between 3 and 15 residents. The prevalence of this type of support is gradually decreasing, however, as residential accommodation is replaced by at-home and community support, which can offer increased choice and self-determination for individuals. Some U.S. states still provide institutional care, such as the Texas State Schools.

Employment Support

Employment support usually consists of two types of support:

- Support to access or participate in integrated employment, in a workplace in the general community. This may include specific programmes to increase the skills needed for successful employment (work preparation), one-to-one or small group support for on-the-job training, or one-to-one or small group support after a transition period (such as advocacy when dealing with an employer or a bullying colleague, or assistance to complete an application for a promotion).
- The provision of specific employment opportunities within segregated business services. Although these are designed as 'transitional' services (teaching work skills needed to move into integrated employment), many people remain in such services for the duration of their working life. The types of work performed in business services include mailing and packaging services, cleaning, gardening and landscaping, timberwork, metal fabrication, farming and sewing.

Workers with developmental disabilities have historically been paid less for their labour than those in the general workforce, although this is gradually changing with government initiatives, the enforcement of anti-discrimination legislation and changes in perceptions of capability in the general community.

Day Services

Non-vocational day services are usually known as day centres, and are traditionally segregated services offering training in life skills (such as meal preparation and basic literacy), centre-based activities (such as craft, games and music classes) and external activities (such as day trips). Some more progressive day centres also support people to access vocational training opportunities (such as college courses), and offer individualised outreach services (planning and undertaking activities with the individual, with support offered one-to-one or in small groups).

Traditional day centres were based on the principles of occupational therapy, and were created as respite for family members caring for their loved ones with disabilities. This is slowly changing, however, as programmes offered become more skills-based and focused on increasing independence.

Advocacy

Advocacy is a burgeoning support field for people with developmental disabilities. Advocacy groups now exist in most jurisdictions, working collaboratively with people with disabilities for systemic change (such as changes in policy and legislation) and for changes for individuals (such as claiming welfare benefits or when responding to abuse). Most advocacy groups also work to support people, throughout the world, to increase their capacity for self-advocacy, teaching the skills necessary for people to advocate for their own needs.

Other Types of Support

Other types of support for people with developmental disabilities may include:

- therapeutic services, such as speech therapy, massage, aromatherapy, or drama or music therapy
- supported holidays
- short-stay respite services (for people who live with family members or other unpaid carers)
- transport services, such as dial-a-ride or free bus passes
- specialist behaviour support services, such as high-security services for people with high-level, high-risk challenging behaviours
- specialist relationships and sex education services.

Assessment and Evaluation of Disabled Learners

Fair Assessment

Assessing students with learning disabilities can be a challenge. However, we must remember that assessing is providing the child with an opportunity to demonstrate knowledge, skill and understanding.

For most learning disabled students, last on the list should be a pencil/paper task. Below are a list of strategies that support and enhance assessment of learning disabled students.

Presentation

- A presentation is a verbal demonstration of skill/ knowledge and understanding. The child describes, shows and offers to answer questions about his/her task. Presentation can also take the form of discussion, debate or purely question/response. Some children will need to speak in a small group or in a one to one setting as LD students are often intimidated in this setting. However, with ongoing opportunities, they will begin to shine.

Conference

- A conference is a one to one between the teacher an the student. The teacher will prompt and cue the student to determine the level of understanding and knowledge. Again this takes the pressure away from written tasks. The conference should be somewhat informal to put the student at ease. The focus should be on the student sharing ideas, reasoning or explaining a concept. This is an extremely useful form of formative assessment.

Interview

- An interview helps a teacher to clarify the level of understanding for a specific purpose, activity or learning concept. A teacher would generally have questions in mind to ask the student to resond to. Very insightful method but this can be time consuming.

Observation

- Observing a student in the learning environment is a very powerful method to assess. It can also be the vehicle for the teacher to change or enhance a specific teaching strategy. Observation can be done in small group setting while the child is engaged in learning tasks. Things to look for include: does the child persist? give up easily? have a plan in place? look for assistance? try alternate strategies? become impatient? look for patterns? Teachers need to be prepared for what they are specifically looking for in an observational setting.

Performance Task

- A performance task is a learning task that the child will do while the teacher assesses his/her performance. For instance: you might want to check some math problem solving by asking if 6 people fit in one car, how many cars will be needed to transport 42 people? During the task, the teacher could be looking for attitudes, skill, ability and evidence of risk-taking.

Self-Assessment

- We always want our students/children to be able to identify their own strengths and weaknesses. Self-assessment will lead the student to a better sense of understanding of his/her own learning. The student may need some guiding questions such as:

What did I do well on?

How can I improve upon______?

Where was my biggest strength/weakness?

There are a plethora of assessment strategies, I've merely focused on the ones that support the learning disabled student.

UNIT-III

Visual Impairment

Anatomy and Physiology of the Human Eye

The human eye is the organ which gives us the sense of sight, allowing us to observe and learn more about the surrounding world than we do with any of the other four senses. We use our eyes in almost every activity we perform, whether reading, working, watching television, writing a letter, driving a car, and in countless other ways. Most people probably would agree that sight is the sense they value more than all the rest. The eye allows us to see and interpret the shapes, colors, and dimensions of objects in the world by processing the light they reflect or emit. The eye is able to detect bright light or dim light, but it cannot sense objects when light is absent.

Process of Vision

Light waves from an object (such as a tree) enter the eye first through the *cornea*, the clear dome at the front of the eye. The light then progresses through the *pupil*, the circular opening in the center of the coloured *iris*. Fluctuations in incoming light change the size of the eye's pupil. When the light entering the eye is bright enough, the pupil will constrict (get smaller), due to the *pupillary light response*.

Initially, the light waves are bent or converged first by the cornea, and then further by the *crystalline lens* (located immediately behind the iris and the pupil), to a nodal point (N) located immediately behind the back surface of the *lens*. At that point, the image becomes reversed (turned backwards) and inverted (turned upside-down). The light continues through the *vitreous humor*, the clear gel that makes up about 80% of the eye's volume, and then, ideally, back to a clear focus on the *retina*, behind the *vitreous*. The small central area of the retina is the *macula*, which provides the best vision of any location in the retina. If the eye is considered to be a type of camera, the retina is equivalent to the film inside of the camera, registering the tiny photons of light interacting with it.

Within the layers of the retina, light impulses are changed into electrical signals. Then they are sent through the *optic nerve*, along the *visual pathway*, to the occipital cortex at the posterior (back) of the brain. Here, the electrical signals are interpreted or "seen" by the brain as a visual image. Actually, then, we do not "see" with our eyes but, rather, with our brains. Our eyes merely are the beginnings of the visual process.

Myopia, Hyperopia, Astigmatism

If the incoming light from a far away object focuses before it gets to the back of the eye, that eye's refractive error is called "myopia" (nearsightedness). If incoming light from something far away has not focused by the time it reaches the back of the eye, that eye's refractive error is "hyperopia" (farsightedness). In the case of "astigmatism," one or more surfaces of the cornea or lens (the eye structures which focus incoming light) are not spherical (shaped like the side of a basketball) but, instead, are cylindrical or toric (shaped a bit like the side of a football). As a result, there is no distinct point of focus inside the eye but, rather, a smeared or spread-out focus. Astigmatism is the most common refractive error.

Presbyopia ("after 40" vision)

After age 40, and most noticeably after age 45, the human eye is affected by *presbyopia*. This natural condition results in greater difficulty maintaining a clear focus at a near distance with an eye which sees clearly far away. Presbyopia is caused by a lessening of flexibility of the *crystalline lens*, as well as to a weakening of the ciliary muscles which control lens focusing. Both are attributable to the aging process.

An eye can see clearly at a far distance naturally, or it can be made to see clearly artificially (such as with the aid of *eyeglasses* or *contact lenses*, or else following a photorefractive procedure such as LASIK). Nevertheless, presbyopia eventually will affect the near focusing of every human eye.

Eye Growth

The average newborn's eyeball is about 18 millimeters in diameter, from front to back (axial length). In an infant, the eye grows slightly to a length of approximately 19½ millimeters. The eye continues to grow, gradually, to a length of about 24-25 millimeters, or about 1 inch, in adulthood. A ping-pong ball is about 1½ inch in diameter, which makes the average adult eyeball about 2/3 the size of a ping-pong ball. The eyeball is set in a protective cone-shaped cavity in the skull called the "orbit" or "socket." This bony orbit also enlarges as the eye grows.

Extraocular Muscles

The orbit is surrounded by layers of soft, fatty tissue. These layers protect the eye and enable it to turn easily. Traversing the fatty tissue are three pairs of *extraocular muscles*, which regulate the motion of each eye: the *medial & lateral rectus* muscles, the *superior & inferior rectus* muscles, and the *superior & inferior oblique* muscles.

Eye Structures

Several structures compose the human eye. Among the most important anatomical components are the *cornea*, *conjunctiva*, *iris*, *crystalline lens*, *vitreous humor*, *retina*, *macula*, *optic nerve*, and *extraocular muscles*.

Low Vision Facts-Anatomy and Physiology of the Eye

The protective outer layer of the eye, sometimes referred to as the "white of the eye" is called the sclera and it maintains the shape of the eye. The front portion of the sclera, called the cornea, is transparent and allows light to enter the eye. The cornea is a powerful refracting surface, providing much of the eye's focusing power (Cassin and Solomon, 1997). Attached to the sclera are six extraocular muscles responsible for movement of the eyes (Bianco, 2002). The choroid is the second layer of the eye and lies between the sclera and the retina. It contains the blood vessels that provide nourishment to the outer layers of the retina (Cassin and Solomon, 1997). The iris is the part of the eye that gives it color. It consists of muscular tissue that responds to surrounding light, making the pupil, or circular opening in the center of the iris, larger or smaller depending on the brightness of the light (Pachler and Rizun, n.d.).

Light entering the pupil falls onto the lens of the eye where it is altered before passing through to the retina. The lens is a transparent, biconvex structure, encased in a thin transparent covering. The function of the lens is to refract and focus incoming light onto the retina for processing (Moorfields Eye Hospital, 2002).

The retina is the innermost layer in the eye. It converts images into electrical impulses that are sent along the optic nerve to the brain where the images are interpreted. The retina can be compared to the film of a camera. It is composed of light sensitive cells known as rods and cones interconnected by a complex mesh of neurons that provide early stage visual processing. Rod cells are primarily in the outer retina, do not discriminate colors, have low spatial resolution, support vision in low light ("night vision"), are sensitive to object movement and provide peripheral vision. Cone cells are densely packed within the central visual field, function best in bright light, process acute images and discriminate colours (Montgomery, 2002). The macula is located in the back of the eye, in the center of the retina. Within the macula is an area called the fovea centralis. This area contains the highest concentration of cones, produces the sharpest vision, and is used to see details clearly (Moorfields Eye Hospital, 2002).

The inside of the eyeball is divided by the lens into two fluid-filled sections. The larger section at the back of the eye is filled with a colorless gelatinous mass called the vitreous humor. The smaller section in the front contains a clear, water-like material called aqueous humor (Discovery Fund for Eye Research, 1999). A circular canal, called the Canal of Schlemm provides a drainage system for the aqueous humor from the eye into the bloodstream. Blockages in the Canal of Schlemm are believed to be contributing factors in the development of glaucoma (Bianco, 2002). The conjunctiva is a mucous membrane that begins at the edge of the cornea and lines the inside surface of the eyelids and sclera, which serves to lubricate the eye. Inflammation of this membrane results in conjunctivitis, commonly known as pink eye (Bianco, 2002; Cassin and Solomon, 1997).

Assessment of Visual Functioning

Visual acuity is by far the most commonly performed measurement of visual function in clinical practice. It is used to determine the presence of refractive error, the adequacy of spectacle corrections, whether a person is fit to drive or enter into some professions such as the police force, whether a person could be registered as partially sighted or blind and is a key indicator of ocular health.

Contrast sensitivity (CS) and glare testing provides additional information about a patient's vision beyond what is provided by visual acuity. Some patients can have normal visual acuity and reduced CS at low spatial frequencies, such as patients with optic neuritis and multiple sclerosis, Parkinson's disease, papilloedema, primary open-angle glaucoma, diabetic retinopathy and compressive lesions of the visual pathways. CS can therefore be used to help screen for visual pathway disorders and to explain symptoms of poor vision in a patient with good visual acuity. Patients with reduced visual acuity could have normal or reduced CS at low frequencies. Patients with reduced CS will have a poorer quality of vision than those with normal CS, despite the same acuity. When used in combination with visual acuity in this way, CS can be used to help explain symptoms of poor or deteriorating vision and to help justify referral of a cataract patient with reasonable visual acuity. Glare testing can also identify visual problems in bright light conditions that are hidden from visual acuity measurements. Reduced CS can also explain a poor response to an optical aid by a low vision patient and suggest the need for a contrast enhancing CCTV. Binocular CS that is better than best monocular, can also suggest the desirability of a binocular low vision aid over a monocular one.

Aims

- To determine chart design(s) and measurement procedure(s) that make visual acuity measurements as accurate and reliable as possible.
- To determine the usefulness of contrast sensitivity and glare tests in clinical practice and to determine the chart design(s) and measurement procedure(s) that make measurements as accurate and reliable as possible.

Nature of Visually Impaired Children with Additional Disabilities

Cortical vision impairment is a complex phenomenon and possibly more common than one would expect. Children with cortical vision impairment are a diverse group whose vision impairment spans a continuum from those who appear to have no vision to those who present with minimal visual perceptual difficulties which are only obvious when they attempt certain tasks (Hughes, 1995).

Cortical vision impairment is not a structural problem of the ocular system, but a disruption in the function of the brain. It is a condition that presents with contradictions. The eyes of children with cortical vision impairment may appear normal. They usually present with normal pupillary response and no nystagmus. Some appear to be blind yet they are able to move around the environment without bumping into anything. Others, appear to have vision which is intermittent. These children are usually attracted to bright shiny moving objects. However while they will reach for an object one moment they may ignore one that is equally as bright the next. They will frequently use one sense at a time, eg they may look at an object but when they touch it they look away.

Groenveld (1997) claims that a multidisciplinary approach is essential in order to obtain a correct diagnosis of CVI and to devise appropriate approaches to learning and management. She recommends intervention by a small group of professionals with a high level of cooperation to ensure continuity. This paper will focus on students with cortical vision impairment. It will define the condition, discuss identification, causes and characteristics, outline behaviours associated with cortical vision impairment, and provide an overview of educational intervention and important pedagogical considerations.

What is Cortical Vision Impairment?

Cortical Vision Impairment is not the result of damage to the eye itself or the optic nerve (it can co-exist) but to the visual systems in the brain which deal with the processing and integration of visual information (Hughes, 1995). It is caused by disturbance of the posterior visual pathways and/or occipital lobes. Jan and Groenveld (1993) emphasise that although changes to visual behaviours and perception can be caused by damage to almost any part of the brain, ìonly damage to the posterior visual pathways, including the visual cortex, can cause cortical visual lossì (p.101).

The clinical definition of cortical vision impairment is a bilateral loss of vision with normal pupillary response and an eye examination that shows no other abnormalities (Good, Jan, DeSA, Barkovich, Groenveld and Hoyt, 1994; Moore 1995). In other words, it is a condition in which the vision is more severely reduced than can be explained by the ophthalmological findings (Steendam, 1989). It may result in a temporary or permanent visual loss (Hein 1995).

The Brain and Vision

Vision has been described Groenveld (1997) as a process. She claims that incoming information is analysed in various areas of the brain. She discusses the findings of Zeki, (1992) and other independent researchers who have identified a number of different areas on the occipital cortex ìwhich respond to distinct attributes of visual informationì (p. 1). She notes that these researchers have demonstrated that the retina is directly linked with the primary visual cortex through the ìlateral geniculate nucleusì (p. 1). The distinct cell layers of the ìlateral geniculate nucleusi respond to different aspects of the visual image, according to Groenveld, and ìexcite corresponding cell groups in the primary visual cortexi (p. 1). Specialisation occurs when information is communicated with the areas of the visual cortex, some of which deal with colour, some with motion and others with shape or a combination of all three. She suggests that information is exchanged between these areas and also the primary visual cortex and that damage to any of them can result in cortical vision impairment.

In addition she explains it could be expected that when the entire primary visual cortex is destroyed, total blindness could realistically be expected. This is not the case, however. Groenveld claims that there is evidence that some signals are ìrouted directly to the specialized areas, bypassing the lateral geniculate bodyi (p, 2). When this occurs, people have, what is referred to as ìblind sighti, and are able to discriminate between motion in different directions or between different wavelengths of light. She adds that these individuals appear to be unconscious of this ability.

Visual Function

The eye is often compared to a camera and the brain to a computer. When light is focused on the retina, it is transformed by photochemical process into electrical messages that are transmitted to the occipital lobes (visual cortex) where they are decoded. Damage to the occipital lobes means that information is only partially analysed, or at times not analysed at all. Jan and Groenveld (1993) explain that the eyes of most children with ocular disorders look abnormal and visual behaviour is usually consistent. They claim thc children with CVI, on the other hand, do not appear blind, they have a short visual attention span, see little, and their visual skills vary from minute to minute. Their visual perception according to Jan and Groenveld (1993) can be ìdramaticallyi impeded by fatigue, ìminor illness, an unfamiliar environment, suboptimal lighting, poor contrast, medications, limited and varying energy levels and innate processing factorsi. The following table taken from Jan and Groenveld (1993) compares some characteristic differences between cortical vision impairment and ocular disorders. Cortical vision impairment frequently exists with ocular vision loss.

It is complex and diagnosis is difficult to determine. It requires thorough medical investigation and careful assessment of functional vision. According to Moore (1995) most children with CVI have some residual vision. He also asserts that the majority of children in developed countries who have cortical visual impairment (10% of CVI cases in the world) have additional neurological deficits, eg, intellectual disability, cerebral palsy, epilepsy, or various spinal and cranial defects (Moore, 1995). This increases the challenge for educators who may find inherent difficulty in differentiating between a visual acuity problem, a perceptual problem, or a delay in vision maturation.

The Role of Vision in Learning

Vision leads to the development of integrative functions such as:

- eye-hand coordination-all visual-motor activities are delayed in infants with CVI, or who are blind
- visual-manual-oral coordination
- visual-object recognition and learning
- visual-spatial recognition and learning. In children with CVI, both visual-object and visual spatial recognition and learning, including the concept of object-constancy are severely impaired
- visual-motor learning and coordination.

Vision is the vital trigger that stimulates head raising. Children with CVI show a developmental delay in head raising functions. Rolling over, raising up on upper limbs, pushing back or forwards and eventually sitting, crawling, creeping, cruising and walking are all believed to be driven initially by visual stimulation triggered by something in the environment, coupled with the drive to obtain objects, explore and manipulate them and thus learn about them. Hence almost all behaviour is visually driven throughout life including all movements, reading, writing, maths, inventing, discovering and creating (Moore, 1995).

Causes of CVI

In the past students with vision impairment have been supported on the basis of ocular conditions alone. With the increase in survival rate of infants and children with damage to the central nervous system and an increase of interest, research and knowledge about cortical vision impairment, this area is now being addressed. One of the major causes of cortical vision impairment that emerged from a study by Groenveld (1997) was asphyxia. This is often referred to in the literature as *cerebral hypoxic-ischemia* (reduced flow of oxygen and blood to the brain which causes extensive brain damage). Groenveld explains that the visual cortex is most vulnerable when the blood supply is interrupted because it is the furthest from the main blood supply, and oxygen is carried by the blood. When this happens, other areas are also affected and, according to Groenveld, this is one of the reasons why CVI rarely occurs in isolation.

Other causes of CVI include head injuries (Kelley, 1998; Groenfeld, 1997; Hughes, 1995), shunt failure in children with hydrocephalus (Kelley, 1998; Connolly, Jan, & Cochrane, 1991), developmental brain defects (Hein, 1995; Groenfeld, 1997), infections of the central nervous system such as encephalitis and meningitis (Kelley, 1998; Groenfeld, 1997) and infantile spasms (Kelley, 1998). Groenveld (1997) claims that about half the cases of head injury found in the infant participants in a study carried out with Jan and Leader in 1990 were due to battery or shaking.

Hughes (1995) describes CVI as being ipermanent to some degree, or transienti (p. 4). She explains that this is dependent on a number of factors such as time of onset of the trauma, the location and the degree of damage to the visual system. Hughes sums up the causes of CVI in the following way:

Associated Diagnosis

A high proportion of children with cortical vision impairment also have additional disabilities with varying degrees of severity which, of course, all interact with each other (Sacks, 1998; Groenveld, 1997). The following conditions are frequently associated with cortical vision impairment:

1. Cerebral Palsy
2. Intellectual disability
3. Hydrocephalus
4. Microcephaly (Hughes 1995).

Characteristics of Children with CVI

The characteristics of students with cortical vision impairment vary considerably. Hughes (1997) comments that few children will present the same characteristics all of the time and this makes the assessment of their visual function and the development of appropriate programmes extremely difficult.

An examination of the literature indicates that the following characteristics may be seen in some learners some of the time:

- eyes appear to be normal (the results of the eye examinations of half of the children who participated in Groenveldís 1990 study were normal: reported in Groenveld, 1997). The other students presented with eye conditions such as optic nerve atrophy, optic nerve hypoplasia, retinal abnormalities and other ocular problems. Groenveld points out that ocular problems may coexist with CVI and this makes diagnosis difficult).
- fluctuating visual abilities/variable visual performance, inconsistent or lack of visual motivation or attention
- stereotypic head positions, tilts or turns. Peripheral vision may be used when looking or reaching for an object, or the child may turn their head away.
- eye closure-the child may blink or quickly close their eyes when visually moving from one target to another, or close one eye in order to see better.
- appears to respond to selective stimuli, eg certain colours, patterns, movement. Some children are attracted by bright lights, or coloured objects. They may ignore black and white objects. Stereotypical searching and staring at brightly coloured objects can be diagnostic for CVI

- navigating vision. Children with CVI who are diagnosed as blind can move about in an unfamiliar environment without bumping into objects.
- photophobia, (abnormal sensitivity to light). I/3 of children diagnosed with CVI may demonstrate photophobia as opposed to attraction to light and colour
- saccadic movement is abnormal. Children with CVI may have difficult in following objects with smooth visual pursuit. In addition they may be unable to comprehend what is seen, whether it moves or where the object is located in space.
- frequent use is made of touch
- will listen rather than look. Hughes (1997) comments that students may avoid looking. She suggests that they sometimes turn away from visual stimuli, opt out, close their eyes, cover their eyes or go to sleep.
- some children have pockets of vision scattered throughout their visual fields. Moore describes this as a ìSwiss cheese effecti (Moore, 1995).
- uses vision as a secondary confirming sense (Hughes, 1995)
- looks away when reaching. The child will locate an object visually, but turn away when touching (Hughes, 1997)
- no nystagmus (unless ocular problems also exist). Groenveld claims that ìa child with pure CVIì will not exhibit nystagmus, although unusual, roving eye movements may bc presenti (Groenveld, 1997).
- *May appear to ësee without looking* (Hughes, 1995).

Identification

It is necessary to assess the level of development of the childís visual skills before commencing an intervention programme. This is to ensure that prerequisite skills have been mastered and the childís programme is pitched at an appropriate level. It is also important to verify the existence of, and qualify the nature of the vision impairment.

Most children with CVI have physical and or intellectual disabilities, but this does not mean that all children with additional disabilities have CVI. However, all children with CVI have a visual perceptual problem (Hein, 1995).

A number of clinical tests can be used to determine CVI. These are shown in the table below which has been compiled from information from Kelley (1998) and Good et al. (1994).

Refractive Errors, Lighting and Field Losses

Refractive errors need to be checked and glasses prescribed if necessary. Appropriate lighting is very important. According to Groenveld Jan and Leader (1990) some children require bright light while others are sensitive to it. Field losses should be taken into account when materials are presented to children. Groenveld Jan and Leader (1990) point out that the side of the field loss does not necessarily correspond to the better hand function. During assessment it is necessary to eliminate other sensory cues as much as possible. This is to ensure that responses are a result of visual stimuli alone (Hughes 1995). In conducting vision assessments Hughes (1995) suggests that vision specialists need to be aware that:

- Children need time to respond. There may be a response delay which could be longer if the child has cerebral palsy.
- Visual response to stimuli may not occur immediately. Teachers need to look for other signs. These may be changes in breathing, ceasing to cry or vocalise, shutting eyes, turning the head away, putting hands over ears/eyes, or blinking Hughes (1995).
- The child may give a visual response, but it may be difficult to interpret, as the child may use peripheral vision or use only one eye while the other wanders. Hughes suggests getting the child to indicate their response in some way, for example, by reaching for the stimulus.
- Avoidance can be another problem. Some children will avoid looking and shut their eyes. With these children it is necessary to persevere.

The emphasis on the collaboration of the various professionals and caregivers to:

- gather information
- interpret data on the student
- use the most accurate information to plan an integrated programme to increase visual functions

are the key components of comprehensive assessments and the development of basic individual programmes (Kelley, Davidson and Sanspree, 1993).

Colour Perception

The colour perception of children with cortical vision impairment is usually intact, even when they have minimal residual vision. Groenveld Jan and Leader (1990) claim that findings from experimental data suggest that the use of colour as a stimulus with forms facilitates the perception of forms by individuals with CVI. They suggest that when teachers introduce simple shapes and letters, it may be helpful to outline them with colour, making sure, of course, that the contrast between the shapes/letters and the background is high. They indicate that yellow and sometimes red are thought to be more easily perceived and recommend that in the initial stages, the identification of objects can be assisted by keeping the colour of the objects constant until the concept has been established. Some children have enough functional vision to deal with picture books and stories. Groenveld Jan and Leader (1990) suggest that for these students it is important to ensure that there is no crowding of material and stress that stories with a single simple picture on a page will be more useful than cluttered pictures and text.

Educational Implications

"Variable visual performance is characteristic of CVI infants/ childreni (Moore, 1995). Since children with CVI often present with fluctuating visual abilities they are frequently described as lazy or malingering. They do in fact function well at times and yet exhibit severe vision defects and operate poorly at others as mentioned previously. Their visual behaviour can be influenced by fatigue, lighting conditions, contrast, context and the environment. It can also be related to medication, and the type and severity of the CVI. Sensory bombardment is considered detrimental to students with cortical vision impairment.

Sensory bombardment is now considered to be detrimental to students with cortical vision impairment (Hein, 1995). Research has proven that busy, stimulating environments may in fact inhibit learning. This is because these students are unable to filter salient information from the mass of sensory information to which they are exposed. Students with CVI may use vision as a secondary or confirming sense.

They may:

- locate objects using tactile cues
- close their eyes when they reach for objects
- behave in ways that suggest that the attempt to process several stimuli is confusing.

Students with CVI Exhibit Changes in Vision

These students may demonstrate differences in vision on an hour-by-hour basis. The frustrating thing for teachers and caregivers is the difficulty in determining whether these changes relate to motivation and attention or to true neurological variations. In addition, according to Groenveld et al (1990), many children tend to improve over time. There are wide variations in educational services, approaches to teaching and treatments applied to these children, and this makes it difficult to draw conclusions about the approaches that influence change.

Students with CVI respond Selectively to Visual Stimuli

Children with cortical vision impairment often respond selectively to visual stimuli.

- colour appears to make objects discernible for many children
- lighting or movement are key characteristics which make certain features of the environment significant for others.

- previous experience with an object or form is a critical characteristic.

Although this varies greatly from child to child, the preference for, and attentiveness to, certain classes of visual stimuli is more notable among children with CVI than among children with other vision problems.

Important Pedagogical Considerations

It is important when students are working on visual perceptual tasks that other handicaps are accommodated as much as possible so that all available energy may be concentrated on the task itself. For example Children with cortical vision impairment may also have epilepsy. Reasonable seizure control needs to be achieved before remediation for cortical vision impairment occurs. Children with multiple disabilities need far more energy to maintain a perceptual continuum than their non disabled peers (Groenveld, Jan & Leader, 1990). This is because they need to analyse visual information in much smaller units and with much greater intensity to interpret its meaning (Groenveld, Jan & Leader, 1990). It is like learning a foreign language. Students find it:

- tiring to keep up with the flow of conversation and overload occurs easily.
- a large amount of energy goes into posture, rather than into maintaining visual perception when they have poor balance
- visual targets are lost involuntarily by students with poor head control if their heads are not supported properly.

Tasks should be repetitive. They should have a clear beginning and end: this helps to conserve energy. When childrenis energy levels are low, they fade in and out of tasks. Their eyes cease to focus for brief periods. Facial expressions should be watched for attending behaviour (Groenveld, Jan & Leader, 1990). Groenveld, Jan and Leader, (1990) suggest that a multidisciplinary approach is necessary to obtain a correct diagnosis and to devise appropriate management strategies. They argue that:

- a small number of people should be involved in the intervention
- cooperation between team members should be high
- the amount of visual stimulation and nonessential information should be reduced to enhance visual efficiency
- visual efficiency may be improved using additional cuing through language, touch, and colour coding
- the accommodation of additional handicaps can assist in maximising available energy for perceptual tasks
- because of the visual complexity of regular classroom settings, full inclusion is not advisable as it may reduce the opportunity for meaningful visual perception. Partial inclusion, however, is important for the social and emotional development of the student.

The contribution of the vision specialists should expand beyond basic programmeming to improve visual functioning. Their role as a member of the transdisciplinary team should include sharing information on:

- the impact of cortical vision impairment on learning
- other specific areas of functioning
- skills of every day living
- orientation and mobility
- ways to increase opportunities to use vision and other sensory information
- ways to use special materials and adaptive techniques
- ways to teach specific skills for protection, safety, and ease of movement.

These are all essential components of any programme for a child with a vision impairment and should be equally available to a child with additional impairments (Kelley, Davidson & Sanspree, 1993).

Teachers of students with cortical vision impairment may need to consider:

- limiting visual input

- using contrasting colours
- identifying visual skills that can be targeted for a particular lesson
- using tactual, gustatory, or olfactory replacements for the use of vision.

Students gain more independence through the use of outline movement, verbal prompting, and cuing. Orientation and mobility instructors are needed to train teachers and caregivers in techniques for the individual child. The emphasis should be on guiding not helping.

Visual and Multisensory Programs

To reduce the specific problems the children have, programmes should be designed with the following guidelines in mind:

- consistency across all learning environments in materials, methods and language
- short frequent periods of work
- much repetition of familiar activities to maintain skills
- learning in a visually uncluttered environment. This will assist in:
  1. limiting the childís spatial and figure ground problems
  2. minimising distractions
  3. encouraging a focus on the work in hand
- ensuring the material to be viewed is well lit from behind the child. Some writers suggest spot-lighting materials in a dim room
- ensuring there is a strong contrast between the material to be viewed and the background
- providing material that is visually motivating and attractive: use shiny, florescent, luminous, coloured, black and white or other starkly contrasting patterns
- presenting material close to the child, level with their eyes and in a position where you expect optimal response. It is very important to be consistent

- reinforcing improved visual performance
- planning a programme using a multisensory approach when a child begins to show awareness to visual cues alone
- using other senses to confirm visual input and aid memory recall. Always presenting the visual information first, then adding the other sensory input otherwise the child may not bother to look
- using every day materials
- trying to involve children as much as possible to decrease passivity
- communicating what is happening to students and showing them the materials you are using Let them feel the objects against their skin, smell and hear them and encourage reaching.
- allowing plenty of time for response
- re-assessing and re-evaluating the programme regularly.

The participation of teachers trained in the education of students with vision impairment (vision consultants) and orientation and mobility instructors is vital to enhance the studentís access to, and participation in the education process. There needs to be an emphasis on collaboration between various professionals and caregivers. Participation in the transdisciplinary team allows the vision consultant to influence the students complete programme and ensure that it is time effective. A collaborative effort allows the vision consultant to educate others about the unique needs of the child resulting from the vision impairment (Kelley, Davidson & Sanspree, 1993).

Conclusion

It is well documented, according to Moore (1995), that infants and children with CVI are delayed to a greater or lesser degree in reaching developmental milestones and in all sensori-motor activities and social development. Direct intervention and stimulation at an early age and support for caregivers is essential particularly in the early years. Moore (1995) reports that 70% of children who have CVI or who are blind have some degree of intellectual disability and/or other disabilities.

In conclusion the problems of children with CVI are usually complex. A multidisciplinary or a transdisciplinary approach is necessary to obtain a proper diagnosis and to devise appropriate management strategies. The number of people involved in the programme should be limited, with a high level of cooperation between them. Visual efficiency can be increased by reducing the amount of visual stimulation and eliminating non-essential information. Additional cuing through language, touch and colour coding may improve visual efficiency also. The level of available energy for visual perceptual tasks should be maximised by accommodating additional disabilities.

Learning Characteristics of Visually Impaired Children

Partners in the IST programme-funded MICOLE project, the teams responsible are working in close contact with national and local associations and organisations of visually-disabled persons, as well as schools. Their main task is to design the system itself. However, project coordinator Roope Raisamo, University of Tampere, Finland, describes several supporting activities emphasising users and their real needs.

> *"We are experimenting with how to use different senses to partially replace missing visual capabilities, especially in tasks that are central in the construction of the system," he says. "Empirical research of collaborative and cross-modal haptic interfaces for visually-impaired children is one of the most important research activities."*

Haptic technology interfaces with the user through the sense of touch. This emerging technology adds the sense of touch to previously visual-only solutions. MICOLE's software architecture and applications are multimodal, that is, they use hearing and touch to complement different levels of visual disability. Their work extends beyond developing an assistive tool. "In addition to MICOLE's immediate value as a tool, the system will have societal implications by improving the inclusion of the visually disabled in education, work and society in general," explains Raisamo.

Initial field studies involved interviews with teachers, children and related user organisations as well as observations of actual group work in schools. The objective was to determine how visually-impaired children collaborate in school with peers and teachers, and to understand to what extent they engage in group work.

> *"The interaction among the pupils, with teachers and with their peers is very important for learning," says Raisamo. "We know that collaborative learning has benefits because the pupils learn through a dialogue with their peers and construct their own knowledge by doing tasks together with others."*

Field study results from Austria, Finland, France, Greece, Ireland, Lithuania, Sweden and the UK showed major differences in the education of visually-impaired children, however, they revealed many similarities regarding aspects of collaboration. Based on these results, a prototyping workshop was held in Stockholm where the school situation for such pupils was addressed. Various hapitc and auditory applications developed within MICOLE were assessed and new designs formulated.

He notes there are no specific requirements for the users of the system. "The system adapts to the users. It is aimed at visually-impaired children, but because it facilitates collaboration among sighted and visually-impaired children, it also supports sighted children." A multimodal system with visual, audio and haptic feedback can support many kinds of users with disabilities because missing one of the modalities does not make the system unusable, Raisamo adds.

Project partners have developed or tested 16 different interfaces and application prototypes, such as explorative learning of the earth's internal layers, rhythm reproduction, a tactile maze game, virtual maracas (percussion instruments), post-its with a haptic barcode, an electric circuit browser, a haptic simon game, memory games, a haptic turtle and a haptic game of the classic first video game, pong. For example, to better teach natural phenomenon, such as seasons, gravity and the solar system, project partners constructed a system using proactive agents that offer the pupil help when necessary. The user decides whether to accept help comprised of visual, auditory and haptic feedback to present content.

Project partners include European and world leaders in the area of haptics and multimodal-human-computer interaction. For example, Reachin Technologies AB is a world leader in haptic technology; France Telecom has experience in developing applications for the blind.

> *"MICOLE offers an outstanding opportunity and the critical mass for the consortium to integrate and realise results of their earlier work and to test the most novel ideas to meet the needs of the visually impaired," says Raisamo. "The results are expected to make a valuable European contribution to the development of the information society and real-world equality for visually-disabled children, empowering them as future citizens."*

Products for Visually Impaired Children

Services for Blind and Visually Impaired Veterans: The VA provides rehabilitation programmes targeting low vision and blind veterans, and is also aggressively pursuing innovative service delivery models. The challenge of helping these low vision and blind veterans has greatly increased, and the Department of Veterans Affairs has made a commitment to provide world-class rehabilitation training by enhancing services, improving access to care and increasing patient satisfaction for veterans with visual impairments. The current estimated number of legally blind veterans in the United States is more than 160,000 (De l'Aune, 2002). Currently, over 35,000 veterans have enrolled for VA care. This number is expected to grow in the coming years as a result of aging of the veteran population, because the most prevalent causes of legal blindness are age-related.

Blindness is considered one of the most devastating disabilities that can affect an individual, striking people of all ages and walks of life. The term legal blindness is, however, a deceiving one. The generally accepted definition of legal blindness is either central visual acuity of 20/200 or worse in the better eye with the use of corrective glasses; or, central visual acuity better than 20/200 in the better eye with visual field deficits in which the widest diameter of peripheral fields is 20 degrees or less. The definition of low vision used to generate estimates of veterans with low vision is central visual acuity equal to or less than 20/70 but greater than 20/200 in the better seeing eye with the use of corrective glasses. In the United States the number of veterans diagnosed with low vision (those individuals who have a significant, uncorrectable visual impairment from 20/70 to 20/190, but who are not legally blind) is currently estimated to be more than one million veterans (De l'Aune, 2002). The most common causes of low vision are age-related as well.

The impact of blindness is very individualized and includes a wide range of eye conditions, from the older veteran whose vision gradually worsens due to macular degeneration or some other age-related eye problems, to the serviceperson who is totally blind from traumatic injury. Veterans who must cope with a significant loss of vision require individualized, specialized care and treatment suited to their specific cause of blindness. Physical and medical condition, age, ability to cope with frustrating situations, learning ability, and the overall needs and lifestyle of the veteran are important considerations. A person confronted with blindness may feel limited and frustrated in performing everyday activities previously taken for granted. Tasks such as dressing, eating, writing, reading, and traveling may become difficult to perform independently. Communication with other people by ordinary means is often hampered, as is the ability to keep up with the daily news and current events. Social interaction, recreation, and hobbies may also be limited or curtailed as a result of vision impairment.

Frequently a person may be forced into premature retirement because of vision loss, often resulting in loss of income and financial security. As a result of the numerous negative outcomes, it is not uncommon for the newly blinded individual to undergo a period of personal stress. Individuals facing blindness and vision impairment may lose self-esteem, or believe the future holds little promise. Spouses, families, and loved ones may experience pressure, strain or uncertainty.

Loss of sight affects each person differently and may hinder overall functioning, including employment, recreation, communication, and social, and family life. To help the veteran cope with these problems the Department of Veterans Affairs established the Blind Rehabilitation Service to provide a wide variety of rehabilitation programmes and services to veterans who are blind.

The rehabilitation programme is designed to improve quality of life for veterans who are blind or severely visually impaired through the development and enhancement of skills and capabilities needed for personal independence, adjustment, and successful reintegration into the community and family environment. Elements of the blind rehabilitation programme include: 10 Blind Rehabilitation Centers, Visual Impairment Services Teams (VIST) and VIST Coordinators located at many VA Medical Centers and VA Outpatient Clinics, Blind Rehabilitation Outpatient Specialist (BROS), National Consultants, and a Computer Access Training (CAT) Program. In addition, there are a variety of low vision services and blind rehabilitation programmes within the Department of Veterans Affairs system including: Visual Impairment Services Outpatient Rehabilitation (VISOR) programmes, Visual Impairment Centers to Optimize Remaining Sight (VICTORS) programmes, Intermediate Low Vision Clinics, Advanced Ambulatory Low Vision Clinics and Advanced Hoptel Outpatient Blind Rehabilitation Programs.

The VA Blind Rehabilitation Service is committed to a continuum of care model that extends from the veteran's home environment to the local VA care site and regionally-based inpatient training programmes encompassing an array of alternative rehabilitative services. The following will describe in detail the programmes offered in Blind Rehabilitation Service, as well as low vision services available at local VA Medical Centers and Outpatient Clinics.

The Blind Rehabilitation Centers

In 1948 the first Blind Rehabilitation Center was opened at the VA Hospital in Hines, Illinois (just west of Chicago). To meet the demand of increasing numbers of blind veterans, additional Blind Centers were later strategically located at VA Medical Centers throughout the United States, including: Palo Alto, California, 1967; West Haven, Connecticut, 1969; American Lake, Washington, 1971; Waco, Texas, 1974; Birmingham, Alabama, 1982; San Juan, Puerto Rico, 1985; Tucson, Arizona, 1994; Augusta, Georgia, 1996; and West Palm Beach, Florida, 2000. Future plans include the addition of new blind centers.

The Blind Rehabilitation Centers provide rehabilitation to legally blind veterans. Comprehensive, individualized blind rehabilitation services are provided in an inpatient VA Medical Center environment by a multidisciplinary team of rehabilitation specialists. A Computer Access Training Program (CAT) is offered as part of the comprehensive training or as a specialized inpatient or outpatient rehabilitation option. Attendance in a rehabilitation programme requires that all veterans participate in ongoing daily activities, and veterans must meet specific travel requirements in order to attend. All medical conditions that a veteran may currently have, in addition to visual impairment, must be stable enough to permit participation in rehabilitation activities. The management of chronic medical conditions is addressed as part of the training regimen, with many veterans experiencing improvement during their stay.

VA's Blind Rehabilitation Program has many years of experience and has found that comprehensive rehabilitation is usually the best course to follow for those who are legally or totally blind. Highly qualified professional staff members guide the individual through a rehabilitation process that leads to maximum adjustment to the disability, reorganization of the person's life, and return to a contributing place in the family and community. To achieve comprehensive rehabilitation, the Blind Rehabilitation Centers offer a variety of skill courses to the veteran, each of which is designed to help achieve a realistic level of independence. The veteran is also assisted in developing a healthy attitude toward himself, blindness, and the future.

Rehabilitation Process for Visually Impaired Persons

Orientation and Mobility

Principles of independent travel (often referred to as Orientation and Mobility) are taught using a cane." Maximum use of any remaining vision to assist travel is evaluated, and in many cases low vision devices are provided and made an integral part of mobility training. Sensory training classes teach the veteran how to more effectively use remaining senses, particularly hearing, as an aid in travel. In addition, exercises in mental mapping serve to enhance the veteran's orientation while traveling through different kinds of environments. Orientation and Mobility instruction in relatively simple routes to increasingly complex routes builds the veteran's confidence in the ability to travel independently. By the completion of the instruction the veteran should have a realistic understanding of his or her travel capacity, and the ability to travel safely and independently in both familiar and unfamiliar areas.

Living Skills

This phase of the rehabilitation programme includes communication, activities of daily living, and independent living.

Communication: Instruction is designed to enhance and restore abilities in written and spoken communication. Opportunities to learn and use strategies and tools for communication are provided to the veteran, such as typing, handwriting, telling time, management of financial records, Braille, recording devices and other electronic equipment. These courses help the veteran to keep up with current events, correspondence and personal files, and help to maintain a normal means of communication with other people.

Activities of Daily Living: Strategies are provided to the veterans to help them accomplish tasks ranging from routine (managing money, making a cup of coffee) to complex activities such as arranging an entire wardrobe, shopping, kitchen organization, and preparation of complete meals. The emphasis is on learning by doing; techniques and methods are taught and then integrated into the veteran's daily routine. By the completion of the programme the veteran should be capable of handling daily living tasks with complete or greatly enhanced independence. Family members often experience a reduction in the burden of care they have been providing to the visually impaired family member.

Independent Living Program: Each Blind Rehabilitation Center has established an independent living programme that is designed primarily for those veterans who will be living alone following their rehabilitation. After extensive instruction, the veteran is given an opportunity to practice newly acquired skills. The veteran can experience countless tasks typically encountered when living independently, and the veteran can devise solutions to many of these problems before returning home. The Living Skills Instructors also arrange consultations with the VA Medical Center dietetic service so veterans have the opportunity to meet with a dietitian. This is particularly important for those veterans who may require special diets and who may require education concerning these diets. Detailed instructions in preparation of special diets can be provided and daily nutrition can be monitored.

Manual Skills

This programme area provides the veteran who has little or no vision with the means to develop and improve organizational skills, awareness of the environment, safe and efficient work habits, spatial relationships, and an understanding and mastery of tactual ability. The manual skills training focuses on the sequential development of skills and builds confidence. Training is generally presented to the veteran in several areas, and may include (but is not limited to) handcrafts, home mechanics, woodworking, metalworking, leatherwork, weaving and ceramics.

The initial training area consists of hand crafting objects in order to develop the individual's confidence in their non-visual senses. The home mechanics training is an introduction to the tools and organizational techniques that allows an individual to perform simple repairs and assembly. Advanced training focuses on the use of adaptive measuring devices, hand tools and power equipment typically used in woodworking.

The manual skills training is not vocational, although some veterans have developed vocational interests or hobbies after participating in this training. Manual skills training may enable a veteran to resume performing home repairs or other related activities at home, further adding to the person's self-confidence and motivation. Veterans who enter blind rehabilitation with minimal abilities in manual skills or those who are slightly skilled in aspects of mechanics or woodworking find this training very beneficial.

Visual Skills

Approximately 85 percent of all veterans who enter a rehabilitation programme possess some level of vision that may be useful in many situations. Each veteran attending the programme is given a comprehensive eye examination, and a thorough visual skills assessment is performed.

Visual skills training addresses the needs of veterans with remaining vision and helps these individuals gain a better understanding of their eye problems through therapy. Instruction focuses on effective use of remaining vision through the development and use of visual motor and visual perceptual skills. Assessment and instruction with special optical and electronic devices that are designed to meet the needs of people who are visually impaired is provided. Ergonomic equipment such as special lighting and positioning devices are provided to assist veterans in using vision effectively. Lessons may employ the use of visual and ergonomic equipment and visual skills that address near, intermediate and distance tasks. This approach allows veterans who have vision to accomplish a variety of tasks, such as reading printed material, and to use their vision to perform routine activities of daily life, independent travel, etc.

An important goal of the visual skills area is to help the veterans to develop a realistic assessment and understanding of their visual capabilities and limitations so that they may better use their vision in daily life.

UNIT-IV

Mental Retardation

Concept, Definition, Classification and Etiological Factors of Mental Retardation

Mental retardation is a generalized disorder, characterized by subaverage cognitive functioning and deficits in two or more adaptive behaviors with onset before the age of 18. Once focused almost entirely on cognition, the definition now includes both a component relating to mental functioning and one relating to individuals' functional skills in their environment.

Alternative Terms

The term "mental retardation" is a diagnostic term designed to capture and standardize a group of disconnected categories of mental functioning such as "idiot", "imbecile", and "moron" derived from early IQ tests, which acquired pejorative connotations in popular discourse over time. The term "mental retardation" has itself now acquired some pejorative and shameful connotations over the last few decades due to the use of "retarded" as an insult. This may in turn have contributed to its replacement with expressions such as "mentally challenged" or "intellectual disability". While "developmental disability" may be considered to subsume other disorders, "developmental disability" or "developmental delay" (for children under age 18), are generally considered more acceptable terms than "mental retardation" among members of the disability community.

- In North America mental retardation is subsumed into the broader term developmental disability, which also includes epilepsy, autism, cerebral palsy and other disorders that develop during the developmental period (birth to age 18.) Because service provision is tied to the designation developmental disability, it is used by many parents, direct support professionals, and physicians. However, in school-based settings, the more specific term mental retardation is still typically used, and is one of 13 categories of disability under which children may be identified for special education services under Public Law 108-446.

- The phrase intellectual disability is increasingly being used as a synonym for people with significantly below-average cognitive ability. These terms are sometimes used as a means of separating general intellectual limitations from specific, limited deficits as well as indicating that it is not an emotional or psychological disability. Intellectual disability may also used to describe the outcome of traumatic brain injury or lead poisoning or dementing conditions such as Alzheimer's disease. It is not specific to congenital disorders such as Down syndrome.

The American Association on Mental Retardation continued to use the term *mental retardation* until 2006. In June 2006 its members voted to change the name of the organization to the "American Association on Intellectual and Developmental Disabilities," rejecting the options to become the AAID or AADD. Part of the rationale for the double name was that many members worked with people with pervasive developmental disorders, most of whom do not have mental retardation.

In the UK, "mental handicap" had become the common medical term, replacing "mental subnormality" in Scotland and "mental deficiency" in England and Wales, until Stephen Dorrell, Secretary of State for Health for the United Kingdom from 1995-7, changed the NHS's designation to "learning disability." The new term is not yet widely understood, and is often taken to refer to problems affecting schoolwork (the American usage), which are known in the UK as "learning difficulties." British social workers may use "learning difficulty" to refer to both people with MR and those with conditions such as dyslexia.

In England and Wales between 1983 and 2008 the Mental Health Act 1983 defined "mental impairment" and "severe mental impairment" as "a state of arrested or incomplete development of mind which includes significant/severe impairment of intelligence and social functioning and is associated with abnormally aggressive or seriously irresponsible conduct on the part of the person concerned."

As behavior was involved, these were not necessarily permanent conditions: they were defined for the purpose of authorising detention in hospital or guardianship. The term Mental Impairment was removed from the Act in November 2008, but the grounds for detention remained. However, English statute law uses "mental impairment" elsewhere in a less well-defined manner—*e.g.* to allow exemption from taxes—implying that mental retardation without any behavioural problems is what is meant.

Signs

Children with mental retardation may learn to sit up, to crawl, or to walk later than other children, or they may learn to talk later. Both adults and children with mental retardation may also exhibit the following characteristics:

- Delays in oral language development
- Deficits in memory skills
- Difficulty learning social rules
- Difficulty with problem solving skills
- Delays in the development of adaptive behaviors such as self-help or self-care skills
- Lack of social inhibitors.

The limitations of cognitive functioning will cause a child with mental retardation to learn and develop more slowly than a typical child. Children may take longer to learn language, develop social skills, and take care of their personal needs such as dressing or eating. Learning will take them longer, require more repetition, and skills may need to be adapted to their learning level. Nevertheless, virtually every child is able to learn, develop and become participating members of the community.

In early childhood mild mental retardation (IQ 60–70) may not be obvious, and may not be identified until children begin school. Even when poor academic performance is recognized, it may take expert assessment to distinguish mild mental retardation from learning disability or emotional/behavioral disorders. As individuals with mild mental retardation reach adulthood, many learn to live independently and maintain gainful employment.

Moderate mental retardation (IQ 50–60) is nearly always apparent within the first years of life. Children with moderate mental retardation will require considerable supports in school, at home, and in the community in order to participate fully. As adults they may live with their parents, in a supportive group home, or even semi-independently with significant supportive services to help them, for example, manage their finances. A person with a more severe mental retardation will need more intensive support and supervision his or her entire life.

Diagnosis

According to the latest edition of the *Diagnostic and Statistical Manual of Mental Disorders* (DSM-IV), three criteria must be met for a diagnosis of mental retardation: an IQ below 70, significant limitations in two or more areas of adaptive behavior (as measured by an adaptive behavior rating scale, i.e. communication, self-help skills, interpersonal skills, and more), and evidence that the limitations became apparent before the age of 18. It is formally diagnosed by professional assessment of *intelligence* and *adaptive behavior*.

IQ below 70

The first English-language IQ test, the Terman-Binet, was adapted from an instrument used to measure potential to achieve developed by Binet in France. Terman translated the test and employed it as a means to measure intellectual capacity based on oral language, vocabulary, numerical reasoning, memory, motor speed and analysis skills. The mean score on the currently available IQ tests is 100, with a standard deviation of 15 (WAIS/WISC-IV) or 16 (Stanford-Binet). Sub-average intelligence is generally considered to be present when an individual scores two standard deviatons below the test mean. Factors other than cognitive ability (depression, anxiety, etc.) can contribute to low IQ scores; it is important for the evaluator to rule them out prior to concluding that measured IQ is "significantly below average".

The following ranges, based on Standard Scores of intelligence tests, reflect the categories of the American Association of Mental Retardation, the Diagnostic and Statistical Manual of Mental Disorders-IV-TR, and the International Classification of Diseases-10:

Class	*IQ*
Profound mental retardation	Below 20
Severe mental retardation	20–34
Moderate mental retardation	35–49
Mild mental retardation	50–69
Borderline intellectual functioning	70–79

Since the diagnosis is not based only on IQ scores, but must also take into consideration a person's adaptive functioning, the diagnosis is not made rigidly. It encompasses intellectual scores, adaptive functioning scores from an adaptive behavior rating scale based on descriptions of known abilities provided by someone familiar with the person, and also the observations of the assessment examiner who is able to find out directly from the person what he or she can understand, communicate, and the like.

Significant Limitations in Two or More Areas of Adaptive Behavior

Adaptive behavior, or adaptive functioning, refers to the skills needed to live independently (or at the minimally acceptable level for age). To assess adaptive behavior, professionals compare the functional abilities of a child to those of other children of similar age. To measure adaptive behavior, professionals use structured interviews, with which they systematically elicit information about persons' functioning in the community from people who know them well. There are many adaptive behavior scales, and accurate assessment of the quality of someone's adaptive behavior requires clinical judgment as well. Certain skills are important to adaptive behavior, such as:

- daily living skills, such as getting dressed, using the bathroom, and feeding oneself;
- communication skills, such as understanding what is said and being able to answer;
- social skills with peers, family members, spouses, adults, and others.

Evidence that the Limitations became Apparent in Childhood

This third condition is used to distinguish it from dementing conditions such as Alzheimer's disease or due to traumatic injuries with attendant brain damage.

Causes

Down syndrome, fetal alcohol syndrome and Fragile X syndrome are the three most common inborn causes. However, doctors have found many other causes. The most common are:

- Genetic conditions. Sometimes disability is caused by abnormal genes inherited from parents, errors when genes combine, or other reasons. The most prevalent genetic conditions include Down syndrome, Klinefelter's syndrome, Fragile X syndrome, Neurofibromatosis, congenital hypothyroidism, Williams syndrome, Phenylketonuria (PKU), and Prader-Willi syndrome. Other genetic conditions include Phelan-McDermid syndrome (22q13del), Mowat-Wilson syndrome, genetic ciliopathy. In the rarest of cases, abnormalities with the X or Y chromosome may also cause disability. 48, XXXX and 49, XXXXX syndrome affect a small number of girls worldwide, while boys may be affected by 47, XYY, 49, XXXXY, or 49, XYYYY.
- Problems during pregnancy. Mental disability can result when the fetus does not develop properly. For example,

there may be a problem with the way the fetus' cells divide as it grows. A woman who drinks alcohol (see fetal alcohol syndrome) or gets an infection like rubella during pregnancy may also have a baby with mental disability.

- Problems at birth. If a baby has problems during labour and birth, such as not getting enough oxygen, he or she may have developmental disability due to brain damage.
- Exposure to certain types of disease or toxins. Diseases like whooping cough, measles, or meningitis can cause mental disability if medical care is delayed or inadequate. Exposure to poisons like lead or mercury may also affect mental ability.
- Iodine deficiency, affecting approximately 2 billion people worldwide, is the leading preventable cause of mental disability in areas of the developing world where iodine deficiency is endemic. Iodine deficiency also causes goiter, an enlargement of the thyroid gland. More common than full-fledged cretinism, as retardation caused by severe iodine deficiency is called, is mild impairment of intelligence. Certain areas of the world due to natural deficiency and governmental inaction are severely affected. India is the most outstanding, with 500 million suffering from deficiency, 54 million from goiter, and 2 million from cretinism. Among other nations affected by iodine deficiency, China and Kazakhstan have begun taking action, whereas Russia has not.
- Malnutrition is a common cause of reduced intelligence in parts of the world affected by famine, such as Ethiopia.

Treatment and Assistance

By most definitions mental retardation is more accurately considered a *disability* rather than a *disease*. MR can be distinguished in many ways from mental illness, such as schizophrenia or depression. Currently, there is no "cure" for an established disability, though with appropriate support and teaching, most individuals can learn to do many things.

There are thousands of agencies in the United States that provide assistance for people with developmental disabilities. They include state-run, for-profit, and non-profit, privately run agencies. Within one agency there could be departments that include fully staffed residential homes, day habilitation programmes that approximate schools, workshops wherein people with disabilities can obtain jobs, programmes that assist people with developmental disabilities in obtaining jobs in the community, programmes that provide support for people with developmental disabilities who have their own apartments, programmes that assist them with raising their children, and many more. The Burton Blatt Institute at Syracuse University works to advance the civic, economic, and social participation of people with disabilities. There are also many agencies and programmes for parents of children with developmental disabilities.

Although there is no specific medication for mental retardation, many people with developmental disabilities have further medical complications and may take several medications. Beyond that there are specific programmes that people with developmental disabilities can take part in wherein they learn basic life skills. These "goals" may take a much longer amount of time for them to accomplish, but the ultimate goal is independence. This may be anything from independence in tooth brushing to an independent residence. People with developmental disabilities learn throughout their lives and can obtain many new skills even late in life with the help of their families, caregivers, clinicians and the people who coordinate the efforts of all of these people.

Archaic Terms

Several traditional terms denoting varying degrees of mental deficiency long predate psychiatry, but have since been subject to the euphemism treadmill. In common usage they are simple forms of abuse. Their now-obsolete use as psychiatric technical definitions is of purely historical interest. They are often encountered in old documents such as books, academic papers, and census forms (for example, the British census of 1901 has a column heading including the terms *imbecile* and *feeble-minded*).

There have been some efforts made among mental health professionals to discourage use of these terms. Nevertheless their use persists. In addition to the terms below, the abbreviation *retard* or *tard* is still used as a generic insult. A BBC survey in 2003 ranked *retard* as the most offensive disability-related word, ahead of terms such as spastic (not considered offensive in America) and mong.

- Cretin is the oldest and comes from a dialectal French word for Christian. The implication was that people with significant intellectual or developmental disabilities were "still human" (or "still Christian") and deserved to be treated with basic human dignity. This term has not been used in any serious or scientific endeavor since the middle of the 20th century and is now always considered a term of abuse: notably, in the 1964 movie *Becket*, King Henry II calls his son and heir a "cretin." "Cretinism" is also used as an obsolescent term to refer to the condition of congenital hypothyroidism, in which there is some degree of mental retardation.
- Amentia has a long history, mostly associated with dementia. The difference between amentia and dementia was originally defined by time of onset. Amentia was the term used to describe an individual who developed deficits in mental functioning early in life, while dementia described individuals who develop mental deficiencies as adults. During the 1890s, amentia was used to describe someone who was born with mental deficiencies. By 1912, ament was a classification lumping "idiots, imbeciles, and feeble minded" individuals in a category separate from a dement classification, in which the onset is later in life.
- Dementia appears to be unique in that it seems to have gone unchanged in terms of meaning over hundreds of years. The term first emerged in the sixteenth century and was used in reference to people who lost mental functioning. In 1912, the classification of dement was

used to identify individuals who had previously functioned normally, but who lost their faculties over time. Today's definition has pinpointed the onset of mental deterioration as occurring after the age of eighteen.

- Idiot indicated the greatest degree of intellectual disability, where the mental age is two years or less, and the person cannot guard himself or herself against common physical dangers. The term was gradually replaced by the term profound mental retardation.
- Imbecile indicated an intellectual disability less extreme than idiocy and not necessarily inherited. It is now usually subdivided into two categories, known as severe mental retardation and moderate mental retardation.
- Moron was defined by the American Association for the Study of the Feeble-minded in 1910, following work by Henry H. Goddard, as the term for an adult with a mental age between eight and twelve; mild mental retardation is now the term for this condition. Alternative definitions of these terms based on IQ were also used. This group was known in UK law from 1911 to 1959/60 as "feeble-minded".
- Mongolism was a medical term used to identify someone with Down syndrome. For obvious reasons, the Mongolian People's Republic requested that the medical community cease use of the term as a description of mental retardation. Their request was granted in the 1960s, when the World Health Organization agreed that the term should cease being used within the medical community.
- In the field of special education, educable (or "educable mentally retarded") refers to MR students with IQs of approximately 50-75 who can progress academically to a late elementary level. Trainable (or "trainable mentally retarded") refers to students whose IQs fall below 50 but who are still capable of learning personal hygiene and other living skills in a sheltered setting, such as a group home. In many areas, these terms have fallen

out of favor in favor of "severe" and "moderate" mental retardation. While the names change, the meaning stays roughly the same in practice.

- Retarded comes from the Latin retardare, "to make slow, delay, keep back, or hinder." The term was recorded in 1426 as a "fact or action of making slower in movement or time." The first record of retarded in relation to being mentally slow was in 1895. The term retarded was used to replace terms like idiot, moron, and imbecile because it was not a derogatory term. By the 1960s, however, the term had taken on a partially derogatory meaning as well.

Perhaps the negative connotations associated with these numerous terms for mental retardation reflect society's ambivalent attitude about the condition. There are competing desires among elements of society, some of whom seek neutral medical terms, and others who want to use such terms as weapons with which to abuse people.

Today, the term "retarded" is slowly being replaced by new words like "special" or "challenged." The term "developmental delay" is rapidly gaining popularity among caretakers and parents of individuals with mental retardation. Using the word "delay" is preferred over "disability" by many people, because that term (delay) encapsulates the core deficit that creates mental retardation in the first place. Delay suggests that a person has been held back from their potential, rather than someone who has been disabled.

Usage has changed over the years, and differed from country to country, which needs to be borne in mind when looking at older books and papers. For example, "mental retardation" in some contexts covers the whole field, but previously applied to what is now the mild MR group. "Feeble-minded" used to mean mild MR in the UK, and once applied in the US to the whole field. "Borderline MR" is not currently defined, but the term may be used to apply to people with IQs in the 70s. People with IQs of 70 to 85 used to be eligible for special consideration in the US public education system on grounds of mental retardation.

Along with the changes in terminology, and the downward drift in acceptability of the old terms, institutions of all kinds have had to repeatedly change their names. This affects the names of schools, hospitals, societies, government departments, and academic journals. For example, the Midlands Institute of Mental Subnormality became the British Institute of Mental Handicap and is now the British Institute of Learning Disability. This phenomenon is shared with mental health and motor disabilities, and seen to a lesser degree in sensory disabilities

Mental Retardation: Definition, Classification, and Systems of Supports

The American Association on Mental Retardation (AAMR) publishes an edited manual approximately every 10 years on terminology, classification, and clinical judgment related to mental retardation and disability. Similar to the 9th edition (Luckasson, 1992), in this 10th edition, mental retardation is defined as:

A disability characterized by significant limitations both in intellectual functioning and in adaptive skills. This disability originates before age 18. Further, five assumptions are essential to the application of this definition:

(1) Limitations in present functioning must be considered within the context of community environments typical of the individual's age peers and culture.

(2) Valid assessment considers cultural and linguistic diversity as well as differences in communication, sensory, motor, and behavioral strengths.

(3) Within an individual, limitations often coexist with strengths.

(4) An important purpose of describing limitations is to develop a profile of needed supports.

(5) With appropriate personalized supports over a sustained period, the life functioning of the person with mental retardation generally will improve.

Mental retardation is described not as an absolute trait, but instead, as an ever-changing interaction between the individual's intellectual and adaptive abilities, participation in activities, interactions with others, social roles, and health. These factors are then considered in the context of the individual's immediate and cultural environment in determining supports. The term mental retardation is retained in this edition because, according to the authors, no consensus could be reached on another term.

The first section of the manual, overview and development, including these definitions of mental retardation, and related terminology, also provides an historical perspective on the definition of mental retardation over a 100-year period. A most notable change in the definition was presented in the 9th edition when the method of classifying levels of severity was redefined. Previously, these levels were determined by IQ score and were classified in categories of mild, moderate, severe, and profound. In the new classification schema, levels are determined by degrees of needed supports. Thus, in the new definition classifications are based on information from a variety of sources instead of results of a single IQ test.

The authors in this edition devote a large portion of book to positive and negative reactions to the definition of mental retardation. Those who voiced positive reactions praised the focus on support needs instead of impairments. Negative appraisals included the subjective nature of intensity of supports. Some feared that those who had been classified with mild mental retardation would no longer be eligible for services.

The authors of this edition respond to critics of the 1992 definition with a model of needs proposed by Greenspan (in press). Greenspan is quoted as saying, "If mental retardation is real, then it must be grounded in the demonstrated incompetencies, needs, and vulnerabilities that cause individuals to be seen as needing supports and protections." He proposes that incompetencies fluctuate across an individual's lifetime. Individuals may be diagnosed with mild mental retardation while enrolled in school, but may have no incompetencies when they leave school. In what appears to be contrary to Greenspan's model, AAMR still proposes that the criterion for diagnosis of mental retardation include test scores that are two standard deviations below the norm on an IQ test and two of three areas of an adaptive behavior assessment.

The second section, diagnosis, covers the assessment of intelligence, adaptive behavior, and diagnosis and clinical judgment. Discussion of adaptive behavior in book, for example, includes three areas of adaptive behavior: conceptual skills, social skills, and practical skills. The interaction of adaptive behavior and diagnosis, specific tests for assessing adaptive behavior, and the role of problem behaviors also are discussed.

In the third section, classification, major classification systems are described and compared with the AAMR classification system. The International Classification of Functioning, Disability, and Health (ICF) developed by the World Health Organization is described as the most compatible with the AAMR system and is particularly useful in etiological classification. The Diagnosis and Statistics Manual: Mental Disorders (DSM), the Developmental Disabilities definition, social security definition, Medicaid Intermediate Care Facility (ICF-MR), and Medicaid Waiver definitions are also described and compared.

The fourth section, supports, includes chapters on supports for individuals with mental retardation, physical and mental health, and public responsibility in the provision of supports. A committee of AAMR recently completed an assessment tool for identifying needs and designing supports plans (Thompson, Hughes, Schalock, & Silverman, in press). Book outlines a generic version of that assessment, beginning with an identification of discrepancies between the individual's abilities and capabilities, and the adaptive skills and competencies required to function in the individual's environment. Discrepancies are evaluated in nine areas: human development, teaching and education, home living, community living, employment, health and safety, behavioral, social, and protection and advocacy. Supports are then determined in order to reduce identified discrepancies. Supports may include teaching, befriending, financial planning, employee assistance, behavioral support, in-home living assistance, community access an d use, and health assistance. Further, supports may be provided by family and friends or by professionals. The final section, implications, provides a summary of the other chapters. Sections of the book are devoted to how the AAMR model will impact current education and habilitation services, research design, eligibility for services, and legal accommodations.

This book will be a useful resource for both professionals and lay persons who are interested in, work with, or are advocates for individuals with either a diagnosis of mental retardation or individuals who score within normal levels on IQ tests, but have significant limitations in adaptive skills. The book can be used as a basic source for terminology, diagnosis of mental retardation and related disorders, and classification systems associated with particular reimbursement and funding streams. It also offers a best-practice approach to intervention and support of those with mental retardation. The entire book can be read in 4-6 hours. Some of the information overlaps across chapters, which allows the reader to skip sections of the text. There are also many tables and figures that summarize information for the reader.

Although this book offers something for everyone, most readers will likely disagree with some of the information conveyed. Families, parents, and advocates are likely to dislike the continued use of the term mental retardation." Others may find the definition too limiting. The authors alluded to "the forgotten generation";. that is, the increasing number of individuals identified who function in the normal range of intelligence but with significant limitations in adaptive behaviors. Others may continue to struggle with the subjective definition for levels of severity. When definitions of levels of severity are based on 10 scores, then classification is very clear. Intensities of support are subjective. Those professionals who assign diagnoses, determine eligibility, or are researchers who use levels of severity to describe the characteristics of research participants typically have little or no experience in designing supports. Another concern of clinicians, teachers, and case managers may be that the AAMR sup ports model is very complex. Assessing nine areas of competence and developing a system of supports that may be natural or service-delivered, and may be one of eight types of support, require time and expertise. Families, parents, and advocates also must struggle to understand the complexities of terminology and the interaction of etiology, health, and cognitive factors in determining prognosis for improving the individual's functioning. A fear that some service providers have voiced is that, given the complexity of the AAMR supports approach, more supports will be in the form of attendant or respite care, not the supports that will truly allow the individual to function more independently and productively.

The AAMR definition of mental retardation is particularly important today because of recent court decisions concerning the legality of the death penalty for persons diagnosed with mental retardation. Fewer individuals meet the definition of mental retardation using the current definition. Prosecutors of violent offenders will likely refute diagnoses of mental retardation if individuals lived independently prior to their conviction. On balance, defense lawyers are likely to point to the requirement that diagnosis includes the results of standardized tests and that such tests offer insight into reasoning and judgment. Whether the AAMR definition will serve both society and the accused remains to be tested.

Classification of Mental Disorders

The classification of mental disorders, also known as psychiatric nosology or taxonomy, is a key aspect of psychiatry and other mental health professions and an important issue for consumers and providers of mental health services. There are currently two widely established systems for classifying mental illness-Book of the International Classification of Diseases (ICD-10) produced by the World Health Organization (WHO) and the Diagnostic and Statistical Manual of Mental Disorders (DSM-IV) produced by the American Psychiatric Association (APA). Both list categories of disorders thought to be distinct types, and have deliberately converged their codes in recent revisions so that the manuals are often broadly comparable, although significant differences remain. Other classification schemes may be in use more locally, for example the Chinese Classification of Mental Disorders. Other manuals are used by those of alternative theoretical persuasions, such as the Psychodynamic Diagnostic Manual. Generally there is a significant scientific debate about the relative merits of a categorical system or a dimensional system (also known as a continuum or spectrum system), as well as significant controversy about the role of science and values in classification schemes and the professional, legal and social uses to which they are put.

Definitions

In the scientific and academic literature on the definition of mental disorder, one extreme argues that it is entirely a matter of value judgements (including of what is normal) while another proposes that it is or could be entirely objective and scientific (including by reference to statistical norms); other views argue that the concept refers to a "fuzzy prototype" that can never be precisely defined, or that the definition will always involve a mixture of scientific facts (e.g. that a natural or evolved function isn't working properly) and value judgements (e.g. that it is harmful or undesired). Lay concepts of mental disorder vary considerably across different cultures and countries, and may refer to different sorts of individual and social problems.

The World Health Organization (WHO) and national surveys report that there is no single consensus on the definition of mental disorder/illness, and that the phrasing used depends on the social, cultural, economic and legal context in different contexts and in different societies. The WHO reports that there is intense debate about which conditions should be included under the concept of mental disorder; a broad definition can cover mental illness, mental retardation, personality disorder and substance dependence, but inclusion varies by country and is reported to be a complex and debated issue. There may be a criterion that a condition should not be expected to occur as part of a person's usual culture or religion. However, despite the term "mental", there is not necessarily a clear distinction drawn between mental (dys)functioning and brain (dys)functioning, or indeed between the brain and the rest of the body.

Most international clinical documents avoid the term "mental illness", preferring the term "mental disorder" However, some use "mental illness" as the main over-arching term to encompass mental disorders. Some consumer/survivor movement organizations oppose use of the term "mental illness" on the grounds that it supports the dominance of a medical model. The term "serious mental illness" (SMI) is sometimes used to refer to more severe and long-lasting disorder while "mental health problems" may be used as a broader term, or to refer only to milder or more transient issues. Confusion often surrounds the ways and contexts in which these terms are used.

Curriculum Development and Teaching Methods in Mental Retardation

Individuals with mental retardation benefit from the same teaching strategies used to teach individuals with learning disabilities, attention deficit/hyperactivity disorder, and autism. It is helpful to break tasks down into small steps and introduce the task one step at a time to avoid overwhelming the individual. Once the student has mastered one step, the next is introduced.

Verbal directions and lectures are not the most effective teaching approaches for any audience, and are especially unreliable methods for teaching mentally retarded students. Mentally retarded individuals do better in environments where visual aides such as charts, pictures, and graphs are used as much as possible. Such visual components are useful for helping students to understand what is expected of them. Using charts to map students' progress is very effective, for instance. Charts can also be used as a means of providing positive reinforcement for appropriate, on-task behavior (e.g., in conjunction with a token economy, as described below).

Individuals with mental retardation require immediate feedback in order to make a connection between their answers, behaviors, or questions and the teacher's responses. A delay in providing feedback may interrupt the connection between cause and effect in the student's mind, and the point will be lost. Most people are kinesthetic learners who learn by doing, by completing a hands-on tasks and appreciating the results. This is especially true for mentally retarded students who cannot comprehend abstract lectures very easily at all.

For example, a teacher who wants to teach the concept of gravity has several options: She can tell students that things are pulled towards the earth by a force known as gravity; she can show students how gravity works by dropping something; or she can instruct the students to drop something while teaching the concept. Chances are that the students will retain more information from dropping an object during the demonstration or by experiencing the act of dropping something, than by simply being told how dropping (gravity) works.

Adult Training and Vocational Placement of Mental Retardation

The passage of Public Law 94-142 in 1975 signaled an increase in the recognition of the educational, socio-emotional, and vocational needs of children with disabilities. Consequently, special education programmes were implemented to provide interventions to accommodate students with identified special needs. Among the 13 disabilities currently addressed by these programmes, specific learning disabilities (SLD) constitute the largest and fastest growing population of exceptional learners in the public schools (U.S. Department of Education, 1994). Although several definitions of SLD exist, it is generally viewed as a psychological processing disorder involving the use or comprehension of written or spoken language.

It manifests itself with problems in listening, thinking, speaking, reading, writing, spelling, or performing mathematical calculations and cannot be better accounted for by another disorder (e.g., mental retardation, emotional disorder, visual or motor impairments) or condition (e.g., cultural differences, lack of educational experiences, economic disadvantage). Most definitions require the existence of a severe discrepancy between intellectual ability and academic achievement (Diagnostic and Statistical Manual-Fourth Edition [American Psychiatric Association], 1994; Public Law 94-142, 1977).

- Healthcare Roundup: Enthoven's Take on Reform, Help For Small Practices, Docs...
- How Private Insurers Could Compete With a Public Plan
- Obama, Insurers Go Toe-to-Toe
- Insurance Is Not The Same as Healthcare Access

Since 1975, numerous studies have documented that SLD is a lifelong condition, continuing and sometimes intensifying in adulthood (Haring, Lovett, & Smith, 1990; Rogan & Hartman, 1990; Sitlington & Frank, 1990). Similarly, adults with SLD should not be viewed simply as children with SLD who have grown into adulthood because the problems associated with SLD change with age. For example, adults with SLD are less likely to graduate from high school (Adelman & Vogel, 1990; Malcolm, Polatajko, & Simons, 1990), exhibit problems finding and retaining employment (Shapiro & Lentz, 1991; Smith, 1992), and are commonly employed in unskilled, entry-level occupations (Haring et al., 1990; Sitlington, Frank, & Carson, 1992; Spekman, Goldberg, & Herman, 1992). As a result, many adults with SLD are financially dependent (Gajar, 1992; Spekman et al., 1992). Lastly, adults with SLD commonly exhibit higher rates of emotional maladjustment and co-morbid psychiatric conditions than the general population (Dunham, Multon, & Koller, 1999).

Based upon the findings that adults with SLD continue to demonstrate significant vocational problems after they leave school, the Rehabilitation Services Administration (RSA) and the state-federal Division of Vocational Rehabilitation (DVR) began public funding of services to this population of consumers in 1981 (Defur & Reiff, 1994). Typical DVR services for adults with SLD include testing/evaluation, guidance and counseling, job training, job placement, and job follow-up (Dowdy & McCue, 1994; Smith, 1992). Studies have shown that DVR consumers with SLD are successfully employed following service provision at rates similar to other populations served by DVR (Berkeley Planning Associates [BPA], 1989; Dowdy & Smith, 1994). Despite these interventions and outcomes, however, few consumer or service variables predict successful vocational outcomes. For example, Berkeley Planning Associates found that only Hispanic ethnicity, on-the-job training, job referral, and job placement services were associated with successful closure. Similarly, Dunham, Koller, and McIntosh (1996) found that persons whose cases were closed as unsuccessful had higher rates of mood disorders and attention problems, and were more likely to have obtained DVR assistance in attending college.

DVR also serves persons with borderline intellectual functioning-those with measured IQs from 70 to 84-when they have concurrent maladaptive problems, such as finding and maintaining employment. Prior to changes in the definition of mental retardation in 1973, children whose measured IQs were within this range received special education (MacMillan, Gresham, Bocian, & Lambros, 1998). Currently, public schools do not provide special programmeming for persons with borderline intellectual functioning under the Individuals with Disabilities Education Act (IDEA). However, they may provide assistance through a Section 504 plan or under another diagnostic label.

Despite differences in how or if services are provided, adults with borderline IQ exhibit characteristics that are similar to those with SLD and mental retardation. The available research suggests that persons with borderline IQ have significant academic, socio-behavioral, and vocational problems (Wittmann, Strohmer, & Prout, 1989; Zetlin & Murtaugh, 1990) and, as children, demonstrate functional limitations similar to those with mental retardation (MacMillan et al., 1998). Although many similarities exist between these two groups, most of the community support services available target those individuals diagnosed with mental retardation. For example, when students with mental retardation leave school they have available a number of options to support their continued personal and vocational development. These include independent living skills programmes, supportive work programmes, sheltered workshops, and adult training centers (Parmenter, 1986). Fewer options are available for students with borderline intellectual functioning when they leave school.

Another population of persons with disabilities that has received little attention in the literature is individuals with both borderline IQ and SLD (B/SLD). In addition to having borderline intellectual ability (approximately 12% of the general population), these individuals also have significant academic skill deficits that are in excess of what is expected given their measured intellectual functioning. Like the definition of SLD, those with B/SLD also demonstrate a severe discrepancy between measured intellectual functioning and academic achievement.

Although past research has focused on the vocational outcomes of individuals with SLD or mental retardation and, to a lesser extent, those with borderline intellectual functioning, no studies have investigated the vocational outcome of adults with B/SLD. It can be reasoned that persons with both conditions have significant vocational adjustment difficulties because of the concomitant subaverage cognitive functioning and severe academic skill deficits. Together, the functional limitations in the cognitive and academic sphere may significantly limit training options and job opportunities. Relatedly, although those with SLD are subject to the training and employment protections under the Americans with Disabilities Act (1990) and Section 504 of the Rehabilitation Act of 1973 (1973), their occupational success may be hindered by their limitations in cognitive ability which are not necessarily protected by legislation. In other words, accommodating the SLD alone may be insufficient to maintain employment.

The primary purpose of the present study was to investigate the vocational outcomes of persons with co-morbid borderline intellectual functioning and specific learning disabilities. A second purpose was to compare the VR training and psychoeducational functioning of those persons successfully employed to those unemployed following DVR intervention.

Method

Participants: Ninety-eight former Missouri Division of Vocational Rehabilitation (DVR) adult clients with B/SLD were included in this study. The data was collected from two consecutive fiscal years and represented all of the closed cases within that time frame meeting the B/SLD criteria. Using the service, demographic, and psychoeducational data compiled from DVR archives, those clients who had measured WAIS-R IQ scores 70 to 84, had no significant difference between Verbal and Performance IQ, and who demonstrated a significant discrepancy between IQ and reading, mathematics, and/or written language were included in the study. These 98 individuals qualified for and received DVR services as consumers with a SLD-not B/SLD.

Their primary diagnosis was SLD as defined by the Rehabilitation Services Administration (RSA, 1985). For purposes of this study, a significant discrepancy between measured IQ and academic achievement was determined by the regression analysis formula used by the Missouri Department of Elementary and Secondary Education (Missouri DESE, 1994). Although a number of regression formulas exist (Berk, 1984; Forness, Sinclair, & Guthrie, 1983), the Missouri DESE formula is used in the State's public schools and by the State's psychological consultants. At the time data was collected, a successful closure was defined by Missouri DVR as at least 30 hours per week of employment for at least two months.

An Instrument for Assessment of Vocational Readiness of Persons with Mental Retardation

Vocational placement of persons with mental retardation has been fraught with many challenges. Amongst the most significant are the identification of an appropriate vocational opportunity, and the determining of the mentally retarded persons' readiness to be placed in the same. This paper details four types of work environments and presents an instrument to select and place them appropriately in these. The vocational environments for persons with mental retardation are comprehensively sheltered employment, sheltered employment, partially sheltered employment and open work employment. We regard comprehensively sheltered work environment as one in which all supportive measures as may be required by the person with mental retardation are made available, and includes home-based employment. The measures would include meeting their emotional, intellectual and physical needs, and the provision of such special facilities as required without causing disturbance to others.

Such work environments would be supervised by personnel who are specially trained to meet the needs of those who working in this environment. Sheltered employment is one where all the facilities mentioned above are available, except that the work environment is away from the homes of the mentally retarded persons. By partial shelter we mean the an environment created within an industrial complex or industry which has been specially made available for persons with mental retardation, using special fixtures, workstations and structures as may be required, and supervised by specially trained supervisors.

Here the mentally retarded person has access to social interaction and the opportunity to earn industry based wages without the challenge of competition. Open employment means the placing of mentally retarded persons in marginally specially supervised open environments, generally without the deployment of specially designed environmental structures.

To assess the vocational readiness of mentally retarded persons in these work environments, an instrument was designed for ease of use, to be handled by teachers in special education as well as those trained in vocational training and employment. The instrument contains a set of behavioural descriptions which every teacher would be familiar with. A set of simple instructions are provided to determine scores that easily position the assessee in the category of employment for which he is likely to be best suited.

An annexure details some of the methods to be adopted for testing in certain specific areas so that identical criteria are used by all examiners. The instrument is so constructed that a minimum level of behaviour is to be present for qualification of placement in a particular category of employment. A higher score than that means placement in areas requiring higher grades of work skills.

Approaches, Methods and Materials for Teaching Persons with Mental Retardation

Individuals with mental retardation benefit from the same teaching strategies used to teach individuals with learning disabilities, attention deficit/hyperactivity disorder, and autism. It is helpful to break tasks down into small steps and introduce the task one step at a time to avoid overwhelming the individual. Once the student has mastered one step, the next is introduced.

Verbal directions and lectures are not the most effective teaching approaches for any audience, and are especially unreliable methods for teaching mentally retarded students. Mentally retarded individuals do better in environments where visual aides such as charts, pictures, and graphs are used as much as possible. Such visual components are useful for helping students to understand what is expected of them. Using charts to map students' progress is very effective, for instance. Charts can also be used as a means of providing positive reinforcement for appropriate, on-task behavior (e.g., in conjunction with a token economy, as described below).

Individuals with mental retardation require immediate feedback in order to make a connection between their answers, behaviors, or questions and the teacher's responses. A delay in providing feedback may interrupt the connection between cause and effect in the student's mind, and the point will be lost. Most people are kinesthetic learners who learn by doing, by completing a hands-on tasks and appreciating the results. This is especially true for mentally retarded students who cannot comprehend abstract lectures very easily at all. For example, a teacher who wants to teach the concept of gravity has several options: She can tell students that things are pulled towards the earth by a force known as gravity; she can show students how gravity works by dropping something; or she can instruct the students to drop something while teaching the concept. Chances are that the students will retain more information from dropping an object during the demonstration or by experiencing the act of dropping something, than by simply being told how dropping (gravity) works.

Therapeutic Applications for Mental Retardation

Physical therapy may be conducted in schools, in the home or institution, or at physical therapy facilities. Physical therapy helps mentally retarded individuals to develop the gross motor skills required for everyday activities. It also promotes flexibility and stimulates mentally retarded individuals' learning abilities through sensory integration activities.

Sensory integration is a natural process used by the body to interpret sensory information concerning the environment. Normally, the various senses work collaboratively to help people navigate their surroundings. However, children with learning disabilities, including some mentally retarded children, often have difficulty coordinating sensory input. Sensory integration activities help these individuals to process their sensory information more effectively.

Children with sensory issues have difficulty filtering sensory input. Their sensory systems may be either hyperactive or hypoactive, and unable to properly block out signals that should be ignored or to amplify signals that should be heeded. Children with hyperactive (overactive) sensory systems may avoid motion, be very prone to motion sickness, and resist engaging in activities like climbing or descending stairs. They may seek support from other people while walking. In contrast, children with hypoactive (underactive) sensory systems may actively seek out motion, enjoy swinging and climbing activities, and not become dizzy after spinning.

Sensory integration activities address children's sensory needs by either lessening or amplifying the intensity of various forms of sensory stimulation they receive. Most sensory integration activities work with children's vestibular, proprioceptive, and tactile sensory systems.

The vestibular sensory system helps people to be able to stand and to coordinate their movements. It involves sensory input from vision and from special sensory organs located in the inner ear. Activities that stimulate the vestibular system involve movement; swinging, jumping, and spinning are good examples. A therapist seeking to help children with hypoactive sensory systems might engage them in structured movement exercises that would meet their sensory needs, such as swinging, jumping, and spinning, while helping them stay within socially acceptable bounds.

The proprioceptive sensory system helps people to have information concerning their body positioning. Proprioceptive feedback helps people coordinate fine motor activities like coloring within lines or buttoning a shirt. It also helps with motor planning, or the ability to coordinate different motor tasks to complete an activity. Activities that stimulate the proprioceptive system include deep pressure, hugging, and climbing.

Only some mentally retarded individuals require physical therapy. Whether physical therapy is beneficial has to do with the underlying condition that has caused mental retardation in the first place. For example, some forms of mental retardation, such as Fragile X syndrome, are often accompanied by sensory challenges as well as intellectual deficits. These individuals are easily distracted by noises or smells. Individuals with Cockayne syndrome frequently need physical therapy to help prevent joint contractions that limit their ability to walk. Individuals who have Prader-Willie syndrome have low muscle tone, which physical therapy helps address.

The primary goal of treatment is to develop the person's potential to the fullest. Special education and training may begin as early as infancy. This includes social skills to help the person function as normally as possible.

It is important for a specialist to evaluate the person for other affective disorders and treat those disorders. Behavioral approaches are important for people with mental retardation.

Genetic: Prenatal screening for genetic defects and genetic counseling for families at risk for known heritable disorders can decrease the incidence of genetically caused mental retardation.

Social: Government programmes to ensure adequate nutrition are available to the underprivileged in the first and most critical years of life. These programmes can reduce retardation associated with malnutrition. Early intervention in situations involving abuse and deprivation will also help.

Toxic: Environmental programmes to reduce exposure to lead, mercury, and other toxins will reduce toxin-associated retardation. However, the benefits may take years to become apparent. Increased public awareness of the risks of alcohol and drugs during pregnancy can help reduce the incidence of retardation.

Infectious: The prevention of congenital rubella syndrome is probably one of the best examples of a successful programme to prevent one form of mental retardation. Constant vigilance, such as limiting exposure to cat litter that can cause toxoplasmosis during pregnancy, helps reduce retardation that results from this infection.

UNIT-V

Hearing Impairment

Hearing and Auditory Processes

Auditory processing is a term used to describe what happens when your brain recognizes and interprets the sounds around you. Humans hear when energy that we recognize as sound travels through the ear and is changed into electrical information that can be interpreted by the brain. The "disorder" part of auditory processing disorder means that something is adversely affecting the processing or interpretation of the information.

Children with APD often do not recognize subtle differences between sounds in words, even though the sounds themselves are loud and clear. For example, the request "Tell me how a chair and a couch are alike" may sound to a child with APD like "Tell me how a couch and a chair are alike." It can even be understood by the child as "Tell me how a cow and a hair are alike." These kinds of problems are more likely to occur when a person with APD is in a noisy environment or when he or she is listening to complex information.

APD goes by many other names. Sometimes it is referred to as central auditory processing disorder (CAPD). Other common names are auditory perception problem, auditory comprehension deficit, central auditory dysfunction, central deafness, and so-called "word deafness."

What Causes Auditory Processing Difficulty?

We are not sure. Human communication relies on taking in complicated perceptual information from the outside world through the senses, such as hearing, and interpreting that information in a meaningful way. Human communication also requires certain mental abilities, such as attention and memory. Scientists still do not understand exactly how all of these processes work and interact or how they malfunction in cases of communication disorders. Even though your child seems to "hear normally," he or she may have difficulty using those sounds for speech and language.

The cause of APD is often unknown. In children, auditory processing difficulty may be associated with conditions such as dyslexia, attention deficit disorder, autism, autism spectrum disorder, specific language impairment, pervasive developmental disorder, or developmental delay. Sometimes this term has been misapplied to children who have no hearing or language disorder but have challenges in learning.

What are the symptoms of possible auditory processing difficulty?

Children with auditory processing difficulty typically have normal hearing and intelligence. However, they have also been observed to

- Have trouble paying attention to and remembering information presented orally
- Have problems carrying out multistep directions
- Have poor listening skills
- Need more time to process information
- Have low academic performance
- Have behavior problems
- Have language difficulty (e.g., they confuse syllable sequences and have problems developing vocabulary and understanding language)
- Have difficulty with reading, comprehension, spelling, and vocabulary.

How is suspected auditory processing difficulty diagnosed in children?

You, a teacher, or a day care provider may be the first person to notice symptoms of auditory processing difficulty in your child. So talking to your child's teacher about school or preschool performance is a good idea. Many health professionals can also diagnose APD in your child. There may need to be ongoing observation with the professionals involved.

Much of what will be done by these professionals will be to rule out other problems. A pediatrician or a family doctor can help rule out possible diseases that can cause some of these same symptoms. He or she will also measure growth and development. If there is a disease or disorder related to hearing, you may be referred to an otolaryngologist—a physician who specializes in diseases and disorders of the head and neck.

To determine whether your child has a hearing function problem, an audiologic evaluation is necessary. An audiologist will give tests that can determine the softest sounds and words a person can hear and other tests to see how well people can recognize sounds in words and sentences. For example, for one task, the audiologist might have your child listen to different numbers or words in the right and the left ear at the same time. Another common audiologic task involves giving the child two sentences, one louder than the other, at the same time. The audiologist is trying to identify the processing problem.

A speech-language pathologist can find out how well a person understands and uses language. A mental health professional can give you information about cognitive and behavioral challenges that may contribute to problems in some cases, or he or she may have suggestions that will be helpful. Because the audiologist can help with the functional problems of hearing and processing, and the speech-language pathologist is focused on language, they may work as a team with your child. All of these professionals seek to provide the best outcome for each child.

What current research is being conducted?

In recent years, scientists have developed new ways to study the human brain through imaging. Imaging is a powerful tool that allows the monitoring of brain activity without any surgery. Imaging studies are already giving scientists new insights into auditory processing. Some of these studies are directed at understanding auditory processing disorders. One of the values of imaging is that it provides an objective, measurable view of a process. Many of the symptoms described as related to APD are described differently by different people.

Imaging will help identify the source of these symptoms. Other scientists are studying the central auditory nervous system. Cognitive neuroscientists are helping to describe how the processes that mediate sound recognition and comprehension work in both normal and disordered systems. Research into the rehabilitation of child language disorders continues. It is important to know that much research is still needed to understand auditory processing problems, related disorders, and the best interventions7 for each child or adult. All the strategies undertaken will need to be suited to the needs of the individual child, and their effectiveness will need to be continuously evaluated. The standard for determining if a treatment is effective is that a patient can reasonably expect to benefit from it.

What treatments are available for auditory processing difficulty?

Much research is still needed to understand APD problems, related disorders, and the best intervention for each child or adult. Several strategies are available to help children with auditory processing difficulties. Some of these are commercially available, but have not been fully studied. Any strategy selected should be used under the guidance of a team of professionals, and the effectiveness of the strategy needs to be evaluated. Researchers are currently studying a variety of approaches to treatment. Several strategies you may hear about include:

- *Auditory trainers* are electronic devices that allow a person to focus attention on a speaker and reduce the interference of background noise. They are often used in classrooms, where the teacher wears a microphone to transmit sound and the child wears a headset to receive the sound. Children who wear hearing aids can use them in addition to the auditory trainer.
- *Environmental modifications* such as classroom acoustics, placement, and seating may help. An

audiologist may suggest ways to improve the listening environment, and he or she will be able to monitor any changes in hearing status.

- Exercises to improve *language-building* skills can increase the ability to learn new words and increase a child's language base.
- *Auditory memory enhancement*, a procedure that reduces detailed information to a more basic representation, may help. Also, informal auditory training techniques can be used by teachers and therapists to address specific difficulties.
- *Auditory integration training* may be promoted by practitioners as a way to retrain the auditory system and decrease hearing distortion. However, current research has not proven the benefits of this treatment.

Teaching Methods Followed in Education of Children with Hearing Impairment

Teaching Methods

Hearing loss occurs along a broad continuum ranging in degree from slight to profound. Individuals with severe and profound hearing loss generally are characterized as *deaf*, whereas individuals with lesser degrees of impairment, including those with unilateral hearing loss (i.e., involving only one ear), are characterized as *hard of hearing*. Childhood hearing loss of any type and degree, if unmanaged, is likely to have a negative impact on the development of spoken and receptive language, the ability to read and write, and academic achievement. For example, a 1998 study of 1,218 children with minimal hearing loss showed that 37 percent had failed a grade. Similarly, studies have shown that children with unilateral hearing loss are ten times more likely than normally hearing children to fail a grade. The vast majority (94–96%) of children with hearing loss are hard of hearing rather than deaf. For these children, speech may be *audible* (i.e., detectable) but not *intelligible* enough to allow them to hear one word as distinct from another.

There are approximately 50,000 school-age deaf children in the United States, a figure representing a dramatic decline since the early 1970s. An additional 5 million school-age children are permanently hard of hearing and at educational risk. An estimated 1.5 million more suffer from conductive, usually temporary, hearing loss. Inclusion of preschool children could put the total number of children with hearing loss close to 10 million.

Historical Overview

Historically, approaches to educating children who are deaf have been based on emotion and personal philosophy rather than positive outcome; in contrast, the education of children who are hard of hearing has largely been ignored. Educational practices in the United States can be linked directly to the teachings of European educators active during the eighteenth and nineteenth centuries. Of note, in 1770 French cleric Charles-Michel de l'Épée founded a school in which he emphasized the use of sign language and finger spelling (i.e., a *manual* approach). Around the same time, schools were established in England by members of the Braidwood family, who emphasized the use of spoken language and speechreading without sign language (i.e., an *oral* approach).

In the United States, the father of Alice Cogswell, who lost her hearing at an early age, commissioned Thomas Hopkins Gallaudet to travel to Europe and learn methods for teaching deaf children. Refused help by the Braidwoods, Gallaudet learned de l'Épée's manual method. In 1817 Gallaudet opened a school in the United States based on the manual approach (now the American School for the Deaf). Gallaudet's son became president of the first college for deaf students in the United States, now known as Gallaudet University.

Oralism took root years later when another young girl from a prominent family, Mabel Hubbard, lost her hearing. In 1867 her father helped establish an oral school. As an adult, Hubbard married Alexander Graham Bell, who became a passionate advocate for oralism. During the late nineteenth century, Bell and Gallaudet often engaged in debate about the merits of the oral and manual approaches. The debate would continue well into the twentieth century.

Education of and Services for Hearing-Impaired Children

Children in the United States who are deaf or hard of hearing are legally entitled to a free and appropriate education. Federal law requires a continuum of educational options, ranging from placement in a self-contained classroom with other children who are deaf to full-time placement in a regular education classroom with normally hearing peers. Most often, the placement involves a variation or a combination of the two extremes. An alternative placement is attendance at a residential school, in which the child can participate fully in the deaf culture.

Perhaps the most important educational decision is the communication method that will be used. The choice lies with the parents, and the best decision is specific to each child and family. Most children who are deaf use one or some combination of three communication modes: American Sign Language, a manual language that is distinctly different from English (i.e., a person does not sign and speak at the same time); a system of manually coded English (i.e., a signed version of English); or hearing and spoken language. A relatively smaller number of children use Cued Speech, a system in which hand gestures enhance speechreading.

Children with hearing loss require support services in order to benefit maximally from a free and appropriate education. For example, it is essential that they receive services from an audiologist, including management of their hearing aids, classroom listening devices, and listening environments. Poor listening conditions can render a hard of hearing child functionally deaf.

Trends and Research Findings

The education of children who are deaf will be revolutionized by two dramatic changes. First, legally mandated neonatal hearing-screening programmes are changing the average age at identification from approximately three years to approximately three months. Research has shown that when appropriate hearing aids and early intervention are in place by six months of age, a child is likely to have age-normal language and learning milestones at kindergarten entry. In this light, the most important educational years are the child's very first years, when the family participates in parent–infant programmeming.

Second, cochlear implants are being made available to increasingly younger children. These surgically implanted devices convert sound into electrical current, which then bypasses much of the hearing mechanism to stimulate surviving nerve elements directly. The coded electrical current creates sensations, which the brain, with considerable listening training, can learn to interpret as sound. Research suggests that children who use cochlear implants surpass children with similar degrees of hearing loss who use hearing aids in the areas of speech recognition, speech production, language content and form, and reading.

Children who benefit from early intervention and improved hearing technology, including cochlear implants, are likely to enter kindergarten ready for the educational mainstream. In the absence of additional disabilities, and with appropriate support services, it is possible that these children may never require special education placements and will choose to use sign language only if it is their cultural preference.

Modes of Communication Used with the Hearing Impaired Persons

Classification of methods of communication used by persons with hearing impairment:

The Auditory-verbal Approach

This is also known as the unisensory mode. The child develops "listening" and speech skills through the use of optimally functioning hearing aids, and auditory training i.e. lip reading is not encouraged. The use of signs is forbidden. The deaf child develops spoken communication skills just like any other child–that is, through the ears.

The Auditory-oral Approach

This mode relies on auditory training and the use of hearing aids to develop spoken language. Lip reading is also used but signs are excluded–that is signing is not allowed.

The Oral Approach

In this mode, lip reading is the primary channel for speech development. Touch is used to perceive acoustic features. Lipreading is also termed "Speech reading." It is the art of understanding what the speaker is saying by watching his or her mouth. It is a skill used by many deaf people. Even the best lip reader cannot see everything that is said, since only about 25 % of all speech is visible on the lips. But lip reading improves when words, phrases and sentences are used in context.

The ability to lipread depends on many factors:

- Visual acuity
- The degree of visibility of the letter/word on the speaker's lips ("f" is easy to see. "h" in not visible at all).
- The speaker's rate of utterance
- Lighting and distance
- The fact that some letters/words look the same on the speaker's lips (e.g. P, B, M).

Training hearing impaired children to use their residual hearing (with the help of hearing aids) along with lip reading improves their lip reading skills.

Other modes of communication:

A gesture is a spontaneous manual expression to communicate one's thoughts.

A sign is a gesture which is used consistently to mean the same thing. A "sign" is the manual counterpart of a "word".

Sign Language is a group of signs joined grammatically (i.e a sentence) to convey meaning. A sign language is the native language of a particular deaf community. In all probability the deaf community of every country has their own sign language. In the UK, the deaf community uses the British Sign Language

(BSL), in the USA the American Sign Language (ASL) is used. The Austrailian deaf community uses AUSLAN. The Indian Sign language (ISL) is well established and is used by the deaf community in India. Sign languages are natural languages and evolve with use.

Sign Language is not written or spoken. It is a complete language and has its own grammar which is very different from the grammar of spoken languages.

The Indian Sign Language (ISL) is used by the deaf community in India. Interpreters are now being trained.

Finger spelling is the use of hand configurations to represent the letters of the alphabet. Each letter is distinctly represented by a specific hand configuration. In India, two systems of finger spelling are used-the two-handed British system and the one-handed American system but the letters they represent belong to the Roman alphabet. Finger spelling is generally used in combination with sign language, especially to spell proper nouns, technological terms and specialist words for which there are no signs.

A signed language or signing system is very different from a sign language. A signed language is a manual code for a spoken language e.g. signed English or signed Hindi or signed Tamil or Signed Japanese. It is not a different language. It uses signs to follow the grammar of a particular language. In the use of this system each word and word-part including grammatical elements of the language are signed. This sign per word system thus adequately supports the fragments of speech. A signed language is not a natural language. It follows the grammar of an existing language. Therefore a signed language is also known as a signing system.

Total Communication is the use of:

- a signed language (signing system)
- hearing aids
- finger spelling
- speech
- lip reading

- any and all mode of communication which ensures effective communication with hearing impaired people. Total communication is considered to be a "philosophy incorporating the appropriate aural, manual and oral methods". The deaf child is taught to perceive the spoken language through a combination the use of hearing aids, lip reading and a signed language.

Monaural and Binaural Speech Perception through Hearing Aids under Noise and Reverberation with Normal and Hearing-Impaired Listeners

Speech perception was studied with normal and hearing-impairedsubjects in a single sound-treated room at reverberation times$T = 0.3$ and 0.6 seconds. Binaural and monaural perception throughhearing aids was compared in quiet and in the presence of ababble of eight voices. The speech and noise sources subtendedan angle of 60° on a circle 11 feet in radius centered atthe listener to give an advantage for binaural perception. Binauralgain was taken as the difference in speech-to-noise ratios forthe same word-recognition score comparing binaural and monauralresults. The average binaural gain was 3 dB for normal subjectsand 1.5 dB for hearing-impaired subjects at both values of reverberation.Only the hearing-impaired subjects showed an advantage for binaurallistening in quiet. The small increase in reverberation causeda substantial decrease in word intelligibility. The hearing-impairedsubjects performed an average of 7% poorer under the longerreverberation in the presence of noise and also in quiet. Thenormal subjects performed 15% poorer at longer reverberationonly in the presence of masking noise. Data are presented describingthe effects of these experimental conditions on perception ofcertain types of consonants and phonetic features of consonants.

Hearing Aid History Through the Years

As you go through a typical work day, consider everyone you speak to: the person who makes your morning coffee; the receptionist at your workplace; your co-workers on the job site; and everyone with whom you come in contact and interact. Have you ever stopped to think that one of those people might be wearing a hearing aid?

In fact, chances are that you encounter someone who is hard of hearing in your everyday life. This person uses a hearing aid to fit in just like everybody else. Today's hearing aids are so small, you probably would never notice them in the people around you. It hasn't always been that way.

Early Hearing Aids

You have probably seen an old black-and-white film where an old person held a horn up to their ear to use as a hearing aid. History shows us that these devices were the butt of many a joke in early films or television programmes. These old hearing aids must not have been very effective; the people using them were always saying, "What?"

Fortunately, hearing aid history moved beyond these big trumpet-like devices. The next generation of hearing aids used transistor radio technology, with a device worn on the body. These aids were a vast improvement over the trumpets and horns of yesteryear. However, they were still bulky, and individuals who needed hearing aids complained that they were uncomfortable to wear.

Behind the Ear Devices and Later

As technology advanced, hearing aids became smaller. History shows that hearing aids were first worn behind the ear, and later inside the ear and in the ear canal. Today, there are even implantable hearing aids, which truly are invisible.

History of Hearing Aid Perception

Hearing aids have come a long way in terms of their perception. They have come from the old-fashioned hearing aids that were ridiculed to being worn with dignity by a sitting president. Presidential hearing aid history includes President Ronald Reagan and President Bill Clinton, two presidents of very different ages who both wore hearing aids.

Future of Hearing Aids

Considering advances in technology, and the ability of science to shrink useful items, the hearing aid of the future is likely to be an implantable device or even a surgical procedure, like the Lasik eye surgery that has become such a popular remedy for nearsightedness. As long as people need help with their hearing, hearing aid development will continue, and hearing aid history will march on.

Perception throught Hearing Aids and Auditory Training and Evaluation of Hearing Aids

Children who are deafblind need to develop skills in using auditory information. Children who are deafblind need to learn to use whatever residual hearing they may have for a variety of reasons including travel safety, identifying people, literacy, communication, and so forth. They also need to learn how to use adaptive devices and equipment such as cochlear implants, hearing aids, and voice output devices. Auditory skills development, just like visual skills development, requires well-thought-out instruction that is provided regularly and consistently throughout the child's school career. Learning to listen, a skill we all need help with, is a skill that is critical for these children.

Steps in Providing Auditory Training

For children with visual impairment or deafblindness the first step in auditory training is to provide access to as much auditory information as possible. If there is a hearing problem, this starts with the use of hearing aids or a cochlear implant. Key to the use of these devices is good behavioral audiological assessment. This is because the best hearing aid or implant fit can't be obtained without behavioral testing.

Any child who is unable to participate in pure tone conventional screening, may need the educational team to compile information about his functional use of hearing before going to the audiologist. Some of the same activities that teach listening can be used to check hearing. By including listening activities at a level appropriate to the child, the child will learn to respond better in more formal hearing assessment situations. The team that knows exactly what behaviors indicate a child with limited communication skills has heard something can be very helpful to the audiologist who may not know what to look for as a response.

The next step is getting consistent use of the device (implant, hearing aid) if the child needs one. A hearing aid or implant is of no help to the child if the child doesn't wear it regularly.

The third step (if the child has some type of device) is to establish a system of daily checks of the hearing aid or implant to make sure it is working properly. Wearing a broken device is an additional impairment to whatever residual hearing the child might otherwise have available to use.

It is important to understand that, even though a child consistently wears an appropriate device in good working condition, he may still not have the same access to auditory information as another child. Each child will have a unique blend of abilities in the areas of hearing, vision, thinking and communication. Some children can become very sophisticated users of a wide range of auditory information while other children may be able to learn to use some, but not as much, auditory information. However, any child will benefit from learning to use any and all auditory information they can.

After the Hearing Aid or Implant, then What?

Auditory training does not end with putting on a hearing aid or implant. The child needs help to learn how to use the device and the information the device allows him to hear. The goal of auditory training is to help a student discriminate sound (in increasingly fine steps from gross sounds to speech) in order to gain meaning from the sounds he hears.

Goals at the highest level of auditory training focus on helping a child use speech. Using speech well requires a person to make very fine discriminations of pitch, loudness, and timing. When we hear a child give an appropriate verbal response to another person's spoken word or phrase (verbal stimulus), we know that he is making those fine discriminations. For most children the social benefits of responding to others' verbal communication is enough reinforcement that they learn quite naturally to make these discriminations and responses. For example, a baby eagerly says "bye-bye" again and again, just to trigger his grandmother's delight and keep her interacting when she announces it's time to go home.

Remember that auditory training is about helping a child make finer and finer discriminations. A gross discrimination is being able to recognize absolute quiet from a very loud sound. The sound is there or not there. A fine discrimination is the difference between the sound "s" like the first sound in "sun" and "f" like the first sound in "fun." Even people who are hearing have trouble hearing the difference between these sounds (especially over telephones!) Moving from a gross discrimination like the presence or absence of sound, one step towards a finer discrimination would be to hear the difference between a loud sound and a quiet sound. The next step from there is to hear the difference between a loud sound, a medium sound, and a quiet sound.

Now, it is not just enough to be able to hear these differences. We want our to children to recognize why these differences are important. We want our children to respond in a way that demonstrates that sounds have meaning. For example, a car horn honking is important to pay attention to; it signals danger. A loud knock at the door or the sound of a doorbell lets you know that someone is outside and wants to come in for a visit. The telephone ringing, the sound of the alarm clock ring, and many other sounds have meaning in our world. Think of other situations where the presence or absence of a sound means something; all of these sounds can be used in auditory training and can be tied to real-life, functional activities for the child.

Of course, it is not fair to ask a child to make discriminations or responses that are beyond their ability. It would be like asking someone without eyes to read print (braille might be ok!) or asking a 6-year-old to play basketball like Michael Jordan. That's why it is important to start with gross discriminations, utilizing sounds you know that the child really can hear. You want the child to have success at each step in learning to use his hearing. When listening becomes too difficult or aversive, the child is likely to shut down. Listening should be a rewarding experience for the child.

Fitting Auditory Training into the Child's Day

It is important to do a quick check of a child's auditory skills every day to make sure his or her hearing aid, cochlear implant, or assistive listening device is working. Doing this type of activity when the student arrives at school can catch problems with technology, but it also serves as a good time to tune the child into listening for voice. A quick way to do this is to use the *Ling Six Sound Test.* The Six Sound Test is used to determine the student's ability to detect and/or discriminate speech sounds.

The six sounds are used because they cover the speech range from low frequency to high frequency. The six sounds are "a" as in "baaaa", "u" as in mooo, `e' as in we, "sh" as in shoe, "s" as in sun, and "m" as in mom. This test is given live every day voiced by the adult with the student's own hearing aids, cochlear implant, and/or assistive listening device.

First, check the student's amplification as you normally would. Then, as the student wears the amplification, say the six sounds either from behind or in front with your mouth hidden from view. Ask the student to respond in some way to the sounds such as clapping, raising his/her hand, jumping up and down, etc. This is done to test for detection. If you ask the student to repeat the sound you can test discrimination. It is important to be consistent. Always say the sounds at the same volume and distance from the student. However, vary the order in which you say the sounds every day.

If, all of a sudden, you notice the child not responding as well as they have been, it may be that the child's amplification is not working or the child's hearing has changed. (As might happen if the child has an ear infection.)

It often works best to have a regularly scheduled time to work on auditory training, especially if you are introducing a new activity. Sometimes this can be scheduled as a small group activity or can be done with an individual child. It is easy to turn listening into a fun experience or a game. A child with very little hearing can sit on the floor near the door and listen for you to knock. He can open the door and pretend to be surprised to see you. She can put the baby doll in a bed "to sleep" and make the baby wake up when the alarm goes off. A group of children can dance to the music and freeze when it stops.

Practice, throughout the day, on listening skills learned in more formal lessons helps the child generalize the skills. For example, the student can listen for the teacher to call his or her name to come line up. For the child with very beginning discrimination skills, the student can listen for a drum sound (off/on environmental sounds). Another child might be asked to listen for his name as you target the skill of off/on awareness of voices. For the child a little farther along, you might ask her to discriminate between names that are very different in length and vowel/consonant structure such as "John" and "Latisha." Another student might be asked to discriminate between a normal voice and a whisper or between two very similar names such as "Bill" and "Will." Letting the child play teacher and have the other children listen can also reinforce their interest in tuning into sounds.

Every lesson in school or every activity at home has potential for working on auditory skills. Have the child listen for a timer to go off to let you know that his oatmeal is ready. Ask the bus driver to honk his horn when he stops out front. Listen for the sound of Dad's truck when he comes home in the evening. (With the help of a cell phone you can even keep the wait short if he gives you a call when he is just down the street.)

Schools have bells and alarms of all kinds; practice listening for the bell to ring before you go to lunch. When the principal makes an announcement over the intercom, encourage the child who hears it first to alert his classmates. As you read "Three Billy Goats Gruff" have one child pretend to be the troll who hides under the bridge and listens for the sound of the goats tramping on the bridge. Have another child listen for the phrase, "Who's that tramping on my bridge?" before responding vocally. Point out sounds as you take a walk and tie them to the objects and events that make that sound such as a loud air conditioner, a noisy cart in the cafeteria, or the sound of a ball bouncing on the floor in the gym.

There is no limit to the number of activities that teach and reinforce listening skills. Every child with a visual impairment, even those without an identified hearing loss, needs to develop good auditory skills. These play a critical role in developing other skills related to literacy, problem solving, following directions, orientation and mobility, and socialization. The auditory channel is a critical sense for learning for a child with deafblindness.

A child may initially only be able to discriminate gross differences between sounds, but with a lot of auditory training he may learn to discriminate very slight sound differences, even with profound hearing losses. Without training, a child with a very mild hearing loss may have difficulty making sense of what he hears.

What Parents should Discuss with their Teams about Auditory Training

Both teachers of the visually impaired and teachers of the deaf and hard of hearing know the importance of listening skills. If your son or daughter is visually impaired or deafblind you should think about how well the child is able to use hearing for learning. Many children should have auditory training goals included in the IEP. As parents, you may need to get some help in determining where to begin with your child.

- Ask your team about how your child uses his hearing in the school setting.
- Observe situations at home or in the community where your child responds well to sounds or seems to have problems and share that information with your team.
- If he has not had a hearing check recently, you may want to consider having one done as soon as possible.

Formal Auditory Training in Elderly Hearing Aid Users

With the progress and improvements achieved in medical technology, there has been an increase in the longevity of the population, and consequently a higher incidence of organic, functional and psychosocial disorders that affect this group. Among them, hearing deterioration is one of the chronic conditions that affect the physical health in aging. Presbycusis is hearing loss caused by aging.

In the hearing rehabilitation of the elderly with presbycusis it is recommended to use hearing aids. With the progress in technology, hearing aids came to the market as increasingly more sophisticated resources, which aim at supplying the needs of the hearing impaired. Nonetheless, some senior citizens can not adapt to the hearing aids and decide against using it or decide for a unilateral fitting, even when they have bilateral hearing loss. The authors also report that a central hearing impairment can negatively impact the hearing aid selection and fitting process. There are good reasons for believing in physiological changes in the central auditory system, stemming from its stimulation after fitting the hearing aids.

Hearing rehabilitation training programmes are used to improve the communication skills of the hearing impaired. There is some evidence that formal hearing training can be efficient in the hearing challenged elderly with sensorineural hearing loss as the one found in most of the people in this age range. It is believed that neural plasticity is not lost with aging. This is an important report, since most users of hearing aids are elderly.

Despite the large number of studies in the area of neural plasticity in the last 15 years, there is still much to study regarding the changes that happen in speech recognition skills because of the reintroduction of the acoustic signal, and if the change magnitude of these changes can be improved with formal hearing training. Based on these concerns, the goal of the present study is to check the efficacy of the formal auditory training programme in elderly citizens with mild to moderately severe bilateral sensorineural hearing loss, users of intracanal hearing aids after three months of their use, by means of speech recognition tests and self-assessment questionnaires.

Meaning of Guidance and Counselling and the Various techniques to Children with Hearing Impairment

Because speech-language pathologists, audiologists, and teachersof the hearing-impaired have contact with parents of the hearing-impairedchild, they are urged to undertake the responsibility of providingsupportive counseling to these parents during the period followingdiagnosis of hearing impairment. Such a service requires a broaderprofessional role than may previously have been envisioned.The authors suggest that the counseling programme be aimed atboth the growth of the family as a whole as well as that ofthe hearing-impaired child. It should promote the successionof stages that parents appear to pass through in the processof acknowledging their child's handicap. The nature of the parents'feelings, the source of their feelings, and ways in which theprofessional involved may deal with these feelings are discussed.Examples from the writers' clinical experience are presented.

Speech Reading Techniques for Hearing Impaired Children

Speech reading is a skill and an art by which children with hearing impairments are provided with speech techniques to understand the verbal message by looking at the speaker's face and bodily gestures. Speech reading skills can help hearing impaired children develop effective communication skills.

Tips for Speech Reading

Speech reading is an effective means of communication for children with hearing impairments. Speech reading helps hearing impaired children in the visual interpretation of the spoken language by other people. Speech reading not only involves focusing on lip movement, but it also involves the observation of other facial expressions and bodily gestures to fully understand the spoken message.

- Speakers should also use visual cues like facial expressions or hand gestures to help hearing impaired children to understand what they are trying to lip read.
- For effective communication it is very important that the environment where the conversation has to take place should be well lit. The light source should not be behind the speaker, rather it should be behind the listener and should fall directly on the speaker's face so that the speaker's face is clearly visible.
- The room should be free from any extra noise. Hearing impaired children can observe and understand better in a quiet environment.

- The topic of the conversation should be told in advance to the children with hearing loss. This will help in them better understanding the objective of the conversation which will greatly benefit hearing impaired children in being prepared to listen and interpret what's being said.
- Teacher should not over-exaggerate. Too much loud speech will be difficult for the children to understand. Therefore in a class with hearing impaired children, teachers should speak softly and slowly.
- There should not be any obstacles in front of the speaker. Any moustache, hands over the mouth should be removed during conversation with children with hearing loss.
- Language is another important factor for good speech reading. It is difficult for children to speech read unusual pronunciations or a different language.
- During the conversation, the speaker should look straight instead of looking down or away from the listener.
- Sounds of some letters e,g, p, b and m look the same when speaking; therefore the speech reader must be able to differentiate between these sounds on the basis of other clues.

Therefore, speech reading skills can help hearing impaired children in developing effective communication abilities when done consistently and with specific techniques used to communicate the message and its meaning.

Caring for Children with Special Needs: Hearing Impairments

Reduce Noise in the Environment

We use hearing to communicate and to hear environmental sounds. Even a mild hearing loss may interfere with clear communication. If a child can't hear speech clearly and consistently, then she will have more difficulty participating fully in activities with other people.

For a child with a mild hearing loss, you will want to make sure that background noise levels and loud music do not compete with conversation. Carpets, area rugs, and soft wall coverings help make a child care environment less noisy. Sound-absorbent material, such as cork board or carpet tiles on the walls, will help minimize noise in a room.

Noisy environments also can be a problem for children who wear hearing aids, especially in understanding conversation. Hearing aids help the child hear better, but they do not restore perfect hearing.

Remember that mild hearing losses may not interfere with communication. If hearing loss occurs at birth or in early childhood, a child will compensate for it. Some conversation may be missed, but with a bit of effort, such as seating the child near you as you read a story, there will be minimal impact. Seating is important in circle time so that a child with a mild hearing impairment can see everyone.

Face the Child when you Speak

A child with a hearing loss needs to see as well as hear what you say to him. You do not need to exaggerate lip movements but you must speak clearly. Do not position yourself so he faces bright light and make sure visual barriers are minimized so that "line of sight" communication is possible. Furniture and bookcases should be low enough for children to see over them. When you show a child with a hearing impairment how to do something, use more demonstrations and gestures than you might with other children, but don't overdo it.

Use Non-Verbal Cues to Communicate

One way to get the attention of a child with a hearing impairment is to tap or thump on the table (if it's not too distracting for other children). She will respond to the vibration. You also can touch her on the shoulder or arm to get her attention if she is busy playing. Other visual cues include waving your arms, stamping your foot, or flashing the lights (flip the switch up and down a few times).

Of course, wild arm-waving is not recommended (it's better to show other children effective, but not theatrical, ways to do this). Depending on the child's age, the child with a hearing impairment can show other children what method works best.

Children in your setting can "role play" interactions so they learn how to communicate with each other. Role-playing in a warm and supportive way can do a lot to explain that the child with a hearing impairment may need to be tapped on the shoulder to get her attention, or see people's faces as they speak. Explain to other children that if she does not respond to a verbal cue, it doesn't mean she's ignoring them. Children often can work out communication difficulties by themselves if they are given an opportunity to practice with each other at first.

Know what to do in an Emergency

Have a clear and effective signal that will get the child's attention in an emergency. Make sure he understands this signal and responds to it. Then practice the procedure. The best solution is to add flashing lights to an existing alarm system because a child with severe hearing impairments may not hear a smoke alarm.

It also is important to establish emergency communication procedures for outdoor play areas, which can pose a difficult situation for children with hearing impairments. Children playing noisily out of the immediate reach of an adult may cause a child with a hearing impairment to miss the call to return to the building. A staff person may need to go to the child when outdoor play time is over or whenever a dangerous situation arises.

Be a Good Role Model

Other children see how you behave and will copy you. If you develop effective communication strategies, other children will, too. If you ignore the hearing-impaired child, other children also may do the same thing. Watch for signs of isolation, such as the child with a hearing impairment playing alone rather than with a group, or other children deliberately turning their backs on that child. If you see problems, handle it the same way you would any social or interpersonal difficulty.

Know how to Care for Hearing Aids

If a child in your care wears hearing aids, you'll want his parents to show you how to care for them. An older child may be able to take care of them himself. Children sometimes take out their hearing aids and "misplace" them, so it is a good idea to ask parents how their child deals with hearing aids.

Other children in your setting need information about hearing aids, too. Invite a local hearing aid vendor or an audiologist to come to your programme with hearing aids that children can see, touch, and listen to.

Keep in mind that sand and dirt can cause problems for children who wear hearing aids. If possible, wood chips are a better choice than sand for outside play areas. Another option is to have the child leave his hearing aids indoors before going outside to play. Set up a specific place for him to put the device so that it doesn't get lost (a common problem for young children).

It is your responsibility to follow whatever communication strategies a child's parents have decided to follow. There are several schools of thought about teaching language to children with hearing impairments. If sign language is part of the child's communication strategy, then it is a wonderful opportunity for all children to learn some signs. Regardless of whether the child uses sign or verbal communication strategies, the hours a child spends with you can be incorporated into active language acquisition. Involve yourself and staff by having the child's speech therapist suggest ways to make your environment language-rich.

Resources for Caregivers

Most communities have people who are deaf. Invite them to your setting to show children how they communicate with Sign Language. Ask them to tell about some of the adaptive equipment that exists for people with hearing impairment. The local telephone company may be able to send a representative to demonstrate amplifying telephones, telecommunication devices for the deaf (TDDs), and flashing signalers. If you have a deaf child in your setting, it would be wonderful to hire a staff person who is deaf.

There are many national organizations that provide services for people who are deaf or hearing impaired. If you are looking for a local organization, contact your nearest audiological center or audiologist. They should be able to refer you to local agencies or organizations. Also contact the special education resource person in your school system.

UNIT-VI

Learning Disability

Types and Factors Affecting Learning

Instructional Design is largely affected by how a user learns:

Meaningfulness Effect: Highly meaningful words are easier to learn and remember than less meaningful words. This is true whether meaningful is measured by:

1) the number of associations the learner has for the word,
2) by frequency of the word
3) or by familiarity with the sequential order of letters,
4) or the tendency of the work to elicit clear images.

An implication is that retention will be improved to the extent the user can make meaning of the material.

Serial Position Effects: Serial position effects result from the particular placement of an item within a list. Memory is better for items placed at beginning or end of list rather than in the middle. An exception to these serial positions is the distinctiveness effect-an item that is distinctively different from the others will be remembered better, regardless of serial position.

Practice Effects: Active practice or rehearsal improves retention, and distributed practice is usually more effective than massed practice. The advantage to distributed practice is especially noticeable for lists, fast presentation rates or unfamiliar stimulus material. The advantage to distributed practice apparently occurs because massed practice allows the learner to associate a word with only a single context, but distributed practice allows association with many different contexts.

Transfer Effects: Transfer effects are effects of prior learning on the leaning of new material. Positive transfer occurs when previous learning makes new learning easier. Negative transfer occurs when it makes the new learning more difficult. The more that two tasks have in common, the more likely that transfer effects occur.

Interference Effects: Interference effects occur when memory or particular material is hurt by previous or subsequent learning. Interference effects occur when trying to remember material that has previously been learned. Interference effects are always negative.

Organization Effects: Organization effects occur when learners chunk or categorize the input. Free recall of lists is better when learners organize the items into categories rather than attempt to memorize the list in serial order.

Levels-of-Processing Effects: The more deeply a word is processed, the better it will be remembered. Semantic encoding of content is likely to lead to better memory. Elaborative encoding, improves memory by making sentences more meaningful.

State-Dependent Effects: State-or Context-dependent effects occur because learning takes place in within a specific context that must be accessible later, at least initially, within the same context. For example, lists are more easily remembered when the test situation more closely resembles the leaning situation, apparently due to contextual cues available to aid in information retrieval.

Mnemonic Effects: Mnemonics-strategies for elaborating on relatively meaningless input by associating the input with more meaningful images or semantic context. Four well-known mnemonic methods are the place method, the link method, the peg method and the keyword method.

Abstraction Effects: Abstraction is the tendency of learners to pay attention to and remember the gist of a passage rather than the specific words of a sentence. In general, to the extent that learners assume the goal is understanding rather than verbatim memory and the extent that the material can be analyzed into main ideas and supportive detail, learners will tend to concentrate on the main ideas and to retain these in semantic forms that are more abstract and generalized than the verbatim sentences included in the passage.

Levels Effect: This effect occurs when the learner perceives that some parts of the passage are more important than others. Parts that occupy higher levels in the organization of the passage will be learned better than parts occupying low levels.

Prior Knowledge Effects: Prior knowledge effects will occur to the extent that the learner can use existing knowledge to establish a context or construct a schema into which the new information can be assimilated.

Inference Effects: Inference effects occur when learners use schemas or other prior knowledge to make inferences about intended meanings that go beyond what is explicitly stated in the text. Three kinds of inferences are case grammar presuppositions, conceptual dependency inferences and logical deductions.

Student Misconception Effects: Prior knowledge can lead to misconceptions. Misconceptions may be difficult to correct due to fact that learner may not be aware that knowledge s a misconception. Misconception occurs when input is filtered through schemas that are oversimplified, distorted or incorrect.

Text Organization Effects: Text organization refers to the effects that the degree and type of organization built into a passage have on the degree and type of information that learners encode and remember. Structural elements such as advanced organizers, previews, logical sequencing, outline formats, higlighting of main ideas and summaries assist learning in retaining information. These organization effects facilitate chunking, subsumption of material into schemas and related processes that enable encoding as an organized body of meaningful knowledge. In addition, text organization elements cue learners to which aspects of the material are most important.

Mathemagenic Effects

Mathemagenic effects, coined by *Rothkopf (1970)*, refer to various things that learners do to prepare and assist their own learning. These effects refer to the active information processing by learners. Mathemagenic activities include answering adjunct questions or taking notes and can enhance learning.

Gifted Children with Learning Disabilities: A Paradox for Parents

Gifted children with learning disabilities present a paradox to educators and parents. The identification and characteristics of gifted children with learning disabilities is outlined. Issues relating to meeting the needs of these students in the New Zealand education system are discussed. The role of parents in supporting these children is explored.

The gifted child with learning disabilities (GCLD) is seemingly a paradox — How can a gifted child be struggling with academic achievement and success in the school system, and yet be focused and passionate about complex interests at home?

How can they seem to learn some things with no apparent effort, and yet in other areas of learning experience so much difficulty? As noted by Sturgess (1997): "Amazing and creative achievements can pale into insignificance if the student is unable to remember what was assigned for homework or where a math book was left. Understandably, parents, teachers, and the students themselves wonder how they could be so capable when it comes to higher level thinking and abstract concepts, and yet so incapable when they are required to organise a written product, sequence ideas, and pay attention to detail."

The recognition of the existence of GCLD children has become an increasing focus for writers, researchers, and educators in the field of gifted education, and this article explorers the characteristics of the GCLD child, and considers some of the issues in the education of these children with a particular focus on the parent's role in supporting their GCLD children.

Definition and Characteristics of "Gifted Learning Disabled"

Significant writing and research on gifted children with learning disabilities began around 25 years ago (Birely, 1995). Much of the difficulty for some educators has been the misguided concept that "learning disabilities" and "giftedness" occur at opposite ends of the learning spectrum (Baum, Owen, & Dixon, 1993), however a strong body of literature now supports the existence of both conditions existing simultaneously (Baum, 1990). Birely (1995) notes that the literature on GCLD can be categorised into four categories:

- case studies,
- articles on educational programmes designed to meet the needs of these children,
- studies of intelligence test patterns, and
- suggestions for teaching strategies to assist these children.

While no absolute definition has been developed or agreed upon, the GCLD can be defined as "a student with an overall IQ score in the superior range or a score on one section of an individually administered IQ test in the superior range... or A student with an exceptional ability in one area (eg mathematics..) and who exhibits a significant discrepancy between achievement and identified intellectual potential...." (John Hopkins University, 1995). Mendaglio (1993) gives three criteria for identification:

- average or above average intelligence,
- significant underachievement, and
- difficulty with skills involving encoding and decoding of language.

GCLD students can be grouped into three categories:

- identified gifted students who have subtle learning disabilities,
- unidentified students whose gifts and disabilities may be masked by average achievement, and
- identified learning disabled students who are also gifted (Baum, 1990).

Estimations of the incidence of GCLD students range from 2–5 percent of the general gifted student population (Whitmore, 1981 cited in Stewart, 1998), while Dix and Schaeffer (1996) estimate somewhere between 5–10 percent of the gifted population are GCLD.

Berk (1983, cited in Mendaglio, 1993) considers that learning difficulties are a category of underachievement. Research by Silverman (1989, cited in Cline & Schwartz, 1999) noted that the characteristics of GCLD students defined in literature are nearly identical to characteristics given for gifted underachieving students. There is no absolute set of characteristics which define the GCLD student (Rivera, Murdock & Sexton (1995); Stewart, 1998), however a common set of characteristics is identified in the literature, and is summarised in Table 1. While some distinguishing patterns are usually in evidence in a WISC III test on a GCLD student, generally the characteristics of GCLD students are defined in terms of behaviours, rather than specific diagnostic tests. Part of the difficulty in defining an absolute list of characteristics is that there are so many types and definitions of giftedness, and so many possible learning difficulties (Maker & Udall, 1983).

Many GCLD children also display attention deficit or attention deficit hyperactivity disorders. While there is an interrelationship between giftedness and these disorders (Cline & Schwartz, 1999; Williard-Holt, 1999) there is also the possibility that GCLD students be misdiagnosed as ADHD or ADD due to similarity in some of the characteristics, especially when a gifted child may be reacting to inappropriate curriculum and exhibiting these behaviours (Webb & Latimer, 1993).

Common symptoms of ADHD (listed by the American Psychiatric Association, 1994, cited in Cline & Schwartz, 1999) include:

- often does not give close attention to details or makes careless mistakes in schoolwork or other activities;
- often has difficulty sustaining attention in tasks;
- often fails to finish schoolwork;
- often has difficulty organising tasks and activities.

These are identical to characteristics often cited for GCLD students and it is thus imperative that such diagnoses are made by well-informed professionals who have a full range of information about the child.

Weaknesses:

- Cannot do simple tasks but can complete more sophisticated activities
- Spells poorly
- Has poor handwriting, reversals of letter and poor formation of letters can be common
- Inconsistencies in reading ability: either good comprehension but poor reading skills, or good reading skills but poor comprehension
- Has difficulty with computation but demonstrates higher level mathematical reasoning
- Transposes numerals in mathematics
- Does well in mathematics, but poorly in language
- Does well in language but poorly in mathematics
- Does not do well on timed tests
- Does not respond well or consistently to auditory instructions/information
- Poor organisational skills, failure to complete or hand in assignments
- Difficulty with rote memorisation, sequential learning
- Poor ball handling skills
- Difficulty copying from the blackboard
- Generalises minor academic failure to feelings of overall inadequacy
- Affective behaviours can include: low self-esteem, unrealistic expectations, reluctant to take risks
- Disruptive in class
- Frequently off task
- Frustrates easily
- Acts out without thinking about the consequences
- Has poor social skills with peers and adults

- A "zig zag" or "scatter" WISC pattern, showing weaknesses the sub tests such as coding, digit span, arithmetic, and freedom from distractibility

Strengths:

- High scores on the WISC in vocabulary, similarities, block design, abstract reasoning and spatial reasoning
- Above average vocabulary
- Great knowledge and passion for subjects of interest
- Can show exceptional skills in mathematical reasoning, geometry
- Divergent thinkers – involving unusual, original, imaginative and creative thought processes
- Active imagination
- Excellent visual memory
- Sophisticated sense of humour

While the term "Gifted Learning Disabled" is in common use in the literature, other terms such as "Twice-exceptional" (Beckley, n.d.) are also in use. Some literature also refers to gifted children with "dyslexia", although this term has not been commonly used in education in New Zealand (Fischer, 1999).

Identification of GCLD Students

Many GCLD students are not identified, and many fail to reach their full potential within the education system (Silverman, 1990 cited in Stewart, 1998). The lack of consensus about a definition of giftedness or LD means that there is confusion over identifying GCLD students (Pendarvis, Howley & Howley, 1990 cited in Stewart, 1998). In addition, recognition of learning disabilities is particularly difficult in some gifted children, as they have a remarkable ability to compensate and hide their weaknesses (Silverman, 1999).

Baum, Owen and Dixon (1993) note that identification often begins when parents or teachers suspect that a student is having a problem. In New Zealand, the WISC lll is not generally used as a diagnostic test within schools, although some children may have had access to such testing through outside agencies and the results have been used in their identification. More commonly, identification will rely on knowledgeable educators or parents identifying a child's mix of abilities and disabilities.

To identify a student as GCLD a wide variety of information should be sought, including indepth assessment of both strengths and weaknesses (Van Tassel-Baska,1992; Baum, Owen & Dixon, 1993; Maker & Udall, 1983). Evaluation should include individually administered intelligence tests, diagnostic achievement tests, evaluation of creative products by experts or teachers, peer evaluations of leadership ability, parent interviews, classroom observation of peer interaction and other performance, and ideally tests of perceptual ability, visual motor coordination, and expressive ability (Maker & Udall, 1993). Such comprehensive evaluation is unlikely to occur routinely in many New Zealand schools at this time.

Parent's Role in Identification of GCLD Students

Sturgess (1999, p 11) notes that parents often indicate that their children were "bright" during their early schooling, "but fell progressively behind other students, particularly in written language, specifically spelling, and sometimes reading". Gifted behaviour before entering school and subsequent failure in school can provide an important indicator of a GCLD student (Rivera, Murdock, & Sexton, 1995), and as parents can provide insight into their children's preschool activities or outside school interests, parental involvement in identification can be key (Rivera, Murdock, & Sexton,1995; Baum, Owen & Dixon, 1993). Delisle (1992) notes that the most efficient way to gain useful parent information for identification is to ask parents specific questions about the traits and behaviours of their children, rather than yes/no type questionnaires.

Parent identification of giftedness and/or learning disabilities can be particularly important in the preschool years when test data is not readily available or appropriate. Research in one study showed that over 70 percent of parents with gifted children first suspected giftedness in their children between birth and three years of age (Gogel, McClumsey, & Hewitt, 1985c sited in Delisle, 1992). A study by Jacobs (1971 cited in

Delisle, 1992) found that 76 percent of parents with gifted kindergarten children had identified them as gifted, compared to the teacher identification rate of only identifying 4 percent of the gifted children.

Parents often know the strengths and weaknesses of their children well, and it is likely that parents are just as accurate in identifying their GCLD children as these statistics suggest for parental identification of giftedness. For example, while a kindergarten teacher may regard a 4-year-old as developmentally normal in being unable yet to identify letters of the alphabet, a parent may recognise a huge contrast between their child's unmastered reading and writing skills, and their child's encyclopedic knowledge of dinosaurs and ability to identify them in great detail.

The Need for GCLD Students to be Identified

It is essential that identification of gifted learning disabled children is made as early as possible, and preferably in the early childhood years to assist GCLD students to succeed in the school system (Williams, 1988). Silverman (1999) stresses the importance of early diagnosis of learning disabilities in order to enable early intervention, particularly in the case of motor delays. Keenan (1994, cited in Sherwood 1998) advocates that "if intervention is begun at the preschool level, these children can enter school with their parents aware of where they will most probably benefit from gifted programmes, where they will experience failure with normal school expectations, and how to allow for and/or remediate the areas of weakness".

Awareness of and identification of GCLD students also allows for the identification of the "hidden" gifted, students whose abilities are masked by their weaknesses. As noted by Johnson, Karnes and Carr, (1997) a barrier to identification of gifted children with disabilities is the expectation that the children will demonstrate the same characteristics of giftedness as children without disabilities who are identified as gifted. So for example, if a teacher believes that all gifted children will express their knowledge and ideas well in their written work, they are unlikely to identify a child as gifted who cannot even form letters correctly. The gifts of GCLD students often remain invisible to teachers and sometimes even parents (Beckley, n.d.). GCLD students may be mistakingly identified as ADD or ADHD, underachieving, "lazy", or "average", and it is therefore important to correctly identify these students using multicategorical information, so that their specific needs are identified.

Vaidya (1993) notes that parents may neglect the importance of nurturing their child's strengths and gifts while concentrating on addressing the difficulties posed by the child's learning disability. Therefore, it is imperative that parents and teachers identify GCLD students and put appropriate strategies in place, which offer enrichment and/or acceleration in the areas of strength, as well as addressing areas of weakness. Sturgess, (1997, p 1) noted that the "use of inappropriate teaching strategies can result in negative attributions and limited learning experiences for GCLD students", and hence it is critical that these students are identified as the first step in meeting their educational needs in an appropriate way.

GCLD students are also at signficant risk for developing negative self concepts as a result of their frustration at being unable to complete simple tasks successfully and yet thinking at high levels, as their intellectual abilities allow them to see clearly what they perceive as failures (Conover, 1996). Whitmore (1980 cited in Delisle, 1992) notes that many gifted children connect their success in school to their worth as a person. Appropriate identification and remediation and counseling can assist in GCLD students in having a more positive understanding of their own strengths and weaknesses.

Baum (1990) notes that in planning for the educational needs of GCLD students, it is important to focus on the development of the strengths and interests, as well as to teach and encourage the use of compensation strategies. Strategies which assist in meeting the needs of GCLD students are outlined.

- Focus on the child's strengths.
- Encourage compensation strategies such as calculator

use, and word processes to compensate for spelling and writing difficulties.

- Find sources of information that are accessible to students who have difficulty reading.
- Teach how to use brainstorming and mind maps to organise their work, and teach formal essay and project planning and presentation.
- Allow the student to use strategies other than writing to communicate ideas and complete school projects eg dictate work to someone else, give a speech, present a video, audio tape, use a computer presentation programme, make a model, use drama, create a mural.
- Use mnemonics to overcome short term memory problems.
- Teach auditory processing skills.
- Provide alternative learning experiences which are not dependent on paper and pencil or reading (puzzles, logic games, tangrams, math manipulatives).
- Give realistic deadlines for completing assignments (often longer than for others). Use contracts.
- Develop routines for daily activities — eg specific times for homework, organising clothing and schoolbooks for the next day, organising class books.
- The use of coloured lenses may may remediate some reading difficulties.
- Encourage awareness of individual strengths and weaknesses. It is imperative that students who are gifted and learning disabled understand their abilities, strengths, and weaknesses.
- Provide mentoring experiences with adults who are GCLD.
- Provide appropriate success feedback.

Silverman (1999) notes that the asynchronous development of gifted individuals is magnified when high levels of intelligence are combined with disabilities. The asynchronous development of the gifted student can raise special challenges as they seek to understand themselves and to make life choices as they enter adolescence. It is important that parents and educators are aware of these issues, and take them into account when developing appropriate learning opportunities.

The GCLD Student in the New Zealand Education System

One of the key issues in the provision for the needs of GCLD students in New Zealand is the lack of a national policy for gifted students and the lack of a national policy that requires schools to provide identification or differentiated education for GCLD students. Official recognition and provision of services for GCLD students is mandatory in other countries (Sturgess, 1997).

Sturgess (1997) identified several issues that contribute to the lack of identification of GCLD students in New Zealand:

- lack of official recognition of either giftedness or learning disabilities as categories of special need;
- identification procedures that fail to identify gifted students who also have learning disabilities;
- limited understanding on the part of many educators of what it means, in academic and affective terms, to be gifted and learning disabled.

GCLD students present a special challenge to schools and educators in New Zealand, as many professional educators have received no training in the identification and provisions to meet the needs of these students (Williams, 1988). It is somewhat difficult for teachers to cater for GCLD students if they have not even recognised that they have specific learning needs. These students may be identified as being lazy and just not trying hard enough. Teachers specifically trained in special education are few and far between in our school systems at this time and while staff such as RTLB's may be trained to teach children with disabilities, few may have knowledge about gifted children and their programmeming needs. Professionals in gifted education may have little knowledge about learning difficulties.

The New Zealand school system is increasingly providing for children from diverse backgrounds, with diverse languages, cultures, socioeconomic levels, and complex family backgrounds that impact on each child's educational needs. These varying needs provide an ever increasing challenge for schools and for the classroom teacher to meet the needs of each child. It is inevitable that with such an array of needs to meet, teachers are will be making choices about which children's needs they can realistically address within their classroom. For some parents, their concern about their GCLD child's needs not being met in the school system becomes so great that they choose to home school their child.

Awareness of the needs of gifted children is however being continually raised in New Zealand, along with the awareness of the needs of GCLD students. The recent publication by the Ministry of Education of *Gifted and Talented Students: Meeting Their Needs in New Zealand Schools* is a strong signal to educators that the needs of all gifted students must be met and should result in many more New Zealand schools developing school policy and progammes for the gifted students including special population such as GCLD students.

The Education Review Office (ERO) is increasingly focusing on the needs of gifted children within schools, however without a national policy on gifted children, ERO can only comment publicly on the fact that a school is not adequately meeting the needs of these students, rather than actually require a school to put appropriate policy and programmes in place. Concerned parents can however draw ERO's attention to the issue by writing to the Board of Trustees and expressing their concerns, as this is likely to "flag" the issue when ERO staff are undertaking their audit (J. Adams, 2000, personal communication, June 19, 2000).

Parental Involvement in Meeting the Needs of their GCLD Child

Stephens (1999) comments that "In order for gifted education to successfully move ahead into the 21st century, parental involvement is essential." Parental involvement can be critical in identifying GCLD students, and in assisting in strategies to assist the GCLD child at home and in school, and in ensuring that appropriate educational opportunities are available to meet the child's needs for extension. Parents of GCLD students also have a role to play in their child's school and community.

Parents' Role in Meeting the Needs of the GCLD Child at School

Fraser (1996) states that "it is essential that parents go to extraordinary efforts to maintain the best possible relationship with the child's school". The New Zealand school system allows for and encourages community input into the running of schools. Elected Boards of Trustees allow for parents to have a significant role in determining staffing, resources, professional development, and in developing the special nature of their individual school. In addition, groups such as PTA, and the openness in some schools towards the use of "parent help" within the classroom allows for substantial interaction between school personnel and parents. While all of these positions offer excellent opportunities for working with and developing a relationship with school staff and offer an opportunity for increasing dialogue for advocacy, they also a draw on parents' time and energy.

In some schools, such parent roles of "helping" within the school are the main opportunity a parent has to build rapport and knowledge about the school and teaching staff. For those parents who work full time, access to school staff can be difficult, especially where no other formal avenues are made easily available for parents to meet with school staff — one 10 minute parent-teacher interview per year is not sufficient for adequate exchange of information between parents and professionals in order to discuss the needs of a GCLD student. While parent involvement within the classroom is common in preschools and primary schools, it is in generally seen as less appropriate at intermediate and secondary schools.

Tolan (1987, cited in Fraser, 1996) notes "when professionals see themselves as the source of all knowledge and information and parents only as receivers of that information, it is perhaps not surprising that they are less aware than they might be of what life may be like for gifted children and their parents". While some educationalists and researchers see meeting the needs of GCLD students purely from a teacher-driven perspective, it remains difficult for parents to contribute towards their child's school education. Silverman (n.d.) notes that parents of gifted children can be placed in a "no-win situation: If they try to develop their children's abilities to their fullest, they often find themselves in an adversarial position with the schools" and until there are government requirements "protecting gifted children and assuring that they get an education commensurate with their needs, parents will have to bear the burden of being their children's advocates — even when it means being branded 'a pushy parent'."

The lack of knowledge exhibited by professionals within the field of education is a major constraint facing parents of GCLD students. In research by Sherwood (1995, cited in Sherwood, 1996) parents expressed the view that "many teachers are not prepared to take anything you say seriously and have a tendency to label the children as being stupid or lazy". Anecdotal evidence suggests that for many parents of GCLD students in New Zealand their experiences are similar. Stephens (1999) identifies that "pre-service teachers should receive special training in effective communication skills so that they might conduct more successful parent-teacher conferences", and further that "it is necessary that pre-service teachers receive sensitivity training to the unique needs of parents of gifted children". Stephens (1999) specifically identifies that pre-service teachers need to gain skills in "effective communication, collaboration with parents, and efficient dissemination techniques".

Mark (1990) notes that when effective parent-teacher communication takes place, this has increased benefits for the child's learning, the teacher has access to information to teach more effectively, and the parents can more appropriately parent. It is still not uncommon for teacher trainees in New Zealand to complete their training with little or no training in how to interact with parents. In addition, schools and teachers have differing ideas about just how much information parents are given about their child's progress at school, which can provide a further barrier to parents wishing to access this information.

While the Official Information Act ultimately means that parents are legally entitled to view their child's school records, in practice this is not always a straight forward process.

For some parents their own experiences of school may not have been positive and may have left them deeply distrustful and skeptical of teachers' abilities and commitment in general, and this may be a barrier to effective communication. For other parents they may have little familiarity with, or understanding of, educational terms and practices, and may be overwhelmed by information. Cultural difference may also result in parents not wishing to be seen to question a teacher's authority or ideas.

In a study by the Javits Centre (n.d.) to determine factors that enable some gifted students to succeed in an academic setting, parents identified the need for constant parental advocacy to ensure their child's academic success, and this advocacy took the form of stressing the importance of education, scheduling appointments with school personnel, constant encouragement and support for their child, seeking help from outside the school, and taking time to work with their child on school work. Delisle (1992) uses the terms "microadvocacy" and "macroadvocacy" to highlight that parents need to be able to separate issues that relate only to their child and those that are more general to all or many gifted children, and notes that both forms of advocacy are important.

Delisle (1992) cites examples of microadvocacy as including parents speaking to their child's teacher about their child's progress; attending a PTA meeting and expressing views on issues pertaining to their child; volunteering in their child's school and writing to the school principal to suggest greater focus on gifted children's needs within the school. Examples of macroadvocacy include forming a parent support group, lobbying government for funding and policy decisions about gifted children, and involving media in promoting the needs of gifted children (Delisle, 1992). As stated by Tolan (1987, cited in Fraser, 1996) "until parents and gifted children come out of the closet and admit (even value) unusual abilities without automatically being accused of arrogance; until professionals are willing to learn from parents and children about the realities the gifted face instead of protecting their own positions as "experts"; until professionals as readily distinguish and serve children functioning several standard deviations above the norm as children functioning several deviations below, it will still be necessary to deal with the gifted as children at risk. There will still need to be advocates who put gifted children at the top of their list of priorities and who continue... to focus on the genuine needs of this real and still neglected minority".

The Needs of Parents of GCLD Students

Parents of GCLD students are certainly likely to suffer from feelings of guilt and question their ability to parent adequately when their children are still unable to perform basic organisational tasks that other children have long since mastered. Eight-year-olds who can still not find their shoes, remember to put their socks or underpants on, and never know where their homework is, provide frustrating challenges for their parents, and such experiences are hardly ones that a parent may wish to share with other parents whose children mastered such tasks at preschool. Parenting is particularly difficult and stressful when children do not measure up to family or community expectations. The need to share such experiences, gain some tips and strategies from parents who have worked on such issues, and just to relax and laugh with other parents who understand, underlines the importance of parent support groups, be they formal organisations or the casual meeting of parents at the school gate.

Stephens (1999) notes that parents often wonder if they are doing enough to cultivate their children's talents and gifts. Keirouz (1990) found that parents of gifted children experience anxiety, confusion, and uncertainty in how to provide appropriate opportunities for their child. Such feelings are likely to be heightened when parents are trying to cater for a "twice exceptional child". Not only do they have to become familiar with issues surrounding "giftedness" and providing enough stimulation for their child's strengths, but they must also deal with the consequences of a "learning disabled" child.

Sayler (1994, cited in Stephens, 1999) notes that parenting a gifted child can be filled with "ecstasy and agony, and everything in between".

In order to fulfill their role as an advocate for their child, and in supporting their child's educational needs, parents need access to information. In New Zealand there has been limited literature aimed at parents of gifted children, although increasingly web sites and listservs are meeting this need for parent information. Some parent organisations provide libraries focusing on gifted education which include some information on GCLD students, as well as local gifted parent organisation newsletters and magazines such as Tall Poppies. There is however a need for more information for parents of GCLD students with specific New Zealand information. Ideally, parent groups can provide both skill training and emotional support for parents of GCLD children (Latson, 1995).

Another significant area of difficulty in meeting the needs of GCLD children in New Zealand is the lack of access to free or subsidised diagnostic services. For many parents, the expense is considerable in the journey to diagnose just what their child's particular needs are. Access to Educational Psychologists, doctor, pediatricians, vision and hearing tests, and tests to establish motor skills delay come at considerable cost in New Zealand, and provide a barrier to those who cannot afford to access such services.

Conclusion

For many gifted children with learning disabilities, academic success is a challenge. It is important that GCLD students are appropriately identified, and appropriate education strategies put in place to meet the needs of both their strengths and weaknesses. While knowledge about the existence of GCLD children and their needs remain relatively unknown amongst New Zealand Educators, parents can be a critical factor in recognising and supporting the needs of these children. Parents have a demanding set of tasks, including a dual role in providing appropriate and stimulating enrichment as well as addressing necessary remediation for their GCLD children. They also have the role of advocate, and take on researching educational options and strategies that may assist their children.

It is important that the needs and issues for GCLD students are acknowledged and acted upon in our schools, in homes, and researched further. In many schools in New Zealand GCLD students are not being recognised, and their different educational needs are not catered for adequately. Awareness of the needs of gifted children is however being continually raised in New Zealand, along with the awareness of the needs of GCLD students.

Of ultimate importance is the necessity to provide an appropriate curriculum and learning opportunities that address the needs of all gifted students and takes into account the needs of all categories of gifted students. Parents have a strong role to play in being advocates for their children to ensure that this happens in New Zealand.

Theories and Models of Learning for the Children with Learning Disabilities

Why should a person with learning disabilities engage in recreation activities? Simply because they can derive many benefits from recreation participation. One benefit is learning from the experience. When the recreation activity experience has captivated the participant, this individual brings particular personality styles of learning, motivation, and expectations about the experience to the setting. The person faced with a specific environment, interpreted by the person or not, promotes one or more learning experiences.

These learning experiences can be motor learning, understanding game directions, or performing a skill, all to meet the demands of that setting. These experiences may come from involvement in a structured recreation programme and may be exhibited as part of the information outcomes of participation. Researchers in the field of learning and educational psychology have discovered a variety of learning outcomes. The following outcomes can be present because of participation in recreation activities: behavior change and skill learning, direct visual memory, information (factual) learning, concept learning, schemata learning, metacognition learning and attitude, and value learning (Roggenbuck, Loomis, & Dagostino, 1991).

The physiological benefits of recreation participation were derived from studies where people engage in physical activity of some kind (e.g., exercise, cycling, swimming,walking, jogging, running, hiking, weight lifting, etc). Specific results from involvement in a physical recreation activity are an increased lung capacity, reduced resting heart rates and lower blood pressure levels. Other benefits consist of decreased body fat mass, increased lean body mass, increased muscle strength, and improved structure and function of connective tissues (ligaments,tendons,cartilage) and joints. Weight-bearing and strength-building activities help sustain bone mass and reduce the incidence of trauma-induced fractures (Paffenbarger, Hyde, & Dow, 1990). Moderate physical recreation activities are known to reduce the symptoms of mild or moderate depression and anxiety through improved self-image, social skills, and mental health (Taylor, Sallis, & Needle, 1985). Noted psychological benefits of recreation activity are as follows:

- perceived sense of freedom, independence, and autonomy,
- enhanced self-competence through improved sense of self-worth, self-reliance, and self-confidence,
- better ability to socialize with others, including greater tolerance and understanding,
- enriched capabilities for team membership,
- heightened creative ability,
- improved expressions of and reflection on personal spiritual ideals,
- greater adaptability and resiliency,
- better sense of humor,
- enhanced perceived quality of life,
- more balanced competitiveness and a more positive outlook on life (Academy of Leisure Sciences & Driver, 1994).

Involvement in recreation activities releases stress and tension from the perils of society. Braum (1991) recalls the findings of researchers that state,"relaxation tends to alleviate many of the symptoms of stress. Activities that fill leisure time, performed within a group, strengthen social support ties known to negate stress" (p. 407). The idea of choice in leisure presents opportunities where one can recreate.

One's environment can be a determinant to stress reduction. Natural environments can be pleasant, relaxing, and stress-reducing for many people, but large urban cities also provide the same experience. Having too much free time and limited access to various recreation activities of one's liking can produce stress. So, for those individuals living out in the country who have access to transportation, the joy of partaking in cultural events in the city on a weekly or monthly basis provides the opportunity for a stress-limited lifestyle. The same can be said for people living in the city who recreate in the country.

Social integration of children and adults with learning disabilities into community recreation programmes offers the chance to develop a positive self-image through successful experiences and satisfying relationships with peers. McGill (1984) reports that integrated play opportunities are stimulating and highly motivating experiences for disabled children, offering them opportunities to imitate and model the play behavior of nondisabled peers. Social integration also enhances relationships between family members. We've all heard of the old adage,"The family that plays together stays together." This adage infers that leisure experiences promote family satisfaction and stability. Recreation activities provide opportunities for couples and families to interact and negotiate individual and collective interests. Orthner and Mancini (1991) state some benefits to the family:

Leisure experiences promote opportunities for developing equity. Unlike many other environments within which people interact, leisure experiences promote opportunities for each individual to maximize her or his own interests and minimize competition. It is during leisure time when husbands and wives, and parents and children, are most apt to practice by negotiating family roles and reaching new definitions of consensuses. When individual interests are promoted over maximum joint interest, family bonds are weakened. Shared leisure experiences encourage opportunities to negotiations and improve the historical comparisons upon which subsequent negotiations are based. (p. 294)

Benefits of leisure in social integration are also noted in people without disabilities. The chance to learn from and to socialize with nondisabled peers has been cited as one benefit for individuals with disabilities participating in integrated and fully inclusive programmes. Research in the 1980's determined that positive attitudes of children not having disabilities toward peers having disabilities were cultivated or increased when involved with an integrated recreation activity (Schleien & Ray, 1988). Recreation service providers also learn from this experience.

Due to the Americans With Disabilities Act of 1990, all private, public, and nonprofit agencies delivering recreation services to the public must supply accommodations and modifications within their programmes to persons with disabilities (as requested). These professionals may not have any knowledge of providing accommodations and/or modifications to participants with learning disabilities. The person with learning disabilities, upon disclosure, thus needs to educate the professional about what accommodations and/or programme modifications should be arranged to enable full participation in recreation programmes. This social interaction not only contributes awareness of this situation to another person but also demonstrates how important it is for individuals with disabilities to participate in a particular recreation activity like everyone else.

Learning Disabilities' Effect on Recreation Participation

This section will focus on its interference with recreation activities. Often, the public and even some professionals who are knowledgeable about learning disabilities forget that everyone has a life after school and after work. Do not let the word learning impede any thinking that problems associated with learning disabilities will only surface during school or work. A person may read during leisure time, and that does not always mean a novel. A person reads directions to complete a craft project, instructions to play a computer game, a description of a recipe, and even the gate number on an airplane boarding pass.

Dyslexia does not cease when one is playing Scrabble(R). Auditory perceptual ability does not suddenly improve because a child receives lower amounts of verbal instruction on the baseball field than in the classroom. Dyscalculia does not go away when playing a card game. Learning disabilities can affect every area of one's life, including participation in recreation activities.

What occurs when learning disabilities interfere with participation in recreation activities? First, the person may only wish to participate in activities that reveal his attributes. For example, an individual who excels naturally in physical activities (e.g., basketball,volleyball,golf, tennis, etc.) may feel more comfortable playing in physical activities than a game of Scattergories(R),which requires the ability to hold information in memory, process written text quickly, recall accurately, and spell precisely. Even when a person excels in physical recreation activities, unexpected obstacles can appear. A few of these obstacles are reading and interpreting written game plays or formations (e.g., basketball, football, gymnastics, marching band, water polo, hockey, etc.), keeping track of a score (e.g. ,golf), and outmaneuvering your opponent through preplanned shots (e.g., racquetball, volleyball, tennis).

In referring to the types of learning disabilities listed in Book, shown is a compilation of illustrations that describes how specific types of learning disabilities affect performance in recreational activities:

- *Dyscalculia:* This can cause one to produce a sum that is incorrect, resulting in losing a game or in misplacement of ranking in golf. This also can cause difficulty in playing games such as dominos; scoring bowling or in any type of card game; casino gambling; calculating dining charges, etc.

- *Dyslexia:* This inability to understand written language poses a problem when reading craft instructions, theater programmes, movie subtitles, travel itineraries, tour guide brochures, and interpreting the directions in learning a new game.
- *Auditory Acuity Difficulty:* This may be the problem if, when playing a game of basketball, a player continually does not respond to a coach's directions from the bench or does not respond to a teammate's verbal play-making messages.
- *Auditory-Vocal Association Problems:* The characteristic is displayed when a person hears what was said, is subsequently able to acknowledge the auditory stimuli in a correct manner, and yet proceeds to perform an incorrect or inappropriate action. In football, upon hearing the signal for an interception, a defensive back stop, turns, and begins to tackle opposing players rather than block (Yellen &Yellen, 1987,p. 51).
- *Auditory Memory Deficit:* This could be the problem if a person finds difficulty remembering directions or instructions that have been previously explained (e.g., just before game or during halftime when new instructions were stated). In volleyball, a player does not remember alterations to a defense play made by the team captain at halftime.
- *Auditory Sequencing Problem:* Here a student experiences the inability to recall a series of auditory instructions. During tap dance instruction the student performs a shuffle step beginning with her left foot instead of her right foot and beforc an eight-count circle to her left.
- *Catastrophic Response:* This can occur anytime when the individual is overloaded with too much visual and/ or auditory stimuli and rcsults in high frustration. A scenario could be that the person misread or did not double check the time to return to the bus from an outing. This resulted in the person and accompanying friend missing the bus to return to their hotel. They are

standing at the wrong bus station surrounded by hundreds of tourists. His friend is yelling, people are everywhere, and the person shuts down for approximately one minute.

- *Cognitive Disorganization:* With cognitive disorganization, a person may often miss or forget steps in a sequence. During a cub scout weekly assignment, 10-year-old Bob never brings all of the materials required to complete a project, or he constantly confuses the steps taken to achieve merit awards.
- *Crossing the Midline and Directional Problems:* These problems become quite apparent during aerobic exercise or dance class, roller or ice skating instruction, driving small motorized vehicles (e.g., scooter, go-cart racing, bumper cars, boats, etc.) and locating a room in a hotel. This individual is unable to smoothly mimic the movements of the aerobic or dance instructor and experiences difficulty mirroring responses. Controlling the steering wheel, judgement of turns on a course, and going in the correct direction may require many practice runs before exhibiting adequate skills.
- *Disinhibition:* A person exhibiting this problem often finds complications with "fitting in" groups, especially team recreation activities. Constant laughing at a teammate when the ball is dropped, always retrieving a shot within someone else's playing zone (e.g., volleyball), and continually talking loudly when silence is expected (e.g., opponent is putting in golf) could lead to dismissal from the team, if the individual is unable to correct these types of behaviors, or could result in peers not inviting this person to accompany them in a recreation activity again.
- *Intersensory Problem:* Trouble using two senses at once could interfere with designing a piece of pottery or hand painting a ceramic dish and holding a conversation with a talkative person who is sitting in the adjacent seat. Individuals exhibiting this dilemma may not

complete the task or may make numerous mistakes during the process due to engagement in conversation.

- *Short-term Memory Problem:* A person with a short-term memory problem does not remember the sequence of a turn taken during a table game, forgets to place a bet before the next poker round, and may not remember what he betted during the current poker round.
- *Visual Acuity Problem:* A player does not exhibit the ability to see clearly and differentiate objects in his visual field. In bowling, the bowler experiences problems in lining the bowling ball up with the range finders on the runway.
- *Poor Visual Coordination and Pursuit:* Here the task of following and tracking objects causes distress. A person has trouble positioning himself to catch a frisbee or misjudges the landing of a spin on a tennis shot.
- *Visual Figure-Ground Differentiation Problem:* With this type of problem the person never identified where the object was from the beginning; she has an inability to distinguish between objects in the foreground and background. In soccer, a player has difficulty seeing her teammates when conducting a "throw-in" to continue the play of game.
- *Visual-Motor, Spatial-Form Manipulation Problems:* An individual finds complications in successfully moving in space and manipulating three-dimensional objects with this problem. Examples are placing jigsaw puzzle pieces in their correct location within a puzzle, maneuvering one's bicycle through an obstacle course, and even parallel parking one's car.

It is common for persons with learning disabilities to employ survival strategies when learning a new skill or interacting in a group situation. Examples of these strategies are as follows:

1. *Learn from Doing:* Jim cannot understand the chalkboard plays so his mind frequently "fades" out during those sessions. Jim feels since he will run that

particular football play three times out on the field before the next game, he'll be fine in learning that game play.

2. *Observe what Others Do:* Sally is always one step behind when Coach Smith verbally explains new jumps she wants the cheerleading squad to try. Sally chooses to stand near the end of the cheerleading squad line. By the time her turn comes, she can successfully perform the jumps just like everyone else in the group.
3. *Develop a Buddy System:* Keith has a problem interpreting what his college football offensive line coach, Coach Green, says during films. During the weekly viewing of football films, Keith may only catch about a third of what Coach Green is explaining. Keith developed a close friendship with George, who is also a member of the offensive line. Keith and George would get together for about an hour after films to discuss what Coach Green wants the offensive team to accomplish for the next game.
4. *Awareness of Instructors' Expectations:* It is common in organized athletic teams that one person's wrongdoings or mistakes can jeopardize the entire team; youngsters and adolescents respond quickly to peer pressure. April immediately became aware of timeliness when the coach made her and her gymnastic teammates run 25 laps around the gym, twice in one week, due to April arriving late to practice sessions. This only occurred the first week of training, and throughout the 16-week training period April was never late again.

These are just a few of the strategies considered "compensation" strategies that individuals with learning disabilities acquire throughout their lives. Some individuals learn them through life experience (the school of hard knocks), while others are fortunate enough to have someone provide them with guidance. It does not matter how compensation strategies are obtained, as long as they are mastered and utilized to render effective participation in a recreation activity of choice. Determining how one can partake in a recreation activity that may demonstrate areas of difficulty is the solution to successful inclusive recreation involvement.

Teaching Strategies in Order to Develop Desirable Skills in Persons with Learning Disability

Some Types of Learning Disabilities – The First Step is Understanding

Some types of learning disabilities can be "treated" through proper testing and training. The key is to identify the specific cognitive weaknesses causing the "disorder" and strengthen those cognitive skills through dynamic, one-on-one training and practice. For the parent, the first step is to understand the types of learning disabilities that may be affecting your child.

Some Types of Learning Disabilities – General Processing Issues

Some types of learning disabilities are categorized by the cognitive processing problem. This means your child may have issues with one of the following:

Attention: The ability to stay on task in a sustained, selective, or divided way.

Working Memory: The ability to retain and process information for short time periods.

Processing Speed: The rate at which the brain handles information.

Long-Term Memory: The ability to both store and recall information for later use.

Visual Processing: The ability to perceive, analyze, and think in visual images.

Auditory Processing: The ability to perceive and conceptualize what is heard.

Logic and Reasoning: The ability to reason, prioritize, and plan.

If there are significant dysfunctions in any of these seven cognitive processes, then your child probably has some type of learning disability. For instance, if "working memory" is deficient, your child may have a problem remembering instructions. If "auditory processing" is deficient, your child may have difficulty with reading and spelling. If "visual processing" is poor, your child may experience issues with reading maps, word math problems, and comprehension. If "logic and reasoning" are weak, difficulties may arise in problem solving, working with abstractions, or interpreting information. If the issue is poor "long-term memory," it may be difficult for your child to recall dates, names, and facts on tests. Of course, some children may experience problems in more than one process category.

Some Types of Learning Disabilities – Specific Learning Disorders

In addition to the cognitive processing categories, some types of learning disabilities are more specifically defined by education-based labels such as reading, writing, language, and math. These more specified types of learning disabilities are categorized as follows:

Dyslexia: A reading disability (the student has trouble reading written words fluently, out loud).

Dysgraphia: A writing disability (the student has difficulty with forming letters and legibility).

Dyscalculia: A math disability (the student struggles with math problems and concepts).

Dyspraxia: A motor coordination disability (also known as Sensory Integration Disorder).

Dysphasia: A language disability (the student has difficulty with reading comprehension).

Aphasia: A language disability (the student has difficulty understanding spoken language).

Central Auditory Processing Disorder: A sensory disability related to processing sounds.

Visual Processing Disorder: A sensory disability related to processing images.

Non-Verbal Learning Disorder: A visual-spatial disability related to body control.

Some Types of Learning Disabilities – The Next Step is Professional Testing

The great news for you and your child is that some types of learning disabilities can be attacked head-on with proper assessment and training. At LearningRx, we've spent nearly two decades developing and testing effective programmes that identify learning weaknesses and strengthen those weaknesses with powerful, one-on-one training programmes. The results have been tremendous and we encourage you to read what others are saying about our system.

Indeed, the first step is to properly test your child and identify the cognitive weaknesses contributing to his or her learning disability. Please contact one of our LearningRx Training Centers today to schedule an appointment.

Types of Learning Disabilities

Learning disabilities can be categorized either by the type of information processing that is affected or by the specific difficulties caused by a processing deficit.

Information Processing Deficits

Learning disabilities fall into broad categories based on the four stages of information processing used in learning: input, integration, storage, and output.

- *Input:* This is the information perceived through the senses, such as visual and auditory perception. Difficulties with visual perception can cause problems with recognizing the shape, position and size of items seen. There can be problems with sequencing, which can relate to deficits with processing time intervals or temporal perception. Difficulties with auditory perception can make it difficult to screen out competing sounds in order to focus on one of them, such as the sound of the teacher's voice. Some children appear to be unable to process tactile input. For example, they may seem insensitive to pain or dislike being touched.
- *Integration:* This is the stage during which perceived input is interpreted, categorized, placed in a sequence,

or related to previous learning. Students with problems in these areas may be unable to tell a story in the correct sequence, unable to memorize sequences of information such as the days of the week, able to understand a new concept but be unable to generalize it to other areas of learning, or able to learn facts but be unable to put the facts together to see the "big picture." A poor vocabulary may contribute to problems with comprehension.

- *Storage:* Problems with memory can occur with short-term or working memory, or with long-term memory. Most memory difficulties occur in the area of short-term memory, which can make it difficult to learn new material without many more repetitions than is usual. Difficulties with visual memory can impede learning to spell.
- *Output:* Information comes out of the brain either through words, that is, language output, or through muscle activity, such as gesturing, writing or drawing. Difficulties with language output can create problems with spoken language, for example, answering a question on demand, in which one must retrieve information from storage, organize our thoughts, and put the thoughts into words before we speak. It can also cause trouble with written language for the same reasons. Difficulties with motor abilities can cause problems with gross and fine motor skills. People with gross motor difficulties may be clumsy, that is, they may be prone to stumbling, falling, or bumping into things. They may also have trouble running, climbing, or learning to ride a bicycle. People with fine motor difficulties may have trouble buttoning shirts, tying shoelaces, or with handwriting.

Specific Learning Disabilities

Deficits in any area of information processing can manifest in a variety of specific learning disabilities. It is possible for an individual to have more than one of these difficulties. This is referred to as comorbidity or co-occurrence of learning disabilities. In the UK, the term *dual diagnosis* is often used to refer to co-occurrence of learning difficulties.

- *Reading dDisability (ICD-10 and DSM-IV codes:* F81.0/315.00): The most common learning disability. Of all students with specific learning disabilities, 70%-80% have deficits in reading. The term "dyslexia" is often used as a synonym for reading disability; however, many researchers assert that there are different types of reading disabilities, of which dyslexia is one. A reading disability can affect any part of the reading process, including difficulty with accurate and/or fluent word recognition, word decoding, reading rate, prosody (oral reading with expression), and reading comprehension. Before the term "dyslexia" came to prominence, this learning disability used to be known as "word blindness." Common indicators of reading disability include difficulty with phonemic awareness — the ability to break up words into their component sounds, and difficulty with matching letter combinations to specific sounds (sound-symbol correspondence).
- *Writing disability (ICD-10 and DSM-IV codes F81.1/315.2):* Speech and language disorders can also be called Dysphasia/Aphasia (coded F80.0-F80.2/315.31 in ICD-10 and DSM-IV).

  Impaired written language ability may include impairments in handwriting, spelling, organization of ideas, and composition. The term "dysgraphia" is often used as an overarching term for all disorders of written expression. Others, such as the International Dyslexia Association, use the term "dysgraphia" exclusively to refer to difficulties with handwriting.
- *Math disability (ICD-10 and DSM-IV codes F81.2-3/315.1):* Sometimes called dyscalculia, a math disability can cause such difficulties as learning math concepts (such as quantity, place value, and time), difficulty memorizing math facts, difficulty organizing numbers, and understanding how problems are organized on the

page. Dyscalculics are often referred to as having poor "number sense".

- *Nonverbal learning disability [this disorder is not listed in the ICD-10]*: Nonverbal learning disabilities often manifest in motor clumsiness, poor visual-spatial skills, problematic social relationships, difficulty with math, and poor organizational skills. These individuals often have specific strengths in the verbal domains, including early speech, large vocabulary, early reading and spelling skills, excellent rote-memory and auditory retention, and eloquent self-expression.
- *Dyspraxia:* Sometimes called motor planning, dyspraxia refers to a variety of difficulties with motor skills. Dyspraxia can cause difficulty with single step tasks such as combing hair or waving goodbye, multi-step tasks like brushing teeth or getting dressed, or with establishing spatial relationships such as being able to accurately position one object in relation to another.
- *Disorders of speaking and listening:* Difficulties that often co-occur with learning disabilities include difficulty with memory, social skills and executive functions (such as organizational skills and time management).
- *Auditory processing disorder:* Difficulties processing auditory information include difficulty comprehending more than one task at a time and a relatively stronger ability to learn visually.

Types of Assessment for Learning Disabled Children

Many normed assessments can be used in evaluating skills in the primary academic domains: reading, not including word recognition, fluency, and comprehension; mathematics, including computation and problem solving; and written expression, including handwriting, spelling and composition.

The most commonly used comprehensive achievement tests include the Woodcock-Johnson III (WJ III), Weschler Individual Achievement Test II (WIAT II), the Wide Range Achievement Test III (WRAT III), and the Stanford Achievement Test–10th edition. These tests include measures of many academic domains that are reliable in identifying areas of difficulty.

In the reading domain, there are also specialized tests that can be used to obtain details about specific reading deficits. Assessments that measure multiple domains of reading include Gray's Diagnostic Reading Tests–2nd edition (GDRT II) and the Stanford Diagnostic Reading Assessment. Assessments that measure reading subskills include the Gray Oral Reading Test IV – Fourth Edition (GORT IV), Gray Silent Reading Test, Comprehensive Test of Phonological Processing (CTOPP), Tests of Oral Reading and Comprehension Skills (TORCS), Test of Reading Comprehension 3 (TORC-3), Test of Word Reading Efficiency (TOWRE), and the Test of Reading Fluency. A more comprehensive list of reading assessments may be obtained from the Southwest Educational Development Laboratory.

Of course, assessment of learning disabilities requires the consideration of more than test scores. The purpose of assessment is to determine what is needed for intervention, which also requires consideration of contextual variables and whether there are comorbid disorders that must also be identified and treated, such as behavioral issues or language delays.

Criticism of the Concept of Learning Disabilities

Some critics of the concept of learning disabilities and of special education take the position that every child has a different learning style and pace and that each child is unique, not only capable of learning but also capable of succeeding. These critics assert that applying the medical model of problem-solving to individual children who are pupils in the school system, and labeling these children as disabled, systematically prevents the improvement of the current educational system.

Describing current instructional methods as homogenization and lockstep standardization, alternative approaches are proposed, such as the Sudbury model of democratic education schools, an alternative approach in which children, by enjoying personal freedom thus encouraged to exercise personal responsibility for their actions, learn at their own pace rather than following a chronologically-based curriculum. Proponents of unschooling have also claimed that children raised in this method do not suffer from learning disabilities.

Gerald Coles asserts that there are partisan agendas behind the educational policy-makers and that the scientific research that they use to support their arguments regarding the teaching of literacy are flawed. These include the idea that there are neurological explanations for learning disabilities.

Marva Collins' Experience

Marva Collins started a low cost private school in inner city Chicago specifically for the purpose of teaching low-income black children whom the public school system had wrongly labeled as being "learning disabled." She once wrote, "I have discovered few learning disabled students in my three decades of teaching. I have, however, discovered many, many victims of teaching inabilities."

One article about Marva Collins' school stated, "Working with students having the worst of backgrounds, those who were working far below grade level, and even those who had been labeled as 'unteachable,' Marva was able to overcome the obstacles. News of third grade students reading at ninth grade level, four-year-olds learning to read in only a few months, outstanding test scores, disappearance of behavioral problems, second-graders studying Shakespeare, and other incredible reports, astounded the public."

Issues and Needs of Children with Learning Disabilities

In the last panel we looked at disabilities funded by the federal government under the Individuals with Disabilities Education Act (IDEA). Here we look at specific learning disabilities (LDs). The graph shows total students enrolled from 1980-2000. Note first of all that students with speech and language impairments are down; as are the mentally retarded. Those with serious emotional disturbance are up — those with specific learning disabilities are *way* up. In the last panel we learned that students with LD appear intelligent yet cannot communicate orally or in written form in line with their evident intelligence, cannot read well or comprehend what they are reading, and cannot do math or reason abstractly.

The causes of LD are unknown. The condition was once thought to be caused by one or more neurological problems, but these explanations have given way to vague speculations suggesting flaws in fetal brain development. These are thought to be caused by toxins in the environment; tobacco, alcohol, and drug abuse; genetic problems; and so on. But it's clear that *no* conclusive answers are offered by science — which is *not* to say that these speculations are wrong. But ignorance prevails.

At the same time, it has been observed that 80% of children with learning disabilities have problems with reading, that this problem appears early—and if not corrected early, is difficult to reverse. As one of the more insightful papers on this subject states: "The poor first-grade reader almost invariably becomes a poor middle school reader, high school reader, and adult reader.

In short, children who get off to a poor start in reading rarely catch up. We wait—they fail." Yet most diagnoses of LD take place at a time when it is already too late to help the students.

Critical Issues in Teaching Young Children with Learning Disabilities

Current issues in teaching young children with learning disabilities reflect significant changes in public policy and professional philosophy. Diverse perspectives are held about these debatable issues.

Developmentally Appropriate Practice (DAP)

The National Association for the Education of Young Children (NAEYC) is the professional association for Early Childhood Education. Guidelines for early childhood programmes developed by NAEYC are called Developmentally Appropriate Practices (DAP. The DAP guidelines recommend a child-initiated curriculum that follows the interests of children and active child exploration.

The DAP guidelines are:

- Activities should be integrated across developmental domains.
- Children's interests and progress should be identified through teacher observations, examination of work portfolios, and (for school-aged children) student self-evaluation.
- Teachers should prepare the environment to facilitate the child's active exploration and interactions on physical, social, and cognitive levels.
- Learning activities and materials for very young children should be concrete, real, and relevant to their experience; the complexity, challenge and abstraction of activities should increase as children understand the skills involved.
- The debatable issue in DAP for teaching young children with learning disabilities is that the DAP guidelines do not consider sufficiently the needs of children who have disabilities. These children may need a curriculum that provides early direct intervention, highly structured learning experiences, and extrinsic motivation, such as high rates of praise, tokens, stickers, or other reinforcements. Modification of the DAP guidelines may be needed for young children with learning disabilities.

Placement Practices

Placement refers to the child's primary setting for instruction. In the past most young children with disabilities were served through special classes. Today, however, more children are placed in inclusive settings that integrate children with special needs with typical children. Inclusive settings offer these educational and developmental benefits:

- It eliminates the stigmatizing effects of segregated programmes.
- It offers services in the least restrictive environment.
- It provides children with the opportunity to learn social and communication skills through being with typical peers.

- It encourages the development of friendships by playing and working with typical children.
- It promotes awareness and acceptance of children of diversity in our society.

An immediate problem in providing integrated placements for preschoolers with learning disabilities is that most public schools do not provide programmes for three-and four-year old children. Schools usually do have kindergarten classes for five-year old children. Administrators must seek integrated settings in the community to include children with learning disabilities, such as nursery schools, Head Start classes, day care centers, and other kinds of early childhood programmes.

Transition to other Placements

Transition involves transferring or moving the child from one type of placement or programme to another. Going to new placement can be a traumatic experience for the young child, as well as his or her family. To make the transition as smooth as possible, it should be carefully planned, coordinated, and monitored. At the completion of the infant-toddler special programme for children ages birth-to-three (Part C of IDEA), the transition would be to a preschool programme for children ages three-to-five with special needs (Part B of IDEA. For the child approaching age six at the completion of the preschool programme, there are several placement options for young children with learning disabilities.

- A regular kindergarten or first grade class
- A transition class (where the child receives additional intervention services)
- A resource room (where the child attends both the regular class and a small special education setting for a portion of the day)
- A special class (which permits a more intensive special education curriculum)

Assessment Practices

Another issue concerns assessment practices. Today we find more reliance on informal, functional assessment measures and less on formal, standardized tests. The authentic assessment measures in early childhood assessment include:

- direct and ongoing observation of the child
- assessment in the natural environment
- the selection of a variety of assessment measures for different purposes.

The issue is whether the informal measures are as reliable and valid as the standardized tests.

Cultural and Linguistic Diversity

In today's society many families and children come to our programmes from diverse linguistic and cultural backgrounds. An increasing number of children come from homes in which a language other than English is spoken. In fact, some 320 different languages are spoken in the United States. Children who are bilingual understand and use two languages — their native language and a second language — English. The duality of languages for bilingual children does not hamper their overall language proficiency or cognitive development.

The problem is that many children whose native language is other than English are not bilingual. They are not fluent in two languages. Instead, these children have limited English proficiency (LEP).They have difficulty using and understanding English. Gaining proficiency in a language requires sufficient time. Young children with learning disabilities may have a basic language disability, in addition to limited English proficiency, that interferes with learning. Teachers must be attuned to both the child's second language problem and to their underlying language disability. Intervention requires practices from several disciplines:

- bilingual education
- special education
- early childhood education

UNIT-VII

Neurological and Locomotor Disabilities

Definitions, Types and Meaning of Neurological and Locomotor Disabilities

Impairment

An impairment in any loss or abnormality of psychological, physiological or anatomical structure or function in a human being.

Functional Limitations

Impairment may cause functional limitations which are partial or total inability to perform those activities, necessary for motor, sensory or mental function within the range or manner of which a human being is normally capable.

Disability

A disability is any restriction or lack (resulting from an impairment) of ability to perform an activity in the manner or within the range considered normal for a human being.

Locomotor Disability

Locomotor disability is defined as a person's inability to execute distinctive activities associated with moving both himself and objects, from place to place and such inability resulting from affliction of musculoskeletal and/or nervous system.

Categories of Locomotor Disability for evaluation

- Guidelines for Evaluation of Permanent Physical Impairment of Upper Limb
- Guidelines for Evaluation of permanent physical Impairment in Lower Limb
- Guidelines for Evaluation of Permanent Physical Impairment of Trunk (Spine)
- Guidelines for Evaluation of PPI in cases of Short Stature/Dwarfism
- Guidelines for Evaluation of Permanent Physical Impairment in Amputees
- Guidelines for Evaluation of Permanent Physical Impairment of Congenital deficiencies of the limbs

Guidelines for Evaluation of Permanent Physical Impairment of Upper Limb

1. The estimation of permanent impairment depends upon the measurement of functional impairment and is not expression of a personal opinion.
2. The estimation and measurement should be made when the clinical condition has reached the stage of maximum improvement from the medical treatment. Normally the time period is to be decided by the medical doctor who is evaluating the case for issuing the PPI Certificate as per standard format of the certificate.
3. The upper limb is divided into two component parts; the arm component and the hand component.
4. Measurement of the loss of function of arm component consists of measuring the loss of motion, muscle strength and co-ordinated activities.
5. Measurement of loss of function of hand component consists of determining the prehension, sensation and strength. For estimation of prehension opposition, lateral pinch cylindrical grasp, spherical grasp and hook grasp have to be assessed as shown in Hand Component of Form A Assessment Proforma for upper extremity.

6. The impairment of the entire extremity depends on the combination of the functional impairments of both components.

Neurological Disabilities

Both nature and severity of neurological disability can vary markedly between individuals. Three distinct categories of neurological disability exist and should not be confused.

- Intellectual disability, which usually occurs at or shortly after birth. This is a generalised intellectual deficit.
- Acquired brain injury (ABI) is as a result of trauma, usually as an adult. This may involve a blow to the head, loss of oxygen or medical events such as stroke (cerebrovascular accident). Symptoms are sometimes very subtle. Standard intelligence tests may not reveal any deficit, but problems such as short term memory loss can affect performance in an educational setting.
- Specific learning disabilities are a group of hidden disorders leading to difficulties in any or some of the processes of listening, speaking, reading, writing, reasoning or performing mathematical calculations. They are inconsistent with a person's general ability.

Specific problems faced by Individuals must therefore be considered when exploring technical solutions.

Curricular Models and Approaches to Teaching the Children with Locomotor Disabilities

The manpower development document of the Rehabilitation Council of India (RCI) (1995) reports that not even five per cent of the disabled population is currently enjoying educational facilities. The reason is that the present educational system is not able to take education to the doorsteps of the children. To provide education to this uncovered population, appropriate strategies need to be adopted for locating them for early intervention services. Early intervention would solve many of the problems of the child later in life. While early identification is of paramount importance in the life of every child, it is more vital in the case of children with disabilities. Research studies indicate that the children identified and provided services early in life find integration in the community natural, real and effective.

As evident from the definitions of various disability conditions, some persons experience difficulties in cognitive functions, some in senses and some others in their physical and bodily conditions. The common approaches in identifying persons with disabilities are as follows :

Cognitive Approach : By adopting the cognitive approach, identification of children may be made as those who are mentally retarded, slow learners, normal learners, academically advanced learners and gifted learners. This identification is purely based on the cognitive functions of the child. For example :

- The child who has an IQ between 50 and 75 will come under the category of educable mentally retarded child.
- The trainable mentally retarded children have an IQ of 25 to 50 and they may find it difficult even to perform manual kind of work.
- Those who have an IQ of less than 25 are called totally dependent category.

In developed countries, not only children with mental retardation, but also children having slow learning skills are also given special attention. For example, slow learners but not mentally retarded children, and academically advanced learners but not gifted are given special opportunities to manifest their abilities. However, the Indian condition is different. Most of the children who have non-observable disability conditions are already absorbed in the system. They are not labelled as children with disabilities. For example, children having IQ range of 70-130 are found in the general classrooms. This is a blessing in disguise. Sometimes, the learning needs of these children go unnoticed and as a result, they become drop-outs from the system. On the other hand, their self-esteem is intact as they are not labelled as disabled children. Of the two, non-labelling has a positive impact on the individual and, therefore, it is better if these children are not labelled as children with disabilities. In order to help them, it is vital to improve the abilities of general classroom teachers to teach children of all categories. Innovative teachers always take care of children with different intellectual abilities. Therefore, the onus lies on the quality of general teacher preparation centres.

Sensory Approach : Through sensory approach, visually impaired, hearing impaired and deaf-blind children can be identified. Out of them, visually impaired children are neither cognitive impaired nor communication impaired. They lack abilities in the orientation of environment. The mobility skills are also affected due to the loss of vision. On the other hand, the deaf child's main problem is in the area of communication skills. Some of them use lip-reading skills whereas some use sign language. It is proper to use total communication system, which uses the combination of both. The deaf-blind children will have a serious disadvantage in both orientation and communication skills. As a result, these children have to be provided compensatory experiences mostly through tactile approach. As blind and deaf children are not impaired cognitively, they can follow the same curriculum meant for the sighted and hearing children. However, certain curricular adaptations have to be made to suit their learning styles.

Ability-based Approach : There are many children who experience difficulty in processing information. Though their intelligence is normal and senses, too, are normal, sometimes they perform poorly due to lack of ability in processing information. Information processing theorists feel that these children lack adequate skills in attention, perception, memory, encoding etc. These children are called as *learning disabled children*. *Dysgraphia*, *Dyslexia* and *Dyscalculia* are some of the defects associated with the learning problems in general. Research indicates that these children can also be made to learn through specific modality approaches such as improving attention skills, perceptual abilities, etc.

Society-based Approach : Among disabled children, some of them are facing emotional problems too. The behaviour disorders in these children may also be a result of social problems such as the state of experience of neglect, over-protection, etc. A disabled child who doesn't have a conducive family support or parental affection is likely to have psychological effects leading to isolation, maladjusted behaviour, etc. These children have to be provided the most appropriate environment for overcoming difficulties. Though educators at present confine to observable cognitive or sensory disabilities, there are many children who experience emotional problems. It is believed that the society and life systems can also lead to depressions resulting in mental illness.

Methods of Identifying Children with Disabilities

Early identification and intervention are imperative to address many problems of children with disabilities before they become complicated. Therefore, teachers and students must be oriented to the methods of identifying children with disabilities. Some of the following methods may be adopted in this connection:

Primary Health Centres (PHCs): The PHC is normally the first contact point for the parents of children with disabilities in rural areas. The doctors of the PHCs need to provide guidance to them regarding facilities for education and rehabilitation of the child. The orientation programme on "Disability Management", being organised by the RCI for the PHC doctors in the country has revealed that doctors are able to refer thousands of persons with disabilities to various education and rehabilitation programmes. Therefore, PHCs are good sources for identifying children with disabilities. As a matter of orientation, teachers and children from schools can visit nearby primary schools to see how children with disabilities come into contact with these PHCs.

Hospitals: Established hospitals can provide reliable information regarding the number of disabled children, the incidence and the prevalence of various kinds of disabilities in the particular locality. The general health camps organised by hospitals and other voluntary organisations can also provide necessary information on disabilities.

Population Centres: The statistics available from population centres may serve as the base for making door-to-door survey to find out the actual number of disabled children for placement in schools.

Voluntary Organisations: Statistical data regarding the disabled population and expertise for implementation of special education programmes may also be available from voluntary organisations which are involved in the services for persons with disabilities.

Through School Teachers: Teachers who work in rural areas have more access to the community and they can obtain reliable information from parents, Parents' Association and Parent-Teacher Association regarding the presence of children with disabilities in the community.

Through School Children: The school teachers may ask non-disabled children of the school to bring information about the children who behave differently while seeing, who fumble over the objects, cannot hear, cannot follow specific directions, etc. On the basis of the information brought by school children, the teacher can pursue the matter for locating disabled children for medical care and placement in school.

Through Village Functionaries: The village head, village administrative officer, village workers, Integrated Child Development Services (ICDS) workers and village nurses can help in the identification of disabled children for placement in schools.

Census Data: The statistics used at present are the projections from the *National Sample Survey Organisation (NSSO) 1991*. These are only projections and the actual data are yet to be available. The Census 2001 has made an earnest attempt to detect persons with disabilities. When the Census report is available, the information on disability, right from national to block levels, may be clear.

The identification techniques discussed in this section are not exhaustive. Local specific techniques may be designed and used for identification of children with disabilities. *It is evident from what has been studied by you so far that definitions have a large impact on the nature of services too. Clear definitions help in the effective identification process. Therefore, it is essential for teachers to know about various categories of disabilities. Though they cannot do clinical assessment, functional assessment procedures can be used by them to identify the children, who can be clearly assessed by doctors and specialists for clinical assessment and for proper educational placement.*

Access to the General Curriculum for Students with Disabilities: A Brief Legal Interpretation

The 1997 reauthorization of the Individuals with Disabilities Education Act (IDEA) introduced important changes in the provision of special education services for students with disabilities. One of the most significant changes concerns the requirement that students with disabilities receive *access to the general curriculum*. Specifically, the new Amendments require that students with disabilities: (1) *have access to* the general curriculum; (2) *be involved in* the general curriculum; and (3) *progress in* the general curriculum.

The purpose of this brief is to define and clarify the meanings of the terms access, involvement, and progress in relation to the general curriculum. These new requirements have the potential to lead to improved educational opportunities and outcomes for students with disabilities.

Students with Disabilities

In order to qualify as a "child with a disability" under IDEA '97 and be deemed eligible to receive special education services, a child must satisfy two requirements: (1) the child has one of the disabilities specified in the law; and (2) the disability results in the need for special education and related services (20 U.S.C. ýÿ 1401(3), 34 C.F.R. ýÿ 300.7). IDEA '97 specifies the disability categories that may entitle a student to receive special education and related services:

- Mental retardation
- Hearing impairments, including deafness
- Speech or language impairments
- Visual impairments, including blindness
- Emotional disturbance
- Orthopedic impairments
- Autism

- Traumatic brain injury
- Other health impairments
- Specific learning disabilities.

In addition, a child aged three through nine who is "experiencing developmental delays," as defined by the State, may be eligible for services under IDEA at the discretion of the State and local educational agency (20 U.S.C. ýÿ 1401(3)(b), 34 C.F.R. ýÿ 300.7(b)).

General Curriculum

The regulations implementing the 1997 Amendments describe the term *general curriculum* as the same curriculum as that established for students without disabilities (34 C.F.R. ýÿ 300.347(a)(1)(i)). The general curriculum can be thought of as "the overall plan for instruction adopted by a school or school system. Its purpose is to guide instructional activities and provide consistency of expectations, content, methods, and outcomes" (Hitchcock, Meyer, Rose, and Jackson, 2002). In recent years, the general curriculum has come to be influenced to a great extent by the adoption of national, state, and district standards (Nolet and McLaughlin, 2000).

Principles and Various Approaches to be Followed for the Children with Motor Disabilities

Renfrew Educational Services offers a programme for children diagnosed with motor disorders such as Cerebral Palsy and meet the criteria for funding through Family Support for Children with Disabilities (FSCD). Our programme is based on a holistic approach that takes into account the physical, social, emotional and cognitive needs of the child.

Focus is on Individual Needs and Goals

Using a multi-disciplinary model, Renfrew brings together a wide range of professionals who work with parents to develop programmes based on the needs and goals of the child.

Renfrew's team approach involves use of motor activities, integration of motor and sensory systems and, when necessary, assistive technology devices.

Developing the child's own internal motivation is a focus of the programme. We do this by fostering confidence, self-esteem and independence, which encourages children to strive to reach their maximum potential.

Our ISMD programme incorporates the following approaches:

- Family centred
- Developmentally appropriate
- Play-based
- Culturally sensitive practices.

The multidisciplinary team may include rehabilitation specialists, child development facilitators, psychologists, occupational therapists, physical therapists, speech-language pathologists, assistive technology specialists and family support.

Programs include:

- Toddler / Preschool (Main School & Sundance Centre)
- After School for Elementary Age Children (Main School).

Intervention Strategies in Education in Different Environments

A child's first word is often marked with photos, video or audio recordings for the baby book, phone calls to grandparents, and multiple opportunities for a repeat performance for everyone who missed the exciting occasion. It is a moment to remember. For infants born with communication delays, however, this moment is delayed.

Communication is the most frequently identified delay for children with developmental disabilities (National Early Intervention Longitudinal Study [NEILS], 2007), and ASHA has just completed new policy documents on early intervention (see sidebar). These documents reflect changes in legislation, social policy, and evidence-based practice that have occurred over the past 20 years. One of the most significant changes is in the area of service delivery. ASHA's new documents (ASHA, 2008a, b, c, d) provide guiding principles to help clinicians provide services that respond to these changes in contemporary practice, with services that are:

- Family-centered and culturally and linguistically responsive (aligned with each family's unique situation, culture, language/s, preferences, resources, and priorities)
- Developmentally supportive and promote children's participation in their natural environments (appropriate for child's age, cognitive level, strengths, family concerns and preferences)
- Comprehensive, coordinated, and team-based (effectively integrated to meet the needs of the child and family)
- Based on the highest-quality evidence available (merger of highest-quality, most recent research with professional expertise and family preferences)

The second guiding principle—providing services in the child's natural environments—focuses on the participants, setting, and context for early intervention.

Natural Environment Intervention

"Natural environments" is the term used in the Individuals with Disabilities Education Improvement Act, Part C (IDEA, 2004) to refer to settings that are typical for infants and toddlers without disabilities or delays. It is used as a contrast to more traditional treatment settings—such as clinical or medical-based programmes—and includes families' homes, early care and education programmes, and other community settings where families spend the most time with their children.

The natural environments paradigm is a consultation-based delivery of supports and services in which the speech-language pathologist acts as consultant, supporting the child and family's communication within their everyday activities and events.

With this change in focus from more traditional treatment settings, families with infants and toddlers eligible for and choosing to participate in their states' Part C early intervention programmes find that services and supports—including speech-language and audiology treatment—are provided in the locations where the families typically spend their time, rather than the families having to go to appointments at multiple locations on different days. The most frequently identified natural environment location for families nationwide is in their homes (NEILS, 2007).

The new set of ASHA early intervention documents address the concept of the natural environment, and include many changes related to providing services. The term natural environment describes much more than a location for the service—it does not mean, for example, that the SLP moves the clinic to the home by taking a bag of toys and treatment materials into the living room. Instead, the concept includes the context for intervention, which is the child and family's typical and valued activities and events, and includes parents and caregivers as partners in the child's communication activities.

In a typical scenario, a partnership develops between the SLP and parents or other caregivers. Family members or caregivers offer information about their typical day, the child's communication opportunities and expectations, the child's and family's preferred activities, and any challenges. In turn, the SLP shares information and resources, and coaches the parents about including communication activities throughout the child's day, with content individualized to meet the specific needs of the child.

In this intervention model, typical routines such as getting dressed, walking the dog, picking up toys, getting the mail, eating a snack, or going to the store, serve as meaningful and functional opportunities for learning communication, social interaction, and other developmental skills. Children practice skills throughout the day as they communicate what they want, see, do, and enjoy during those common and repeatable exchanges.

A Process, Not a Place

Although "natural environment" seems to refer to a location, it is actually the process that is most important. Central to the process is the tenet that children learn through participating in their everyday activities and meaningful experiences with their family and caregivers. Authentic interactions that are interesting and fun result in more frequent and longer engagement, with subsequent positive outcomes for the child and family. When caregivers maximize learning opportunities in the child's daily routines and activities, the child has many opportunities for intervention every day, throughout the day, and in a meaningful and responsive manner.

Families realize benefits from the emphasis on natural environments. They don't have to set aside special treatment time or acquire special materials when intervention is accommodated within the family's daily routine. No matter how many unexpected events come up or activities change in any given day, the same familiar and necessary routines involving communication take place and can be used to enhance the child's growth and development.

Team-Based Services

Multiple professionals work together on a team with the family to develop the individualized family service plan (IFSP) and provide early intervention services in the natural environment. The team is responsible for selecting the most appropriate service delivery model based on the specific needs of the child and family.

In some instances, one professional on the team is designated as the primary service provider (PSP); this model helps avoid fragmentation of services and frequent home visits from multiple professionals (e.g., audiologists, educators, occupational and physical therapists). With this approach, which involves "role release" and "role extension," one professional is designated to provide services across disciplines, and the other professionals provide consultation to this designated primary provider. An SLP on such a team may serve as either the primary provider or consultant; when the child's main needs are communication or feeding and swallowing, the SLP should be designated as the primary service provider (ASHA, 2008b).

The designation of the PSP should be a team decision and individualized for each child and family. It is a viable model if it includes careful consideration of which team member offers the best match of expertise and relationship with the family, and is not based only on logistics, such as availability or cost. When using the PSP model, the team must communicate regularly to support one another—as well as the child and family—to ensure maximum progress.

All team members, whether acting as the primary service provider or as a consultant, focus on the interactions between the caregiver and child, rather than only on delivering services directly to the child. Embedding intervention into the family's identified routines throughout the day is the core feature of service delivery in the natural environment.

Facilitating Learning for Caregivers

Clinicians may want to adopt the following five adult learning strategies, based on the work of Malcolm Knowles, noted theorist and writer in the field of adult education. These strategies are consistent with a natural environment process and support interaction between the caregiver and the early intervention provider.

1. *Agree on learning priorities and roles.* Functional and meaningful child communication goals reflecting the family's priorities are critical. A thorough exploration of the caregiver's objectives for the child will enhance the development of goals for consultation and lead to clear, relevant, and jointly established expectations. Agreeing upon the learning priorities promotes collaboration.

   Establishment of goals, however, is not the only learning support needed for caregiver-implemented intervention. It is equally critical to clarify the role of the caregiver as intervention provider. It is important for SLPs to describe and demonstrate their role as consultant (rather than direct-service provider) to caregivers at the beginning of the relationship; a thorough understanding of the concept will decrease miscommunication later.

2. *Join in rather than take over.* SLPs should look for ways to join in the caregiver-child interactions, rather than expecting the caregiver to observe or join the SLP-

child activities. Active learning opportunities set the stage for informed discussion and problem-solving. Join a dad as he and his son walk the dog, or the child care teacher as she and her group play with building blocks. Your observations of how the caregiver provides and uses opportunities for communication enhance your ability to share evidence-based and individualized strategies, such as environmental arrangements or contingent imitation.

3. *Build on the caregiver's strengths.* Learners keep and use new information more easily when they integrate the new ideas with what they already know (Bransford, Brown, & Cocking, 1999). Maintaining the caregiver's current routine or activity sequence will facilitate ease of learning. Anchors for learning are plentiful when the family or caregiver participates in identifying opportunities to embed different intervention strategies or outcomes. The routine sequence and use of everyday materials serve as learning anchors for the adult. Incorporating limited modifications or additional opportunities is easier within a familiar and comfortable framework.
4. *The relationship does matter.* SLPs should not expect the caregiver to take risks early in the process of developing a relationship. Although there are some "just do it" learners who are ready to try anything, most benefit initially from supports. Confidence and motivation will grow from success in embedding intervention, improvement in the child's skills, and positive experiences with the consulting process. As trust in the consulting relationship increases, so does the likelihood the adult learner will try new ideas.
5. *Provide specific and meaningful feedback to enhance competence.* Adults tend to prefer to learn one concept at a time, and they learn the concept best by applying it to relevant problems (Knowles, 1995). This tendency becomes more pronounced with age, during periods of illness or exhaustion, and when dealing with multiple

priorities. "More isn't better" when the adult can't remember how or when to use the information. Learning to embed intervention opportunities in daily routines is a complex process, and caregiver competence typically will not result after a single brief conversation or demonstration. Parents and caregivers may not have had training in child development, disabilities, intervention strategies, data collection, and principles of instruction and reinforcement, or had multiple opportunities to practice intervention strategies with feedback from mentors and teachers. Help parents and caregivers to build competence by using instructional techniques that build their confidence. Feelings of inadequacy resulting from the complexity of the task inhibit learners and reduce the frequency of their attempts.

Working in the Natural Environment

SLPs working in early intervention need to have training on teaching adults, coaching caregivers, and providing consultative services. The ASHA early intervention documents identify multiple knowledge and skill sets that support the SLP in the roles of consultant, family educator, and team member. These knowledge and skills are in addition to—not replacements for—skills in other, more traditional, roles.

For example, traditional practice emphasizes child-focused intervention; in natural environments intervention, the SLP must be fluent with child-focused intervention and have skills in teaching other adults, using effective and relationship-enhancing instruction.

Much of what SLPs are sharing or demonstrating about early intervention is new and often complex information for parents. Information may need to be shared more than once, in a variety of formats, applied to multiple settings and situations, and revisited as new circumstances occur. It's not sufficient, for example, to model an activity with the expectation that parents will then be able to repeat the activity after observing it.

The presentation of information should always be meaningful to the caregivers and individualized for their priorities and interests, their daily routines and activities, and their preferred places for the child to learn and play. There are no "one-size-fits-all" handouts or activities that will support all adult learners. The SLP should use aids that help the learner organize the information and relate it to previously stored information; for example, a visual schedule for bath time with key vocabulary helps the caregiver remember "when" in the routine to label and offer choices, as planned during a session with the SLP.

SLPs also must present information at a pace that supports implementation. Systematic presentation of one concept at a time, demonstration and practice of that concept, and opportunities for feedback and problem-solving will help the adult learner build from knowledge to application and, more importantly, to generalization of the concept. Comprehension and use of the concept or strategy are further enhanced when competing demands (e.g., new or unfamiliar routine or activity, need to engage other children or siblings, limited time) are initially minimized. Often, caregivers learn the mechanics of a specific strategy that could be embedded in a child's routine, but are unable to use the strategy fluently because they have not had adequate practice and feedback on how, when, and where to use it. The learning curve for adults is maximized when the environment is arranged for their success.

Building the Evidence Base

As SLPs have gained familiarity with the concept of natural environments, questions about implementation have evolved from basic information about the meaning of the construct to more challenging issues. They seek solutions to real-world situations: What works best for which children? How do I support caregivers so that intervention occurs throughout the day? What environmental arrangements support early interactions?

The early intervention knowledge base increases when researchers and providers seek answers for "how-to" questions generated from practice. And answers are beginning to emerge. As summarized in the new ASHA guidelines (ASHA, 2008b), the evidence base is expanding and consensus is building on recommended early intervention methods and strategies. Increasing evidence supports parents as effective communication and play partners, with improved child outcomes as the result (Kaiser, Hancock, & Trent, 2007).

As the field advances, multiple intervention approaches are available for replication (see sidebar). Early intervention in the natural environment differs based on theoretical perspectives (developmental or behavioral), role of the clinician (primary service provider or consultant), contexts (embedding in routines or natural learning opportunities), strategies for child intervention (responsive interaction or applied behavior analysis), and ways of facilitating caregiver participation (modeling with feedback or conversations). SLPs need to vary approaches for different children and families based on disorder type, age, other individual needs, and available evidence.

Adaptations in Various Areas for the Children with Neurological and Locomotor Disabilities

There are many types of seizures a child can experience that are not related to having the disability called epilepsy, or seizure disorder. Convulsions, or febrile seizures, sometimes occur in babies and young children who have high fevers. Others are caused by chemical imbalances in the body, including babies born to drug addicted or alcoholic mothers who suffer withdrawal after birth.

Seizures are often symptoms of other conditions or diseases. Children who develop type one insulin dependent diabetes may have convulsions due to extremely high blood sugar before they are diagnosed, or seizures due to low blood sugar if they miss a meal, have unexpected exertion or exercise, or too much insulin. Some children have a dual diagnosis of type one diabetes and seizure disorder.

If you suspect your child is having a seizure, it is important to report the symptoms you observe to your doctor. The doctor will want to know the movements you saw-head dropping, shaking, hands moving, or a period of not being aware or staring, movement by movement. Make a note of any uncharacteristic or unusual behavior, and any sensation that the child reports before or during the seizure.

Give your best estimate of how long the seizure lasted, what the child was doing before and after the suspected seizure, including how responsive, alert or drowsy the child was, and if there was loss of bladder control in a potty trained child. In an 'absence seizure' the child will not remember what happened during the event, so fill in that information for an older child who is unaware of that time period.

Remember when you are talking to others about your child's seizure or seizure disorders in general, it's important to talk positively about the event as well as the future when your son or daughter can overhear the conversation. It can be embarrassing to hear details and disturbing to hear about your fears ~ our children are dealing with enough without the extra drama of our concerns.

It can be reassuring for children to hearus tell family and friends about older successful people who live with seizure disorder, and that it is just a small part of who he or she is or what they will accomplish in life. Brothers and sisters should have basic information and reassurance that adults in charge take on whatever responsibility is needed to care for all the children in the household. It will also be helpful to educate others about how to recognize a seizure and what they could do to help.

A child having a violent seizure does not need to be tightly restrained or to bite on something to protect them from biting or swallowing the tongue. The most important thing they can do during a child's seizure is to stay calm.

It's good to try to help the child lie down to reduce the risk of injury from falling down, and put something soft under his or her head.

To reduce the risk of choking, they may want to gently turn the child to rest on one side, loosen tight clothing, remove (or cushion) hard or sharp objects nearby, and/or remove eyeglasses.

It is important to remain nearby until the child is fully alert, and to listen to as well as reassure them.

Medications and other treatments available for children who have seizures or seizure disorder should be discussed with the child's specialist, usually a pediatric neurologist, and your family practice doctor.

If one medication does not work well within a certain amount of time, it's important to adjust the dose according to your doctor's advice, and to follow directions carefully during a change in medications or addition of a new medication. A special diet known as the Ketogenic Diet should be attempted only under medical supervision and may be dangerous for some children.

Children who have seizure disorders qualify for individual education plans (IEPs) and/or 504 plans at school that will accommodate their special needs and give them opportunities to be successful in class and on the playground. Many people talented in different fields have learned to live with epilepsy and contribute daily to their communities and the world.

Children with Muscular Dystrophy

Before hearing a family member's diagnosis of Muscular Dystrophy, most people are unaware of the many types of MD and other neuromuscular diseases.

As with any diagnosis, families have different emotions, ways of coping, and stages of response to the information. What our children need most is our attention, our humor and our love, and reassurance that we will be there with them through whatever happens.

Finding support, encouragement and comfort for ourselves is also important, including our circle of friends and family and kindred spirits we may meet in parent groups, hospitals or online, while also respecting the privacy and considering the wishes of the child with MD.

If your child has been diagnosed with Muscular Dystrophy, you can find information on the specific type from a list of at least 40 neuromuscular diseases discussed at the Muscular

Dystrophy Association web site. Every child with Muscular Dystrophy is a unique individual who deserves to live his or her best possible life being recognized and celebrated, and allowed to consider whatever dreams, goals or plans they can imagine.

The MDA website features a booklist for children, booklets for adults, and archives of the MDA Quest magazine, and offers many other resources.

Information in Spanish is also available, much of it translated from English articles so that family members and professionals who speak each language can read the same information.

The Muscular Dystrophy Association offers information about Muscular Dystrophies, Metabolic Diseases of Muscle, Diseases of Peripheral Nerves, Inflammatory Myopathies, Diseases of the Neuromuscular Junction, Myopathies Due to Endrocrine Abnormalities, Other Myopathies, and Motor Neuron Diseases like Spinal Muscular Atrophy.

Children with Spina Bifida

When my newborn son was diagnosed with Down syndrome, I called a pregnancy support hotline for information. The counselor I met there was a bright and funny young woman who put my mind at ease like few people I have met since. She admired my son, complimented both of us, and enjoyed the time we spent together without seeming to be bogged down with concern over the diagnosis or how I might be adjusting to it.

As I left I told her that she was the first person to treat my baby and me like my daughter and I had been treated when she was brand new. She claimed that it was easier for her to look past the diagnosis because she had been born with spina bifida herself, and her life was turning out just fine.

I had not noticed any physical signs of a disability while we had talked, and she said her diagnosis was very late because she did not have obvious symptoms, a blessing in some ways because she had all the opportunities and support she needed growing up as if she did not have a diagnosis at all. On the other hand, she did not have the intervention and support that might have helped with what she called 'some discomfort' related to spina bifida.

Most children with spina bifida are diagnosed at birth, and some, prenatally. Support groups and knowledgeable professionals are available where parents of newly diagnosed children can find information that might be relevant to their sons and daughters. There are several associated conditions that may be present in newborns with spina bifida that require treatment or intervention, including hydrocephalus, Chiari syndrome, bladder and bowel complications, and orthopedic problems.

Tourette Syndrome Explored on Oprah

Tourette Syndrome, also known as Tourette's Syndrome, is a neurological condition whose symptoms can be seen in some children as early as the age of 2. The age range of onset for Tourette's is often described as two to fifteen years, when children's symptoms can easily be diagnosed as behaviorally based, or overlooked when other neurological conditions or learning disabilities are diagnosed. Parents of very young children may be concerned about behaviors that can easily be dismissed as their child's unique interpretation of The Terrible Twos.

The discussion episode about the Oprah book club selection, _Icy Sparks_, was a wonderful opportunity to promote awareness of Tourette Syndrome and its affects on children and families.

Some years ago popular fiction characterized everyone with Tourette Syndrome as having uncontrollable verbalizations of obscenities or epithets. Because these are much less common than the initial repetitive movements, like blinking or facial twitches, and less common than other verbal and sound 'tics' that first challenge most individuals with Tourette Syndrome, children may have had a missed or delayed diagnosis.

Some of the conditions that may also be diagnosed in children with Tourette's are Attention Deficit Disorder-ADD,

Attention Deficit Hyperactivity Disorder-ADHD, Obsessive Compulsive Disorder-OCD, and Oppositional Defiant Disorder-ODD.

Many individuals with Tourette's are more mildly affected, and most learn to control their symptoms even though it is a great challenge. A young person with Tourette Syndrome who I first met as a preschooler grew up to be one of the most popular young men in my daughter's high school graduating class.

Children with Tourette Syndrome are beautiful young people with a great deal of talent and potential who are being raised by attentive, caring parents who seek the best opportunities for them. Treatment, support and accommodations now available give them a much better chance for successful adult lives.

UNIT-VIII

Curriculum Development

Concept and Principles in Curriculum Development

Early intensive behavioral intervention (EIBI) for children with autism is a non-linear, multi-component endeavor concerned with complex instructional contingencies and curriculum content. It might be useful to think of EIBI in terms of three general elements: curriculum protocol, analysis, and implementation and programme structuring. These elements are interdependent and when discussing the clinical field of EIBI all three elements must be considered. Curriculum content and instructional contingencies interact in complex ways as numerous skill domains are addressed in a systematic and incremental manner. In directing this process of cumulative hierarchical learning, a strong focus on maintaining intrinsic programme coherence is imperative. The present paper discusses some important aspects of the intricacies of EIBI.

From a behavior analytic perspective autism is not viewed as a central deficit but rather the condition is conceptualized as a constellation of many individual deficits to be treated separately (Lovaas & Smith, 1989). This pragmatic stance is shaped by extensive research that shows that improvement in one domain does not necessarily facilitate improvement in another. For instance, acquisition of prepositions does not necessarily facilitate acquisition of pronouns (Lovaas & Smith, 1989). No aspect of skill development can be taken for granted and intervention must proceed in incremental steps addressing multiple skill domains simultaneously.

Continuous time analysis of typically developing children shows that language development proceeds in incremental steps with an abundance of structured and fine-tuned environmental support. Acquisition of any complex skill requires many levels of accomplishment and higher skill levels can be acquired effectively only after lower levels have been mastered (Moerk, 1992). As such, learning is cumulative and hierarchical (Staats, 1981, 1994). These facts are amplified dramatically with respect to young children with autism. Children with autism require considerable time, numerous levels of accomplishment, incremental steps and highly attuned environmental support (i.e., contingency arrangements) in order to acquire even basic skills.

This poses significant conceptual and analytical challenges when designing effective intervention. Staats (1994) has pointed out that "applied behaviorists, acquainted only with the principles of reinforcement, are limited in their ability to analyze many problems of human behavior, thus shortchanging the value of the behavioral approach". The clinical field of early intensive behavioral intervention (EIBI) transcends the basic principles of behavior analysis (i.e., basic conceptual calculus and learning principles) and must strive to establish concepts and principles that are effective in dealing with tremendous behavioral complexity and development. Whereas learning is concerned with the formation of new response patterns and response functions, development is concerned with "the emergence of new kinds of behavioral organization as the outcome of transformational sequences from previous conditions" (Ribes, 1996).

A Non-linear Endeavor

The skill building process is not a linear endeavor in which individual repertoires comprise isolated and unrelated units independently controlled by environmental variables. Rather, skill building is encompassed by a complex and dynamic system in which behavioral units and repertoires are related and interdependent. Complex behavior is not a matter of straight lines that can be adequately accounted for in terms of linear logic. Rather, there are "snags and snarls" and multiple "lines" of progression characterized by confluence, overlapping and convergence. Furthermore, there are complex hierarchies (e.g., category structure) and dynamic networks to consider. According to the concept of cumulative and hierarchical learning, one repertoire provides the basis for learning another repertoire, etc. (Staats, 1981, 1994).

As such, the current behavioral repertoire of the child might be considered both a dependent variable, as a function of contact with past contingencies, and an independent variable with respect to subsequent learning. Current behavior and present learning contingencies act in conjunction to produce further learning. Staats (1981, 1994) refers to a repertoire that is necessary for later learning as a Basic Behavior Repertoire (BBR). The concept of BBR is heuristically valuable to the field of curriculum development for young children with autism since it surpasses the three-term and four-term contingency and incorporates the existing repertoire of the child as an independent variable in the skill building process. The total behavioral repertoire of the child (i.e., the collection of repertoires and their dynamic interactional properties) emerges as an important focus of analysis.

Typically, numerous individual components combine to yield a BBR and these in turn must be related to each other in systematic ways to yield coherent behavioral repertoires and emergent or generative behavior. EIBI is characterized by a complex curriculum protocol consisting of several hundred individual programmes or steps organized according to more general or broad domains (i.e., macro skills) exemplified by memory, imagination, and understanding the implications of social behavior (McEachin, 2001).

An important task is to analyze the "internal structure" of each domain. By "internal structure," we refer to a constellation of components and the relationship between them. For instance, labeling (i.e., tact relation) constitutes a skill where the internal structure consists of at least three elements. These elements can be described, as opposed to explained by, the whole object assumption (the word refers to the whole object not one of its parts, features or other aspects of the naming context), mutual exclusivity (an object can only have one name unless there is overwhelming evidence to the contrary) and the taxonomy assumption (the name is extended to objects of the same kind not thematically or by some other form of extension) (Markman, 1989). Naming constitutes a BBR for the acquisition of abstract concepts and super-ordinate categorization skills.

Each macro-skill consists of a constellation of BBR's and it is critical to analyze (1) the constellation of behavior comprising a BBR, (2) the specific learning strategies necessary to establish a BBR, (3) the importance of the elements in the BBR as prerequisites for the acquisition of subsequent skills, (4) how the BBR and the situation (i.e., teaching contingencies) exert joint influences in producing behavior, and (5) how the BBR will interact reciprocally with the environment to determine subsequent learning (Burns, 1990).

Concepts and Principles

The A phase of the Planning Guide establishes the basic principles of the curriculum planning process in these areas:

A1 Ideas of health and lifestyle learning.

A2 The nutrition education curriculum – family, community and school environment.

A3 The nutrition education curriculum – the classroom.

A4 The pedagogical approach to nutrition education.

The suggestions made in these areas are not controversial, but neither are they universally applicable in practice. They should be discussed and agreed before going on to the situation analysis in Phase B.

The Reader in Phase A outlines and illustrates the concepts.

The Activities in Phase A clarify the concepts, open them up for discussion and comparison with existing ideas and attitudes, and lead to a summarizing of the group's conclusions. Finally, the principles and ideas agreed in Phase A are presented by participants and put on permanent display, to sum up the areas of agreement, and to serve as reference points for Phases B and C.

Unit A1: Note For National Curriculum Developers

The four units of Phase A enable readers to agree the principles and concepts on which the development of the curriculum will be based. These will affect all other parts of the process and will ensure that nutrition education has the best chance of making a real impact on health. It is recommended that these principles and concepts form the introductory book of a curriculum planning document. National curriculum developers should read and discuss the units one by one and look through the Activities. The Summing Up at the end of each Activities unit will help to focus the essential points. They can then come to an outline agreement on the concepts and principles which should guide the development of the national curriculum, and draft a policy statement outlining agreed positions on:

1. the concept of health
2. principles of curriculum development
3. appropriate learning approaches.

This can serve as the first book of the curriculum planning document.

Review: If the national group is reviewing the Planning Guide for local use, they should indicate to schools, teacher education colleges and local education authorities how far they endorse the principles outlined in Phase A.

Curriculum Development for Mentally Handicapped Children

Process of Curriculum Development for Mentally Handicapped Children: In Hong Kong, mentally handicapped (MH) children generally go to the following three types of schools: schools for mildly MH children, schools for moderately MH children and schools for severely MH children. The Services Division of the Education Department is responsible for the assessment and placement of these children in the type of schools most suited to their intelligence and learning needs, so that they can develop their potential in an appropriate learning environment.

During the past years, curriculum development for MH children in Hong Kong was undertaken jointly by the Education Department, heads and teachers of schools for MH children and related professionals. A wide range of curriculum outlines, teaching programmes, teachers' handbooks, etc. have been developed for the reference of schools for MH children.

However, curriculum development is a continuous process: what is taught and how it is to be taught are subject to ongoing review. In view of the everchanging needs of society, it is considered necessary that the curriculum for MH children, which includes the aims of the special education curriculum, the curriculum goals, curriculum content, strategies for curriculum implementation, etc. should be reviewed and revised. Some general principles for a broad, balanced curriculum for these children should be formulated and laid down in a guide to provide schools with a general direction for implementation.

Overview of Curriculum Development: The Curriculum Development Council has therefore prepared this Guide to Curriculum For Mentally Handicapped Children to provide schools with a framework of the MH curriculum to help develop the children's potential. Within this framework, the curriculum is subject to adaptations to meet the specific learning needs of individual children.

The curriculum for MH children falls into the following six areas of learning:

(1) Language
(2) Mathematics
(3) Personal and Social Development
(4) Perceptual Motor
(5) Aesthetics and Creativity
(6) Practical Skills.

These six areas of learning encompass twelve basic subjects as follows:

(1) Language
(2) Mathematics
(3) Computer Learning

(4) Self-Care
(5) General Studies
(6) Perceptual Motor Training
(7) Physical Education
(8) Music
(9) Art and Craft
(10) Home Economics
(11) Design and Technology
(12) Independent Living Skills.

Each of these subjects consists of several modules. Book in the Guide will give a brief description of the combinations and content of the modules in these subjects. A series of twelve syllabuses on the above subjects will be prepared for the reference of schools at a later date. These syllabuses will provide, in practical terms, subject-specific guidelines, including teaching samples, to show how the principles spelt out in the Guide can be put into practice. These twelve syllabuses, together with this Guide to Curriculum for Mentally Handicapped Children, will replace the existing three curriculum guides used with mildly, moderately and severely MH children since 1984.

MH children generally have difficulties in learning and social adjustment. They need educational programmes specially designed to prepare them for living and functioning in their homes, the neighbourhood and the community; to equip them with good work skills and habits and a positive work attitude in preparation for future vocational training. They also need educational programmes to equip them with self-care skills, independent living skills and communication skills so that they can integrate into the community as contributing members.

Curriculum Approach

In fact, the aims of education are basically the same for all children, irrespective of their abilities and learning needs. Therefore, in designing a curriculum for MH children, while their learning characteristics need to be taken into consideration, the general framework of the mainstream curriculum should also be kept in view.

The Target Oriented Curriculum (TOC) is one of the modes of curriculum development presently adopted in Hong Kong. It emphasizes the importance of setting clear learning objectives, on which teaching, learning and assessment can be based; designing learning materials according to learning objectives set; using assessment and records of progress to monitor progress and motivate further learning, etc. In this case, the characteristics of TOC are comparable to those of the MH curriculum. In fact, one could say that the spirit of TOC is embodied in the MH curriculum. The two syllabuses on Chinese Language and Mathematics intended for MH children are being prepared along the same line.

The effective utilization of resources, especially human resources, is another important factor contributing to successful curriculum development and implementation. Current trends in education emphasize the joint involvement of the teaching and specialist staff of the school and parents in curriculum development. This joint involvement would enable the curriculum to be appropriately tailored to meet the abilities and specific learning needs of individual children. The whole-school approach to curriculum development currently adopted in special schools is the manifestation of this spirit of joint involvement.

Curricular Approaches in Special Education

Special education is the education of students with special needs in a way that addresses the students' individual differences and needs. Ideally, this process involves the individually planned and systematically monitored arrangement of teaching procedures, adapted equipment and materials, accessible settings, and other interventions designed to help learners with special needs achieve a higher level of personal self-sufficiency and success in school and community than would be available if the student werc only given access to a typical classroom education.

Common special needs include learning differences, communication challenges, emotional and behavioral disorders, physical disabilities, and developmental disabilities. Students with these kinds of disabilities are likely to benefit from additional educational services, different approaches to teaching, and use of technology. Intellectual giftedness is a difference in learning and can also benefit from specialized teaching techniques or different educational programmes, but the term "special education" is generally used to specifically indicate instruction of students whose special needs reduce their ability to learn independently or in a classroom, and gifted education is handled separately.

The opposite of *special education* is *general education*. General education is the standard curriculum presented with standard teaching methods and without additional supports.

Provision of Individualized Services

Special education is not a location, but the act of educating students in a way that is "special", or different from the usual methods. A special education programme should be customized to address each individual student's unique needs. Special educators provide a continuum of services, in which students with special needs receive services in varying degrees based on their individual needs.

The provision of education to people with disabilities or learning differences differs across countries and (in the US, Canada, Germany, and other federally organized countries) across states. The ability of a student to access a particular resource depends on the availability of services, location, family choice, and government policy. For example, in some poor countries, students with disabilities simply cannot attend school.

In most countries, educators are being challenged to modify teaching methods and environments so that the maximum number of students are served in typical educational environments. In the US, the President's National Council on Disability has called for special education to be regarded less as a "place" and more as "a service, available in every school." Inclusion reduces social stigmas and improves academic achievement for many students.

Additionally, improved teaching methods and early intervention programmes such as response to intervention are being implemented by general education teachers to reduce the need for special education through prevention.

Special education programmes need to be individualized so that they address the unique combination of needs in a given student.

Students with special needs are assessed to determine their specific strengths and weaknesses. Placement, resources, and goals are determined on the basis of the student's needs. Modifications to the regular programme may include changes in curriculum, supplementary aides or equipment, and the provision of specialized physical adaptations that allow students to participate in the educational environment to the fullest extent possible. Students may need this help to access subject matter, to physically gain access to the school, or to meet their emotional needs. For example, if the assessment determines that the student cannot write by hand because of a physical disability, then the school might provide a computer for typing assignments, or allow the student to answer questions orally instead. If the school determines that the student is severely distracted by the normal activities in a large, busy classroom, then the student might be placed in a smaller classroom.

The education of students with developmental disabilities, who require more time to learn the same material, frequently requires changes to the curriculum. Successful special education programmes for developmentally disabled students focus on "only what is necessary for them to know and what they are capable of learning," so that all of the child's time is spent learning high-priority skills, and so that the child is not inappropriately frustrated by advanced subjects that are beyond their capabilities. By contrast, most students with a specific learning disability primarily need changes to the method of instruction, rather than to the skills and information being taught.

Support can be provided for short periods or long-term, and the kinds of support may change over time. For example, a child that required a one-on-one instructional aide for safety reasons while very young might outgrow this need when older.

What Qualifies Children as Special Ed Students?

Special Ed children have a wide range of disabilities that qualify them for special education programmes, such as "specific learning disabilities, speech or language impairments, mental retardation, emotional disturbance, multiple disabilities, hearing impairments, orthopedic impairments, visual impairments, autism, combined deafness and blindness, traumatic brain injury, and other health impairments".

Criteria: In order to receive special education services a student must meet the following two criteria:

1) *Must have one or more of the following disabilities listed above.*
2) *The child must require special education and related services.* Not all children who have disabilities need to be in a special ed classroom, some can perform well in a mainstream classroom. Therefore, there is additional research to assign each child to the best learning environment for them specifically.

What is the next step if the child has a disability? When a child is suspected of having a disability a team is called upon to evaluate what the education of this child should be. The team consists of at least one teacher and at least one specialist in this field to evaluate the particular student. The team evaluates the student and decides whether they need to be placed into a special ed classroom or would be fine being a part of mainstream classrooms.

IDEA:Individuals with Disabilities Act.: Section 614: "Schools may place children with disabilities in separate classrooms or schools only when supports and services are not enough to help the child learn in a regular classroom"

Differentiating Curriculum for Special Education Children

An array of Special Education Services exist so that children with a wide variety of learning disabilities and different education plans can be placed in a programme that works for them.

1. *General Education Classroom Placement:* for some students with learning disabilities their learning needs can be met in a general education classroom with no additional outside help.
2. *Collaboration:* students with disabilities who are in general education classrooms meet outside the classroom with professionals such as the school psychologist, resource room teacher, language specialists, or others.
3. Resource Room Placement: in this programme students spend most of their day in general education classrooms but then participate in resource room programmes for the other part of the day. REsource room usually includes a small number of students working with a special ed teacher on reading, language, and math.
4. *Special Education Placement with Part Time Inclusion:* in this programme special ed students are taught by a special education teacher for most of the day but join their peers for subjects such as phys ed, art, and music.
5. Self Contained Special Education: in this programme students are in a class that is located in a separate school, they are taught by special education teachers and have very little contact with the general education programme.
6. *Related Services:* IDEA '97 guarantees that children with disabilities benefit from general education or special education.

Differentiating Beneficial for All Students

There is a lot of controversy and dispute as to whether differentiating curriculum for special ed students is beneficial to all students. The advocates for this programme suggest that inclusion and adjusting the lesson plans to the individual students need creates positive results to all the students in the classroom. The opponents of this argument inquire that targeting different levels of academic ability in one classroom at the same time creates negative consequences to the students who are not learning disabled.

Due to the new standards of school's academic success, by the No Child Left Behind Act (NCLB), schools are being challenged to produce students with a very high level of education. This push for success academically is even further challenging the inclusion of special ed children into mainstream classrooms. Schools have as far as planning field trips for special ed students on the day of the test so that they cannot "negatively effect the scores".

PRO-Differentiation: Supporters of differentiation in classrooms understand the fact that most students with learning disabilities can function and learn as well as their non disabled peers. Segregating these students is a thing of the past and with new laws such as NCLB and IDEA, we are in a new era that allows students with learning disabilities to be a part of the general education programme. More specifically supporters believe that differentiation greatly closes the achievement gap and benefits all students in the classroom.

From the unique learning style to promoting students' sensitivity and acceptance of all of their peers this process has shown many positive results. A great deal of research indicates that moderate gains occur in students' academic achievement when teachers adopt practices from gifted education pedagogy, such as ability grouping, curriculum modification, differentiation (Renzulli, 1994; Tomlinson, 1995, 1999), strategies to enhance higher level thinking skills, concept-based instruction, problem-based learning), and constructivist pedagogy, to improve student achievement. "Because it is unlikely that one strategy operating in isolation is as effective as multiple interventions, it is recommended that school personnel investigate the combined effects of grouping practices and differentiated curriculum" (Tieso, 2003).

Anti-Differentiation: The idea of differentiation is essentially grouping students in ability level. There has been much research that has shown that grouping is not effective for low ability children because they are discouraged to do well whereas the high ability children are motivated to succeed because "they are both academically and socially superior". (Sandholtz, 2004)

Studies that support Anti-Differentiation:

1) Study done by Anita Stevens at SUNY Albany researchers the effects of tracking on students at a high school level. Tracking students is in essence the same thing as differentiation and as this study shows it ends up increasing the achievement gap. She discusses how tracking students by ability and placing students in ability based groups was originally intended to accommodate the growing and increasingly diverse student population. Even though the intentions of tracking seemed good it ended up counteracting its goal and perpetuating existing inequalities among students instead of equalizing their opportunities for success. (Stevens, 1999)
2) Study done that interviewed 16 year old teens that have learning disabilities and were placed in general education classrooms with paraprofessionals. The results of this study showed that the respondents to the research stated that the vast majority expressed powerful messages of disenfranchisement, embarrassment, loneliness, rejection, fear, and stigmatization. What these students sought was so simple and yet foundational to quality education. They wanted to belong. They wanted to feel that they were worthy of the teacher's time. They wanted to have friends. They wanted to go about their school day without fear or embarrassment. They wanted to learn. In too many cases they did not experience these basics, despite the fact that they attended general education classes and had the support of paraprofessionals. This study suggested to go back to segregated classrooms because inclusion was not beneficial my any means. (Broer, 2005)

Need based Curriculum in the Field of Special Education

The field of special education has made tremendous progress within the past 30 years. It is an ever-changing field with the ultimate goal of helping all students, but specifically students with disabilities, achieve independence. The question of which direction special education takes is an important one and this study is based on the philosophy that teachers should lead the way. Beliefs and best practices, especially regarding special education curriculum, is an area that will continue to change and grow. Special education curriculum has historically been drawn from the Individualized Education Program (IEP) (Pugach & Warger, 2001). Many special educators feel that it is a documentation of the curriculum for students with disabilities, and use the goals and objectives from the plan as the primary source when programmeming for these students. Thus each student's curriculum is developed based on his or her needs as recorded on the document.

Other educators see the IEP as more of a reference point in the context of a standard curriculum. They feel the primary function of the plan is to document recommendations for curricular accommodations and modifications (Adelman & Taylor, 1993). This view, however, assumes that the mission of schooling is the same for all students, those with and without disabilities. Further compounding the disagreement about the nature and content of special education curriculum are the concerns of teachers and administrators alike, that the training of special educators is inadequate in the broad areas of curriculum development (McKenzie, 1991), as well as in content subject areas (Cline & Billingsley, 1991). Sands, Adams, & Stout (1995) found that teacher training in curriculum development and modification was most likely to take place through "on-the-job" experiences and that teachers wanted more training in the areas of curriculum for teaching compensatory skills and life skills.

Teachers' beliefs and practices can influence both curriculum practices in the classrooms and reform issues about curricular implementation (Conley, 1991). Also, due to the shift towards more inclusive schools, special education educators need to have more input into what is required in general education curriculum (U.S. Department of Education, 2003). Inclusive programmes continue to transform the role of the special education teacher and collaboration between the regular educator and the special education educator is and will become increasingly more important (Agran, et al., 2002). Pugach and Warger (2001) indicate that by targeting the curriculum rather than the student deficits, educators will have a better chance of eliminating barriers to student success. This exploratory study was designed to collect data from special education teachers regarding variables such as curricular training, philosophy, and practices.

Purpose of the Study

The findings are primarily descriptive in nature, and investigated whether special educations teachers preferred Individualized Education Program-based teaching versus a more standard curriculum-based approach. In addition, special educators were asked if they felt the need for further curriculum training and if so, in what specific area(s). The first research hypothesis was that the majority of the participating teachers use the Individualized Education Program as their primary source of special education curriculum. The null hypothesis was that there will be no statistical significance in favor of the Individualized Education Program or the curriculum. The second hypothesis was that there will be a difference based on gender when it came to which method of curriculum they prefer. The null hypothesis was that there will be no statistical significance between genders. The third hypothesis was that teachers will prefer to receive future training in the areas of basic skills. The null hypothesis was that there will not be a statistical significance for future training. Although the emphases in this study were the three hypotheses, because of the nature of the background of the participants, it was decided that other questions would be asked as well, for personal and professional study. From those data, questions and concerns were generated that would guide further inquiry into special education curricular practices at the local, state, and national levels.

Description of the Survey

A Special Education Use of Curriculum Survey was developed based on a study by Sands, Adams, & Stout (1995).

A subsection from another survey designed by Ysseldyke, Thurlow, Wotruba, and Nania (1990) was also used as a template. The three hypotheses were addressed by asking participants to respond to three specific questions on the survey and the rest of the questions were primarily exploratory in nature; it was felt that the teachers' responses would be important in determining future questions and practices.

The survey was a compilation of different assessment types. Participants were asked to choose a singe item, rank primary choice, and fill in the blank. The survey also contained one open-ended question. There were three major sections of the survey: demographics, special education curriculum, and future training needs.

Definition of Children with Special Educational Needs

Children are considered to have special educational needs if they cannot benefit fully from the curriculum provided for children of their age or if they cannot be catered for adequately in an ordinary educational setting. Children with one or more of the following characteristics can be considered as children with special educational needs (SEN children):

- hearing impairment
- visual impairment
- physical handicap
- mental handicap
- maladjustment
- learning difficulties.

Aims of the Special Education Curriculum

All children, whether or not requiring special educational services, have basically the same needs and should not be distinguished from each other. Therefore, the aims of the special education curriculum should basically be the same as those of the mainstream curriculum in that great emphasis is put on the development of children's potential to the full. Accordingly, children should be exposed to similar experiences, skills, concepts, values, etc. However, the means to achieve these aims may be different and the rate at which to achieve them may also vary according to the abilities of individual children.

General Aims: The general aims of the special education curriculum are:

(1) To help the children achieve personal development according to their individual differences.

(2) To prepare the children for living and functioning in their homes, the neighbourhood and the community.

(3) To develop in the children study skills, a positive study attitude and good study habits for self-learning or for further studies.

(4) To develop in the children work skills, a positive work attitude and good work habits for vocational training or for work.

(5) To help the children achieve as much independence as possible and become contributing members of the community.

Specific Aims: For purposes of practical curriculum planning, these general aims may be broken down into the following specific aims:

(1) *Aims Related to Intellectual Development:*

(a) To help the children make sense of their environment and construct within their minds a framework of knowledge.

(b) To develop in the children a positive attitude towards learning.

(c) To develop in the children lively, enquiring minds and to encourage in them independent thinking and rational judgements.

(d) To help the children acquire, generalize and apply knowledge and skills in daily life and to train them in habits of rational thinking with all its components, e.g. observation, systematic information gathering, analysis, synthesis, deduction and induction.

(2) *Aims Related to Communicative Development:* To develop in the children the ability to express their

thoughts and feelings through speech or other modes of expression.

(3) *Aims Related to Social and Moral Developments:*

(a) To help the children acquire social skills, learn to make friends and co-operate with others.

(b) To help the children acquire social and moral values and to develop in them a sense of responsibility, respect and tolerance for others, including their views, beliefs and ways of life.

(c) To help the children understand the interdependent nature of individuals and the world.

(d) To encourage the children to participate actively in different kinds of activities and to contribute to the school and to society.

(4) *Aims Related to Personal and Physical Developments:*

(a) To foster in the children self-esteem, self-confidence and a positive, realistic self-image.

(b) To provide perceptual motor training for the children.

(c) To encourage the children to pursue physical and recreational activities.

(5) *Aims Related to Aesthetic Development* : To foster in the children imagination and creativity and to develop in them an appreciation for beauty.

Flexibility in Curriculum Planning

This Guide aims to provide heads and teachers of special schools and special classes with a general curriculum framework to accommodate the learning needs of SEN children and is written with the majority of these children in mind. As schools differ in terms of the abilities and learning needs of their children as well as resources available, they should tailor the centrally designed curriculum to meet the abilities and learning needs of their children, taking into account the given curriculum aims and broad areas of learning.

One way to adapt the centrally designed curriculum is through the development of a school-based curriculum. To facilitate this development, support from the head of school and co-operation among the staff are indispensable for sharing of knowledge and experience. Regular channels of communication such as case conferences, staff seminars, bulletins, informal discussions, etc. should be established to facilitate such sharing. It is also important that initiative and participation should be encouraged at all levels, whether at the level of the head of school, panel co-ordinators, teachers, or other professional staff concerned, to develop curriculum materials to supplement the centrally designed curriculum.

Another way to adapt the centrally designed curriculum is through the development of Individual Educational Programmes (IEP). Children have individual differences and therefore individual learning needs. To meet these individual learning needs, teachers are encouraged to design, where feasible, IEPs for their children, based on assessment given by all those working with these children and in collaboration with their parents. An IEP ensures that a child receives teaching materials specifically tailored to meet his individual learning needs. It is a programme whereby he can work on appropriate tasks over a period of time at his own pace under motivating conditions. In designing an IEP for a child, a number of factors should be considered: his level of development in the motor, cognitive, psychological and educational aspects, his previous learning experience, his special environmental needs,his special educational needs, etc.

Special Education Co-ordinating Committee

The Special Education Co-ordinating Committee (SECC) was established in September 1988 under the Curriculum Development Council (CDC). It comprises of representatives from the Education Department, the University of Hong Kong, the Hong Kong Institute of Education, the Vocational Training Council, heads and teachers of special schools and a head of school with intensive remedial services. In effect, the SECC taps the expertise and experience of a cross-section of the special education sector in Hong Kong so that comprehensive and objective views can be ensured. Various working groups and subgroups with co-opted members from related professions have also been formed to assist in curriculum development.

(Curriculum Development Council was restructured in September,1999 and the Special Education Co-ordinating Committee is renamed as Committee on Special Educational Needs.)

Curriculum Guides for Children with Special Educational Needs

The first task of the SECC is to formulate and review educational aims for SEN children. The next task is to design a series of curriculum guides for specific categories of SEN children. Heads and teachers of special schools and special classes and all those concerned with the education of these children may refer to these guides for specific advice on the teaching of different categories of SEN children.

Curricular Skills related to Special Education

On the principle of "one curriculum framework for all', students with special educational needs (SEN), like their able counterparts follow the mainstream school curriculum and are offered essential life-long learning experiences. To put in place the above objectives, the Committee on Special Educational Needs (CSEN) under the Curriculum Development Council is responsible for formulating policy and overseeing curriculum development for students with SEN. In this connection, various ad hoc committees were set up to promote the following work:

To develop programme of study; learning objectives; learning and assessment exemplars for students with SEN;

To conduct surveys in exploring the way ahead of curriculum reforms in special schools; to work in collaboration with schools on the development of school-based curriculum so as to enhance students' learning;

To design and produce reference materials;

To conduct seminars, workshops and experience sharing sessions for enhancing teachers' professionalism;

To encourage schools to participate in the "Seed Project" on issues which are in line with the aims of curriculum reform.

As curriculum development is a continuous process. It should be updated and improved from time to time to meet new needs of society and students. It is expected that during its ongoing enhancement process, participation and support from schools; frontline personnel as well as parents are essential elements that contribute to its success.

The education of children with special needs in Pakistan is an area which is grossly neglected and in need of urgent attention. The Seventh National Plan (Pakistan Planning Commission 1988), while quoting WHO figures for disability (10 to 15% of the population), and recognising the need for special schooling and rehabilitative services, notes that existing facilities are few and inadequate. These facilities come under the Ministry of Health, Special Education and Social Welfare, which is responsible for providing both special schooling and integrated and comprehensive rehabilitative services. In consequence the Economic Survey (Pakistan Planning and Development Division 1991-92) has it that major current emphasis is upon improving the provision of schooling, enhancing the performance of the executive agencies, and strengthening and consolidating social welfare and rehabilitative services.

A constraining circumstance is that, as recent reports indicate, Pakistan's children face poor performance on social indicators, and have a health status that continues to be deficient. In fact poverty keeps an estimated eight million children at work and out of school, and there is in addition a high rate of childhood disabilities. The problems faced by girls are particularly severe, restricting their access to health care, and to both education and recreation (UNICEF cited by the daily newspaper DAWN April 29 1993).

However, the UNICEF Programme in Pakistan for 1992-96 is aimed at placing children's concerns high on the political and development agenda, and supporting the implementation of the World Summit Declaration (United Nations 1981), and of the Convention on the Rights of the Child (United Nations

1989). It is explicitly stated by the Declaration and the Convention that the UNICEF Programme will also promote the integration of disabled and socially disadvantaged children, thus providing them with social services and basic education. The Directory of Special Education and Welfare Services for Disabled Persons in Pakistan (Pakistan National Institute of Special Education 1994) shows an increase in special education provision, though this nevertheless remains minimal in terms of current needs and of the pattern of provision.

Services for children with special needs in Pakistan are subdivided into four categories of handicap. These are, with estimated percentages: physical 40%, mental 30%, visual 20% and hearing impairment 10% (Pakistan Ministry of Health, Special Education and Social Welfare 1981).

The National Policy (1986 a) estimated that in 1992, 4.6 million children and young people in Pakistan would need special education. Of these, 3.7 million were said to have mild learning difficulties and to be capable of integration into ordinary schools, and 0.9 million were considered to require special schooling.

Historically, educational policy and practice in Pakistan has been influenced by the legacy of the British (1757-1947). Independent philosophy on special education is therefore in its infancy in Pakistan, and even so is still clearly influenced by the Warnock Report (1978). More recent curriculum and other interventions recommended by key documents published in Britain, such as The National Curriculum, SEN Code of Practice or the Green Papers will not affect the planning or implementation of special education in Pakistan in the foreseeable future. The terminology used in special education is also in need of attention. However, this is a separate issue not addressed in the present paper. For a detailed discussion of the historical development of special education in Pakistan see Lari (1988, 1996).

Curriculum Issues

The National Policy (1986 a) is primarily concerned with issues such as organising services for the disabled and the implementation of programmes, and pays insufficient attention to the crucial matter of the curriculum. The 1988 Review of Policy also fails to specify curriculum objectives or the appropriate teaching methodology to be followed, although it does state that the aims of education for children with special needs must be seen as the same as those for mainstream children, and that the curriculum in special schools should therefore reflect the broad pattern of the curriculum in ordinary schools.

The Review of Policy also states however, that the detailed design and implementation of the curriculum, though subject to centrally issued guidelines, should be the responsibility of the heads of special schools. It recommended that pupils in special centres who are able to follow the curriculum and examination system of the federal capital or the province should do so, while for some other pupils the content of such a curriculum may need to be adapted or modified to meet their special needs. It is stressed that the fundamental difference in the curriculum for children with special needs must lie in the methods employed by teachers in response to the type of disability experienced by children, and that this difference must moreover be reflected in all related in-service training courses.

Vocational Training

The National Policy stresses the need for improving post school vocational courses in special education, but maintains that one of the functions of such courses is to promote independent living, and to prepare the recipients of special education for employment. Such a function, in the view of the National Policy, requires that in addition a vocational emphasis be placed across the curriculum at all stages of the development of special needs children.

The National Policy also proposes that training centres be set up in each provincial capital to provide job specific training along the lines of the National Training Centre for the Disabled which currently operates in Islamabad. It further proposes that opportunities for experiencing a range of activities and for short-term job placements before making a final training choice should also be provided. It is emphasised that centres should be organised by a senior member of staff designated as the Employment Co-ordinator, and that for the severely disabled for whom open employment is not a viable option, sheltered workshops should be set up wherever possible.

Method

In order to clarify the current situation in the wake of these policy documents, the present research conducted a survey of special school headteachers in Pakistan, using a purpose-built questionnaire. Target schools included all four of the categories of handicap referred to earlier and situated in each of the provinces of Pakistan, namely Punjab, Sindh, North West Frontier Province, and Baluchistan. The main objective was to sample headteacher opinion on the curricular content and needs of special schools in Pakistan and to determine what problems, if any, they encounter in designing and implementing an appropriate curriculum for pupils with special educational needs. The importance of the teacher's role as the active agent in handling and communicating the curriculum is generally acknowledged (for example, Barrow 1984), and is a particularly important area of investigation for future research in special education in Pakistan. However, for the purposes of the present investigation, the headteacher was the appropriate authority to supply the kind of information which we were seeking.

The questionnaire used in the present Study, as explained in more detail below, was designed to obtain basic information on such variables as headteachers' qualifications, training and experience; institutional data including the number, ages and principal disabilities of pupils enrolled, the incidence of pupils with behavioural and personality problems, and the percentage of pupils with special needs following respectively the *normal*, *modified* or *special* curriculum.

Main Objectives of the Questionnaire

The overall aim of the Study was to provide a coherent picture of the state of special education in Pakistan. Accordingly, the objectives of the Questionnaire were to secure from a sample of headteachers information in the following areas:

1. The course content in the curriculum in special schools in Pakistan in the light of the National Policy, and concepts relating to the formal/informal curriculum in special schools.
2. Information on the identity of the authorities responsible for planning special education in Pakistan, and the extent of headteacher and teacher participation in this planning.
3. The identification of differences, if any, in the curricula in special schools offered to the four disability groups already identified, namely the:
   a. mentally disabled
   b. hearing impaired
   c. visually impaired
   d. physically disabled
4. The identification of difficulties experienced by headteachers in achieving a balance in the curriculum for pupils with special educational needs between:
   a. subjects specific to children with special needs
   b. subjects which appear in the national/provincial curriculum in *normal* schools.
5. Areas in the curriculum particularly in need of attention in a design of the school curriculum.

Constraints and Difficulties of the Research Exercise

Considerable difficulties were experienced in obtaining what was considered to be an adequate response from headteachers in Pakistan. In many cases the Questionnaire was mailed to some of the headteachers several times, and many reminders were sent. Postal delays caused difficulties of communication, and some of the schools had moved premises without leaving forwarding addresses. These problems indicate some of the difficulties of conducting educational research in a developing country. In addition, as Phillips (1986) points out, institutions such as special schools are often hypersensitive to investigation of their pedagogical authority. But ultimately persistence and gentle reminders paid off, and a reasonably large and representative sample of schools was obtained.

Administration of the Questionnaire

This sample included special schools in all four provinces of Pakistan (i.e. Sindh, Punjab, Baluchistan, and North West Frontier Province). The initial mailing was to all schools listed in the Directory of Special Education Programmes in Pakistan (1986 b), though repetitions in the Directory were discounted as also the Adult Centres for Rehabilitation. Lists of special education centres established after 1986 were obtained from both Directorates of Special Education in Pakistan, at Islamabad and Lahore respectively.

A total of 70 questionnaires were eventually returned, which represents a response rate of 52 percent. A number of questionnaires were returned undelivered due to the fact, as mentioned earlier, that several schools have moved without leaving forwarding addresses. In one instance it was confirmed that a school had closed for lack of finance and perceived need after a government centre for special needs had been established in the same area. It is also possible that some of the schools listed as having opened since 1986 had not yet commenced to function in an organised manner.

Taking into consideration these difficulties and constraints on research in developing nations, the response obtained to the questionnaire was considered adequate, particularly in view of the non-availability of many of the schools to which the questionnaire was sent. When those schools that had moved or closed were eliminated, the response rate from the actual, as opposed to the hypothetical sample, was just over 75 percent.

Functional Skills Curriculum

VCOE special education programmes for students ages 3-22 with moderate to severe disabilities utilizes a functional skills curriculum that fosters independence in seven curricular domains.

These domains are:

- Communication
- Community Access, Motor Skills
- Functional Academics
- Recreation, Leisure
- Self care, Independent Living
- Social, Emotional
- Vocational.

Depending on the programme in which a student is enrolled, the student may be participating in a standards-based functional skills curriculum or a standards-based general education curriculum, such as the Phoenix School, with accommodations & modifications.

This curriculum has been aligned to the Essential Learning Standards for students with Moderate/Severe Disabilities established by the California Department of Education in 2002 as follows:

Communication

These skills are related to the ability to comprehend and express information in a variety of ways, which may include the development of receptive and expressive language skills, including non-verbal and gestural communication, the use of augmentative communication systems, and the ability to comprehend and express emotions.

Community Access, Motor Skills

These skills are related to gross motor development and ambulation, including strength, balance, and coordination and are related to physical activities and increase independence and physical access to both the school campus and the community.

Functional Academics

These skills are related to academics that also have direct application in one's life. The programme focuses on the acquisition of academic skills that are functional in terms of independent living. Core curriculum material is modified to meet the cognitive levels of the students within the special education classroom and through attendance within general classrooms/activities as appropriate. Many academic areas require the development of prerequisite skills, including fine motor development, cognitive skills and pre-operational activities.

Recreation, Leisure

These skills are related to pursuing hobbies, interests, sports activities, or other appropriate activities undertaken in free time. They may include activities done alone or with others.

Self-Care, Independent Living

These skills are related to toileting, eating, dressing, hygiene and grooming. Additionally, skills are taught that are related to functioning within a home, maintenance of one's health, and purchasing or obtaining goods and services

Social, Emotional

These skills are related to regulating behavior, social exchange, coping with demands and controlling impulses. It may include the development of social skills, responding to situational cues and making choices.

Vocational

These skills are related to procuring and holding a job in the community and the development of specific work skills. The instruction may include task completion, self-management, and job-related interactions with peers and adults.

Social Skill Curriculum

Deficits in social skills affects a child's emotional well being which might lead to problems in academic achievement as well (Mercer &Mercer 1998). The three ares are interconnected, however no one assessment instrument can address all the areas adequately. The parents, siblings, teachers, peers and the child herself/himself can furnish information about the functional level of the student. Direct observation is another valuable data gathering tool, it must be done in areas that are nonacademic and triangulation involving all the concerned people should be done to get an accurate baseline. Older students can complete a checklist that present a strength and weakness profile.

The four areas covered under Social skills Curriculum are: Conversational skills, making friends, Understanding the "Hidden Curriculum".

Trends in Special Education

Researchers have conceptualized the history of special education in stages that highlight the various trends that the field has experienced. Although some of these conceptualizations focus on changes involving instructional interventions for students with disabilities, others focus on the place of interventions. The focus on placement reflects the controversy in which the field of special education has found itself throughout history. Samuel G. Howe was one of the first to assert–in the nineteenth century–that instructional settings had inherent qualities that alone insured effective interventions. Belief in the essential curative powers of place spurred the late nineteenth century crusade for bigger and better institutions, as well as the mid-twentieth-century movement for deinstitutionalization. Exclusive focus on the importance of place distracted many professionals and prevented them from recognizing that dramatic changes in philosophy were accompanying the movement for deinstitutionalization. In the late nineteenth century, social Darwinism replaced environmentalism as the primary causal explanation for those individuals with abilities who deviated from those of the general population, opening the door to the eugenics movement of the early twentieth century, and leading to the segregation and sterilization of individuals with mental retardation. At the beginning of the twentieth century, the debate had suddenly shifted from *whether* the disadvantaged should be helped to *where* these individuals should be served. As the institutionalization versus deinstitutionalization debate raged, many individuals were given custodial treatment, which is contrary to the mission of special education.

Almost a century after the placement debate began, special educators still focused on the importance of place. Many were calling upon the field to create not one perfect setting for the delivery of services, but a continuum of placement options that would address the needs of all students with disabilities. The civil rights movement had reconceptualized special education as a case of access of minorities to the educational privileges of the majority, and the least restrictive environment clause of EAHCA/IDEA prompted advocates for people with disabilities to call for *mainstreaming*–the return of students with disabilities to the regular classroom whenever and wherever possible.

In the 1980s the Regular Education Initiative (REI) was an attempt to return responsibility for the education of students with disabilities to neighborhood schools and regular classroom teachers. In the 1990s the full inclusion movement called for educating all students with disabilities in the regular classroom with a single, unified and responsive education system. Advocates for full inclusion, following in the footsteps of Howe, argued for appropriate instruction in a single, ubiquitous place, contrary to the mandate of IDEA.

Recent Trends, Issues in Field of Special Education

Special education has been the target of criticism throughout history. Some of the criticism has been justified, some unjustified. Some criticisms brought to light ineffective practices, such as the inefficacy and inhumanity of relegating all persons with disabilities to institutions. Other criticisms were distractions with disastrous repercussions, such as the singular focus on the importance of place while ignoring other inappropriate practices.

The beginning of the twenty-first century found new criticisms being launched at special education. Some argue that the use of diagnostic labels is potentially stigmatizing to students, others that minority students are overrepresented in some disability categories, and still others that education of students with disabilities in special classes and schools, even pulling students out for instruction in resource classes, is akin to race-based segregation. Some of these criticisms may expose ineffective practices, others may only distract educators from the effort of finding and implementing effective instructional practices. Professionals must develop the ability to learn from history and differentiate between unimportant criticisms and those with merit.

One valid criticism repeatedly launched against special education involves the implementation of ineffective educational interventions. Although great concern about the *where* of instruction was expressed in the 1980s and 1990s, little attention was given to the *what* of instruction. Throughout the twentieth century the field of special education repeatedly adopted instructional strategies of questionable efficacy–interventions that have little to no empirical basis. Additionally, special educators have adopted, with "bandwagon" fervor, many practices that have been proven ineffective and have thereby repeated the mistakes of history. If special education is to progress, professionals will need to address and remedy the instructional practices used with students with disabilities.

Special education has also been validly criticized for the way in which students with disabilities are identified. In the early nineteenth century, physicians and educators had difficulty making reliable distinctions between different disability categories. In fact, the categories of mental retardation and behavioral disorders are inseparably intertwined. Many of the disability categories overlap to the extent that it is hard to differentiate one from the other. Additionally, some of the categories–learning disabilities and behavioral disorders, for example–are defined by the exclusion of other contributing disabilities. Thus, at the beginning of the twenty-first century, much work remains on the identification of students with disabilities.

Perhaps the largest, most pervasive issue in special education is its relationship to general education. The relationship of special to general education has been controversial since the beginning of universal public schooling. However, in the late twentieth and early twenty-first centuries, the question of whether special education should retain a separate identity or be fused with general education such that it has no separate identity (e.g., budget, personnel) was made prominent by proponents of a radical restructuring of special education. Proponents of radical restructuring and fusion argue that such integration is necessary to provide appropriate education for all students regardless of their disabilities and without stigma or discrimination. In their view, special education suffers primarily from structural problems, and the integration of two separate systems will result in a flexible, supple, responsive single system that will meet the needs of all students without "separating out" any. All teachers, according to this line of thinking, should be prepared to teach all students, including those with special needs.

Opponents of radical restructuring argue that special education's problems are primarily the lack of implementation of best practices, not structural. Moreover, they suggest, special education will not survive to serve the special needs of exceptional students if it loses its identity, including special budget allocations and personnel preparation. It is not feasible nor is it desirable, they contend, to prepare all teachers to teach all children; special training is required to teach students who are educationally exceptional. Arguments about the structure of education (special and general), who (if anyone) should receive special treatment, how they should be taught, and where special services should be provided are perpetual issues in special education. These issues will likely continue to be debated throughout the twenty-first century.

In the late twentieth and early twenty-first centuries, another issue became the basis for conceptual or theoretical bases for special education practices. Postmodern and antiscientific philosophies have been put forward in both general and special education. These ideas have been challenged by others who have noted the importance of the scientific method in discriminating among ideas and assertions. Likely, postmodern ideas and attempts to apply them to or refute them will be perpetual.

More than two hundred years after Itard began his work on the education of the wild boy of Aveyron, special educators are being asked to make decisions concerning such issues as placement and delivery of services. The inclusion debate, although important, has the potential to distract the field of special education away from issues of greater import–issues such as the efficacy of intervention and the accurate identification of students with disabilities.

If special educators are to avoid the mistakes of the past, they will need to make future decisions based upon reliable data, evaluating the efficacy of differing options. Since the inception of what is now known as IDEA, significant progress has been made in applying scientific research to the problems of special education. In the twenty-first century, special education need not remain a field of good intentions, but can fully employ the scientific child-study techniques begun in the late eighteenth century to provide free and appropriate educations to all children with disabilities.

UNIT-IX

Educational Technology in Special Education

The Role of Technology in Education and Special Education

Technology has found its way into every aspect of our culture today. It's in medicine, it's in social work, and no even more than it use to be, it's in our education systems. Teachers are continually being encouraged to take technology classes so that their students can benefit from their knowledge. In Education, technology plays are role in the classroom, in assistive technology products, and software that is brought into the school. So what exactly is the role of technology in Education? What is it doing for our students and children? Or is it doing anything? Let's take a closer look.

Advantages to having Technology in Education

There has been substantial evidence around the world that technology has become one of the most important and vital components to the success of a child's education. Here are some of the advantages that technology helps provide for children today:

1. *Student Achievement:* Technology has been proven to help students achieve in reading, writing, and arithmetic. Each year teachers are instructed and challenged to meet AYP's (Adequate Yearly Progress) under the No Child left Behind Act of 2001. Technology

gives educators one more tool to help them reach those goals. Students become engaged and can often times facilitate parent involvement at home.

2. *Professional Requirements:* Not only does technology benefit students in the education system, it also benefits the educator. There are so many opportunities for teachers to learn and acquire new skills over the internet, keep up with credentials and in return help them improve their teaching abilities.
3. *Meeting Special Needs*: Technology, more specifically with assistive technology special needs students, and student with disabilities have been able to achieve in areas and ways that would not have been possible. Technology creates individualized learning environments for students and really can play a major role in special needs ones.
4. *Continuing Education*: Technology has also made it possible for those who didn't finish college or high school to get back into things without having to even leave the comfort of their own home. And technology has made it possible for continued education; those wanting to reach a little higher and gain more knowledge in something new or old. Technology brings the learning right to your students; wherever they may be.
5. *Workforce Skills:* And last, but certainly not least, technology has served students well because it has provided them with the skill and knowledge they need to enter the workforce.

It is becoming increasingly difficult for teachers to reach every child in the classroom. Class sizes keep getting larger, but teachers remain still one of the lowest paid salary jobs in America. Yet the need is still there to teach and prepare the children for the future; the need to prepare them for the "real" world. And the real world today is a world full of technology. So if we don't provide technology in our education system then when will students have a chance to get familiar with it? How will they train themselves for the "real" world?

So what exactly is the role of technology in education? Technology is making it possible for teachers to reach more students, allowing students the time they need to succeed, and providing our future workforce with competent, knowledgeable employees.

In the current age we live in, technology has become an important component. Every day there is some new gadget or software that makes lives easier and improves on the technology and software that already exists. Making lives easier is not, however, the only role technology plays in our lives.

Technology is playing an increasing role in education. As technology advances, it is used to benefit students of all ages in the learning process.

Technology used in the classroom helps students adsorb the material. For example, since some people are visual learners, projection screens linked to computers can allow students to see their notes instead of simply listening to a teacher deliver a lecture.

Software can be used to supplement class curriculum. The programmes provide study questions, activities, and even tests and quizzes for a class that can help students continue learning outside the classroom.

Technology has also become part of many curriculums, even outside of computer and technology classes. Students use computers to create presentations and use the Internet to research topics for papers and essays.

Students also learn to use the technology available to them in computer and tech classes. This ensures that after graduation they will be able to use the technology in a work setting, which may put them ahead of someone who didn't have access to a particular technology or software in their own school setting.

As technology advances, students have better access to educational opportunities like these. When something new and "better" is revealed, the "older" technology becomes more affordable, allowing it to be used in educational settings, even when schools are on a tight budget.

Technology has also advanced to help children even before they've started school. Educational video games and systems for young children helps them prepare for school and in some cases get a head start on their education.

There are people who may say children are "spoiled" by technology. Instead of being able to add a long column of numbers in their heads, for example, they turn to a calculator. Regardless of these arguments, technology is an important part of today's society. By incorporating it into the classroom, students will be better equipped to transition from the classroom to the work place.

Use of Computer in : Educational Management, Library, Assessment and Evaluation of Persons with Disabilities, Assistive Devices and Computer Aids, Information Handling, Graphics

Technology has opened many educational doors to children, particularly to children with disabilities. Alternative solutions from the world of technology are accommodating physical, sensory, or cognitive impairments in many ways.

Much of the technology we see daily was developed initially to assist persons with disabilities. Curb cuts at streetcorners and curb slopes, originally designed to accommodate people with orthopedic disabilities, are used more frequently by families with strollers or individuals with grocery carts than by persons with wheelchairs or walkers. The optical character reader, developed to assist individuals unable to read written text, has been adapted in the workplace to scan printed documents into computer-based editable material, saving enormous amounts of data entry labor.

Technology—An Equalizer

Technology can be a great equalizer for individuals with disabilities that might prevent full participation in school, work, and the community. This is most evident in the case of individuals with mobility, hearing, or vision impairments, but is also true for individuals with limitations in cognition and perception. With technology, an individual physically unable to speak can communicate with spoken language. Using a portable voice synthesizer, a student can ask and respond to questions in the "regular" classroom, overcoming a physical obstacle that may have forced placement in a special segregated classroom or required a full-time instructional aide or interpreter to provide "a voice."

Improvements in sensor controls enable subtle motor movements to control mobility devices, such as electric wheelchairs, providing independent movement through the school and community. Text and graphics enhancement software can enlarge sections of a monitor enough to be seen by persons with vision impairments. Text can be read electronically by a digitized voice synthesizer for a person who is blind. For persons with hearing impairments, amplification devices can filter extraneous noise from the background or pick up an FM signal from a microphone on a teacher's lapel.

Word processing, editing, spellchecking, and grammatical tools commonly found in high-end software facilitate the inclusion of students with learning disabilities in regular classrooms by allowing them to keep up with much of the work. Not inconsequentially, the children often feel better about themselves as active learners.

Technology is providing more powerful and efficient tools to teachers who work with children with disabilities. These tools enable teachers to offer new and more effective means of learning while individualizing instruction to the broad range of student learning needs. Educators are using computers as tools to deliver and facilitate learning beyond drill and practice, to provide environments that accommodate learning, and to ensure enhanced and equitable learning environments to all students.

Access to the World Wide Web, email, listservs, and other electronic learning environments is common in many classrooms. In these environments, students around the world can interact in real time via onscreen messaging or video and audio transmissions. In most of these learning situations, a disability makes no difference at all.

Assistive Technology Defined

The definition of assistive technology applied to education is extremely broad, encompassing "any item, piece of equipment, or product system whether acquired commercially off the shelf, modified, or customized, that is used to increase, maintain, or improve functional capabilities of individuals with disabilities."

As a result, the potential range of AT devices is incredibly large, and both "high-tech" and "low-tech" devices are included. High-tech devices may be computers, electronic equipment, or software. Although electronically operated, high-tech devices need not be expensive, a simple low-cost switch that controls a battery-operated toy can be considered a high-tech device, as can a tape recorder. Low-tech devices are manually, not electronically, operated. This group includes devices such as pencil grips, mouth sticks, and mechanical hoists.

This definition also expands the consideration of potential educational applications with its focus on devices "used to increase, maintain, or improve the functional capabilities of persons with disabilities." As educators, we try to increase or add new academic, social, and daily living skills and knowledge to the functional capability of all children. This is a basic goal as we prepare children to take their place in society.

In the case of children with degenerative impairments, such as muscular dystrophy, educators may be working to keep children functioning at their current level. They may be striving to help students maintain their capability to function in the world. Teachers work with students to improve skills and knowledge, making existing skills and knowledge even more functional and improving fluency so that functional capabilities may be generalized into different settings.

It is critical to understand the implications of this definition to comprehend its effect on children with disabilities in our schools. It is fairly easy to understand how the definition is applied with regard to children with physical or sensory disabilities. To see a young child who had been unable to speak for her first five years say her first sentence with a speaking computer device presents an exciting and clear picture of assistive technology. The benefit of AT is also easy to comprehend when a child who cannot hear can understand his teacher's directions because real-time captioning converts the teacher's speech to text projected onto his laptop computer.

The definition of assistive technology also applies to the more difficult-to-gauge tools that teachers use to deliver and facilitate learning, including instructional applications of technology. These applications range from drill and practice tutorials to facilitated learner-based environments provided through the Internet or interactive hypermedia and multimedia-based instruction.

It is important to understand that virtually all applications of technology — tools for children to learn, as well as tools for teachers to provide learning opportunities — can be defined as assistive technology. This is true for individual children with disabilities whose disability has a primary impact on academic performance (e.g., learning disabilities) or functional performance (e.g., multiple physical and visual disabilities).

Legal and Moral Requirements

The mandate to provide assistive technology to children with special needs is grounded in the moral concerns protected by the U.S. Constitution and its amendments. *The Education for All Handicapped Children Act* (P.L. 94-142) was based on the Supreme Court's 1954 *Brown vs. Board of Education* decision that separate education was not equal education under the 14th Amendment to the Constitution. At the time the law was passed by Congress in 1975, nearly 2 million children were excluded from schools in the United States. With the legislation, the president and the Congress established a legal requirement for a "free appropriate public education in the least restrictive environment" for children with disabilities and, as a result, the field of special education began to flourish for the first time in nearly seventy-five years.

Many controversies surfaced, however, about the extent of the required educational services and the cost to society for those services. The major debates have focused on the need for a clear definition of an "appropriate" education in the least restrictive environment and the requirement to provide assistive technology devices and services to all individuals with disabilities.

'Appropriate' Education

The requirement for an "appropriate" education in the least restrictive environment has led to the development of a separate educational system designed to meet the needs of children with disabilities. Some educators contend that this is the same type of separate system that the Supreme Court found unconstitutional in 1954. These individuals suggest that all children, regardless of ability, should be educated with their neighborhood peers in their local school.

Others in favor of the special education system argue that it is necessary to meet the educational needs of all children with disabilities, particularly in the "continuum of services" mandated by the Individuals with Disabilities Act (IDEA). In their view, children must have specific intervention designed to "mainstream" them back into regular education. Without the intervention, these individuals believe that students will be doomed to continued and more significant failure. They also note that, while the goal of mainstreaming is reasonable, some children may not benefit appropriately from a full inclusion programme.

Although there are many arguments on both sides of the issue, it is apparent that new technologies can provide the tools to bring more children with disabilities into "regular" educational settings. In my opinion, assistive technology will certainly mainstream more and more children in wheelchairs, children who cannot physically speak, see, or hear, and children who need computers to write, organize, think, and function educationally.

The AT Requirement

The second debate centers on the requirement to provide assistive technology to all students. The initial legislation, the Education for All Handicapped Children Act, did not require schools to provide assistive technology devices and services to individuals with disabilities. The current assistive technology mandate was created by later legislation and prompted by the technological revolution resulting from the development of the microcomputer.

Subsequent legislation passed by Congress encouraged states to develop services designed to provide assistive technology to all persons with disabilities and required provision of AT as a special education service (trained special education teachers in special classes), related service (occupational, physical, speech therapies, and other services needed to access education) or supplemental service (services necessary to maintain a child in regular education classes).

Many states have not addressed the AT issue, since assistive technology devices and services were identified as requirements only recently. This may be due to a fear of "breaking" instructional budgets by purchasing high-cost equipment in already cash-short school systems. Concern also exists that the rapid evolution of technology creates the potential of costly investment in devices that may have a relatively short life span. A close look at the situation will show that these concerns are not well grounded, however. Schools already use extensive amounts of AT, and need only to identify it as such. Nearly any use of computers falls into this category, as do tape recorded instructions or homework, copies of notes from a classmate or teacher, switch-operated toys, drawing paper taped to table tops, as well as large pencils and crayons. All of these could be noted, as required, in Individual Education Plans (IEPs) and Individual Family Service Plans (IFSPs).

Assistive Computer Technology for Persons with Disabilities

The personal computer (PC) can be the backbone of independence for millions of individuals with sensory, physical, and learning disabilities. Computersand information technology can be modified with alternative input, alternative output, and other assistive technology to empower consumers who have disabilities. Computer vendors support persons with disabilities by incorporating accessibility utilities into operating systems such as Microsoft Windows, Apple Macintosh, and UNIX. PCs equipped with assistive technology permit individuals to function independently at school, work, and home, and allow access to great quantities of information from diverse sources such as compact disks, networks, electronic mail, instant messaging, the World Wide Web, and other Internet resources. For the purposes of this discussion, the term "assistive technology" will be used to describe any hardware device or software programme that permits individuals with disabilities to operate PCs and access information technology independently. Moreover, this article uses the definition of disability as outlined in the Americans with Disabilities Act in the United States, and the Disabilities Discrimination Act in the United Kingdom—any permanent condition that impairs a major life function such as seeing, hearing, walking, or speaking.

Personal Computer Platforms

Since their advent in the early 1980s, PCs have become a vital tool for business and education applications, and are now common in many homes. Personal computer platforms are a combination of hardware and software, working together in synergy. The hardware is the physical structure of the system, and software is the set of instructions that control the hardware. PC hardware consists of several fundamental components, including the central processing unit, memory units, disk drive storage, keyboard, and video monitor or screen.

For persons with disabilities, the keyboard, mouse, and monitor are of prime concern. PCs employ input devices like keyboards and mice for entering information and for controlling the system. Output devices, like monitors and printers, display processed information. Adapting PCs for use by persons with disabilities involves the modification of these standard input and output devices with assistive hardware or software. For example, adapting a computer's output systems to use speech or Braille printouts can make the computer accessible for persons with visual disabilities.

Technology for Persons with Vision Impairments

The video monitor is a standard output device for PCs. By its nature, the monitor relies on the visual sense to convey information. For persons with vision-related disabilities, the monitor can present a significant barrier, depending on the nature of the vision loss. The output of a standard computer printer is also fundamentally inaccessible for persons with vision impairments. Several assistive technologies that can help compensate for visual impairments include video magnification, screen readers, Braille displays and printers, and optical character recognition systems.

Magnification software enlarges text and graphics displayed on PC monitors. Magnification programmes are widely used by persons with poor vision or who have difficulty reading. They focus a larger image on the retina, making text and graphics more visible. Most magnification programmes can magnify either the whole screen, or just a select region of the screen. Some basic magnification utilities magnify just the mouse pointer or cursor.

Mostcomprehensive packages allow the user to change the screen contrast and font or adjust the magnification in steps. Some programmes provide speech output and magnification at the same time. Magnification software can enlarge the output from commercial applications such as word processors, databases, spreadsheets, browsers, e-mail, and other applications. Some magnification programmes can also display books, magazines, and other printed materials magnified on the monitor using an external camera or scanner.

Screen readers are software programmes that provide either speech or Braille output, and are commonly employed by persons who are blind or visually impaired. Screen readers require a computer sound card and speakers to provide voice output. For Braille output, a screen reader requires a Braille display. Braille displays connect to the PC and contain a row of mechanical Braille dots that pop up and down under computer control. The user employs arrow keys to scroll text for reading. Braille displays allow vision-impaired users to control the operating system and application programmes.

For persons with vision impairments, the printed word can present a formidable barrier to independence. Optical character recognition (OCR) software can help overcome this barrier.

OCR software requires a flatbed or handheld scanner to be connected to the host PC in order to function.

OCR systems are used to scan printed materials directly into the PC to accommodate many types of disabilities. Once scanned, the text can be read using a screen reader, magnification software, or Braille display or printer. OCR software can also help users with learning disabilities scan and format information in ways that help them process the information. In addition, the technology empowers those with motor-related disabilities to process and access information.

Technology for Persons with Motor Impairments

For persons with motor-related disabilities, the computer keyboard and mouse can present a significant barrier. There is a wide range of assistive technology available to compensate users who have motor disabilities. Several common input modifications include adapted keyboards, on-screen keyboards, alternative communication programmes, and voice recognition.

Keyboard adaptations designed to assist users who have difficulty using the standard keyboard come in many different forms. Models exist that can be used with one hand, or with another part of the body. There are adapted keyboards that allow the keys to be rearranged to suit the user's needs. Some models allow the keyboard to be adjusted for the most suitable ergonomic fit. These can be adjusted to lay flat on the desk in the traditional manner or they can be used in a vertical configuration, if that best suits a user's preferences and needs.

On-screen keyboards are software programmes that display a pictorial representation of a standard keyboard on the computer screen. The on-screen keyboard can be configured to scan through the keys one at a time through software. When the desired key is highlighted, a user can select the key by striking an adapted switch connected to the computer. Adapted switches come in many configurations; they can be controlled by breath, by hand, or by another part of the body. Some adapted switches can also be activated using voice commands.

Many motor disabilities can impact one's ability to speak, so alternative communications systems have been developed to assist persons with communications tasks at home, school, or in the workplace. Alternative communications systems range from picture boards to notebook computers equipped with speech synthesis systems capable of an unlimited vocabulary. Such systems can be used to communicate with friends, family members, and co-workers, and for tasks such as delivering presentations.

Voice recognition and dictation systems are powerful assistive technologies that allow persons with disabilities to control a computer and dictate documents verbally using spoken commands. Voice recognition software requires a computer with a sound card and a microphone to accept verbal input. Voice recognition software must be trained by the user to recognize the speaker's voice accurately, a process that takes about an hour. The software stores recorded voice patterns from the training process, and matches these stored templates against the incoming verbal command stream from the microphone. Voice recognition can be used for applications such as e-mail, web browsing, and word processing.

Technology for Persons with Hearing Impairments

Numerous forms of adaptive and non-assistive technologies are available to increase independence and quality of life for individuals who are deaf or hard of hearing. For persons with hearing-related disabilities, access to the spoken word can often present a significant barrier. Assistive technology to support users with hearing-related disabilities focuses on accessing the spoken word at home, in the classroom, or at the work site. Technologies to assist the hearing-impaired include such systems as TTYs, amplification systems, and applications like e-mail and instant messaging.

TTYs, or text telephones, allow people to type messages back and forth over the telephone. These devices allow individuals to send text messages using a keyboard and printer or visual display. They access the telephone system using standard connectors, and can be used for home, school, or business applications. There are also portable TTYs that can be used in a mobile environment.

Amplification systems increase the volume and clarity of the spoken word, making it more accessible for persons with limited hearing ability. These devices range from hearing aids that fit inside the ear to assistive listening devices that can be carried in a pocket or purse and used for large gatherings.

Users can also adjust the speaker volume on most computer platforms to increase access for persons who are deaf or hard of hearing. If the speaker volume is adjusted to zero, this causes the visual display to flash and alert the user to the presence of audio output.

Non-assistive computer programmes like electronic mail and instant messaging empower individuals with hearing-related impairments to communicate over the Internet. The widespread availability of electronic mail contributes greatly to the independence of persons with hearing impairments. Instant messaging allows for expanded communication in much the same manner as electronic mail does, with an immediacy similar to that of a telephone conversation, and its wide availability to all computer users, regardless of disability, makes it attractive as a means of communication.

Technology for Persons with Learning Disabilities

The term "learning disabilities" covers many impairments that impact the ability to process information. Technologies to assist persons with learning disabilities include speech systems that read printed material aloud, digital assistants to maintain schedules and lists of tasks, software to correct spelling, and task management software to guide users through the successful completion of projects. Many of these are standard productivity software programmes used in business and education.

The Internet

The Internet is a vast network of computers that spans the globc. This important network allows persons with disabilities to share and exchange information in an accessible form. The Internet supports applications like e-mail, instant messaging, and the World Wide Web. PCs connected to the Internet, or a private Intranet, can be adapted with a wide variety oftechnologies to allow access to applications such as e-mail, web browsers, and online databases. The Internet and Intranets empower persons with disabilities to access information using speech, Braille, magnification, or some other form of assistive technology. The Internet increases independence for people with mobility issues to interact, work, and socialize. Assistive software can be loaded onto a network to allow that software to be shared by all users belonging to the network.

Assistive Technology and Computer Operating Systems

Accessibility utilities are being integrated into computer operating systems such as Windows, Macintosh, and UNIX. While these accessibility utilities differ from one platform to another, most operating systems include utilities to magnify text and graphics, convert text into synthesized speech, and help users control the keyboard and mouse functions.

Operating systems are growing more compatible with assistive technology in general, and this is evidenced by Microsoft's Active Accessibility, which helps assistive technologies work together with the operating system and application programmes.

Future Technology

Legislation such as the Americans with Disabilities Act in the United States and the Disabilities Discrimination Act in the United Kingdom is fostering the development of assistive technology for persons with disabilities. Section 508 of the Rehabilitation Act in the United States is helping to make the World Wide Web more accessible as well. The development of computer platforms of increasing speed and power also contributes to the ongoing evolution of assistive technology. As computers get more powerful, assistive technology also increases in capacity and potential, driven by the advancement of microprocessor-based technology.

The increasing miniaturization of powerful computer components will lead to assistive technologies that are more portable, lightweight, and cost effective, allowing for increased independence and improving the overall quality of life for persons with disabilities.

Use of Computer Assistive Instructions in Tutorial, Self-study and Distance Learning

What is an Assistive Technology Device?

An assistive technology device is any item, piece of equipment, or system that is used to help improve or keep the skills of a child with a disability. Examples of assistive technology devices include, but are not limited to:

- Electronic communication aids
- Computer software
- Voice recognition system
- Touch-sensitive computer screens or tablets
- Switches or battery-operated toys.

How does Assistive Technology Help?

Many different devices can help people with disabilities in everyday life. Assistive technology can give children access to school, social, and sports activities, with chances to learn and play with children who do not have disabilities. Assistive devices can help children learn and give them confidence and independence.

What is an Assistive Technology Service?

An assistive technology service is any service that helps a child with a disability in finding, buying, or using an assistive technology device. Examples of assistive technology services include, but are not limited to:

- Testing your child's needs in school or everyday life
- Buying, renting, or otherwise acquiring assistive technology devices for your child to use
- Choosing, designing, fitting, adapting, maintaining, repairing, or replacing assistive technology devices
- Combining the use of assistive technology devices with other therapies, interventions, or services
- Training or technical assistance for your child and/or family, if needed
- Training or technical assistance for service providers that work with your child.

What Laws Require that my Child with a Disability Receives Assistive Technology?

There are two major Federal laws that require assistive technology services for a child with a disability:

- Individuals with Disabilities Education Act (IDEA)
- Section 504 of the Rehabilitation Act.

Individuals with Disabilities Education Act (IDEA)

The IDEA requires States to provide a free and appropriate public education (FAPE) in the least restrictive environment (LRE) for children with disabilities ages 3 through 21 and early intervention services for infants and toddlers birth through age two and their families.

Section 504 of the Rehabilitation Act

Section 504 of the Rehabilitation Act protects the rights of people with disabilities in programmes and activities that receive federal financial assistance.

Section 504 protects the rights of individuals:

With visible disabilities.

With disabilities that may not be apparent.

Who are treated as if they have a disability because of a history of a disability or have been misclassified as having a disability.

Who have disabilities, such as orthopedic impairments or hepatitis, but do not qualify for special education services.

Section 504 requires that schools provide assistive technology devices to your child if the device or service:

Is a related aid or service to your child's appropriate education.

Allows your child to go to a regular classroom with other students who do not have disabilities.

Allows your child to be with children without disabilities for sports, social activities, and / or other activities outside the classroom.

Section 504 requires a "504 Plan" that describes all reasonable accommodations. It should also include assistive technology devices and services.

What Rights does my Child with a Disability have in Receiving Assistive Technology?

Individuals with Disabilities Education Act (IDEA)

Free and Appropriate Public Education (FAPE)

Least Restrictive Environment (LRE)

Related services

Individualized Education Plan (IEP)

School districts are required to provide a free and appropriate public education to students with disabilities based on their individualized educational needs. A child's individualized educational needs may include special education and related aids and services such as physical therapy. Modifications to the regular education programme, including adjustments in test taking procedures and to rules regarding absences when a student's absences are due to a disability may also be included. Any special education and related services should be written in your child's IEP.

504 of the Rehabilitation Act of 1973.

Free and Appropriate Public Education (FAPE)

Transportation

Non-academic services

School districts and other recipients of federal funds are required to provide a FAPE to students with disabilities based on their individualized educational needs. The services under Section 504 also include FAPE, but also require that schools provide non-academic services. Schools must provide transportation to and from these services. Again, any special education and related services should be written in your child's 504 Plan.

What is an Assistive Technology Referral and Evaluation?

An assistive technology referral is actually another term for an assistive technology evaluation for your child.

You can ask for an assistive technology evaluation at any time, such as when you request a special education evaluation or if your child already receives special education services.

All activities before, during, and after school should be evaluated to determine if assistive technology would help your child. The assistive technology evaluation should include eight areas:

- Health
- Vision
- Hearing
- Social/Emotional
- General Intelligence
- Academic Performance
- Communication
- Motor.

What Happens after the Assistive Technology Device and Services are Provided?

After an assistive technology service or device is given to your child, the school must also make sure that your child is learning appropriately with the assistive technology service or device.

The school does not have to give your child the best assistive technology service or device. The school must provide the assistive technology service or device that your child needs to learn or function in school.

Is the School Responsible for Providing Personal Devices?

Usually, no. Schools usually do not have to provide devices to persons with disabilities in everyday life. Assistive devices can help students learn more easily and can give them more confidence and independence. Assistive technology can give children access to school, social, and sports activities, with chances to learn and play with non-disabled children.

However, a school may have to buy a personal device for a child if the IEP team decides it is necessary for the child to receive FAPE. The child may be allowed to take the personal device home if it is necessary for the child to continue learning at home, such as doing homework with the assistive technology device.

Where and When Can My Child Use the Assistive Device?

Your child can use the assistive technology device wherever the IEP says it can be used. Your child should be able to use the assistive technology device as they move from grade to grade. If you change school districts, the new school district can buy a new assistive technology device or buy the old one from the former school. If you own the assistive technology device, your child may use it at home whenever it is appropriate.

Who is Responsible for Maintenance and Repair of Assistive Devices?

The school is responsible for buying, repairing, and maintaining assistive technology devices. The school must repair and replace assistive technology devices that are broken in school.

However, if an assistive technology device is brought home and broken at home, then parents may have to pay for the repair if the device was not used properly.

Make sure your child's IEP explains:

- What needs to be done when any assistive technology device is broken or needs to be fixed
- Where your child will get another device until the broken onc is fixed or replaced
- What other assistive technology device your child could use until the broken one is fixed or replaced

Writing Assistive Technology into Your Child's IEP Goals and Objectives

The IEP must explain how and why your child should use the assistive technology device to achieve each goal and objective. The IEP should include goals for your child to learn how to use the assistive technology device.

The IEP should have specific objectives to make sure your child learns how to use the assistive technology device. Examples of objectives include, but are not limited to:

- What tasks your child will use the assistive technology device to do
- How the school will train your child to use the assistive technology device
- How many times the school will train your child to use the assistive technology device
- Who will train your child to use the assistive technology device
- When and where your child will use the assistive technology device.

How do I Help My Child Learn How to Use an Assistive Technology Device?

Training is when information is provided to your child, the child's family, or the child's teacher or professionals on how to use or operate an assistive technology device. The school should pay the costs of training.

Transition Services and Plan

The IEP should also include and explain transition services for your child when they move from each school and then when transitioning into the community. The IEP must include a list of different agencies or service providers outside of school that may be needed to help your child. The IEP should also explain what assistive technology your child needs to live in the community and how the assistive technology will be provided. For more information about transition services, see Nebraska Advocacy Services, Inc. information sheet entitled "Tips on Transition Services."

What if a New Assistive Technology Device is Available?

If a new assistive technology device becomes available you may wish to ask your child's school to evaluate the new assistive technology device. The school will determine whether it will give your child more opportunities to be with students who do not have disabilities in the classroom or non-academic school activities.

Self-Study—Distance Learning

Back in the last century people were learning languages from books. Then as technology moved on, audio cassettes were added to practise listening. The next advance was to use video so that learners could appreciate the cultural environment of the language.

Computers started to be widely used for language learning only in the last 20 years. At first they were limited to text and the benefit of the computer was the interactivity that allowed immediate feedback to the learner. This enabled plenty of drilling on grammar and vocabulary but was not the most exciting of methods. The launch of the Windows 95 operating system opened the door to full multimedia programmes that could offer all that the traditional materials could do plus the innate computer feedback.

Today technology has moved on further. The development of the internet has now turned the computer into a communication centre. The general use of email has created new opportunities for teachers to assist learning at a distance.

This development of learning materials is naturally having an impact on traditional learning structures. Self-study used to mean trying to learn from books that were often little more than phrase books. Since learning a language is a hard task for the great majority of us, it is not surprising that self-study on its own was not very successful. Teachers were needed to provide information, motivation and guidance.

As learning materials become more comprehensive and motivating, you can make more and more progress on your own. The role of the teacher is changing. Basic information and drill can be provided by computer; the teacher is then free to concentrate on the more important aspects: motivation and production of language in speech or writing. Timing and degree of interaction between you and your teacher can be flexible. Of course in most educational institutions the curriculum and timetable are still very structured. But if you are learning in your own time, and probably at your own expense, you now have much more flexible options.

The latest development is a direct email link from self-study CD-ROMs to an online teacher. Now you can get personal one-to-one tuition from any multimedia PC with an internet connection.

One leading publisher has just launched a range of courses, not just for English but for French, German, Italian and Spanish as well. These courses are on CD-ROM and each language has 3 levels-beginner, intermediate and advanced.

When you need more help you simply email the tutor. The tutor will know which course you are following and your results to date so he is able to provide good, relevant advice. All you do is buy the CD-ROM at normal price and then get additional tuition as you feel the need. So the self-study becomes distance learning with all its advantages of flexibility and low cost.

Distance Learning Challenges

How to Overcome the Difficulties of Self-Study?: Distance learning students and tutors face unique challenges which must be overcome to ensure success. Students who plan to address the following challenges will help make achievement certain.

Isolation

The effects of feeling isolated are often underestimated. Support is always available, but students have to be proactive and seek it out. Look for support in the following areas:

- Other students on the course
- Tutor
- The institution
- Other students in the institution.

Keeping on Track

It can be difficult to stay on track as there's often something more interesting or more important to do. Make sure the complete study calendar is available and diarize key dates. Many institutions ensure that there are key deadlines, such as assignment hand-in dates or tutorials, as this helps students to stay on track. If not, then commit to some.

Make these dates as important as institution imposed deadlines. Include target dates for completing activities (not for starting them) and allow plenty of time to revise for any exams. Writing up assignments and final reports can be stressful so allow extra time for these. Check when holidays fall and adjust schedules accordingly.

Using a Library

These days a lot of information is available on the internet, but it still may be necessary to visit libraries to follow up reference material – either physically or online. Make sure access is organised ahead of time. Many distance learning institutions have agreements in place with local physical libraries so students can visit. Libraries are great places to study; quiet, with few distractions and an atmosphere conducive to learning.

Assignments and Feedback

An important part of learning is feedback and review of progress. Most distance learning institutions provide a feedback mechanism, such as assignments marked by tutors or online quizzes. Receiving feedback can be difficult. It's not just about "passing" or gaining a high score, as comments made by tutors can provide valuable help in how to move to the next level. If no feedback is given, students could ask for it. Being prepared for feedback in the right frame of mind will allow students to progress – feedback is rarely critical.

Reflection and Review

Start any distance learning course by thinking about the reasons for undertaking the course and what results are required. Write these down and keep them. Throughout the course, regularly check back to ensure progress is being made as this helps with motivation when the course gets tough. When feedback is received, review it in light of these learning objectives; to achieve the objectives, take the feedback on board. Work out what needs to change for next time.

Distance learning provides an extra set of challenges for students. Being aware of the challenges and planning to overcome them will help ensure success for both students and tutors.

Computer Assisted Instructions in Reading English at Higher Secondary Level

Technology is an ever-increasing part of the English Language arts classroom Today's teachers are developing new and exciting means of integrating Language writing and literature with innovative technologies.

The President of India, A.P.J. Abdul Kalam, formally launched the India-U.S. Edusat Network at Rashtrapati Bhavan on 8th December 2005. His advocacy for a knowledge grid connecting educational institutions, research facilities and industries is the logical follow-up of a series of measures that have been undertaken by Anna University to ensure that tele-teaching reaches even to the remotest corners of the state. This will enable the knowledge users to have access to high-performance computing environment, virtual reality, simulation systems, parallel/clustered servers, and super computer infrastructure from any end of the grid.

According to him, the whole purpose of education in a country was to develop and enhance the potential of human resource and progressively transform it, into a knowledge society. Every Nation wants to produce students who ultimately become the knowledge workers in their own economy to be global citizens. In the 21st Century, the need for competitiveness, in the field of Higher Education knows no bounds. In the words of Dr. Kalam, "The competitiveness is powered by knowledge power. Knowledge power is powered by innovation. Innovation is powered by science and technology and technology is powered by resource investment". (The Hindu, Friday, December 9, 2005).

The progress and growth of Technology in Higher Education is significant and it can be measured in terms of the excellent output in research – teaching – research cycle leading to societal transformation. Gartner has projected that the total Indian enterprise IT spending (not including consumer IT spend) including hardware, software, telecommunications and IT services will reach Rs. 1,903 billion in 2006, growing at a compounded annual growth rate (GAGR) of 20.8 per cent from 2004 to 2009. The aim of this paper is to focus on the 'Impact of Technology on Teaching and Learning in Higher Education'.

Education is facing a significant challenge in preparing students and teachers for future" knowledge based society". In recent years the educational access to digital information and communication technology (ICT) has grown dramatically. ICTs are quickly becoming more accessible, like computer, internet and WWW. ICTs are not single technology but it is a combination of hard'vare, software, media and delivery systems. ICT can influence much in developing teaching and learning environment in the following ways, which is quite different from older technologies.

Integration of multiple media : into single educational application.

Interactive and include the capacity to control, manipulate and contribute to information learning environment.

They are flexible offering freedom from rigid scheduling and from barriers of time and location.

Through connectivity they provide access to every other person on the planet who has a internet account, to hundreds and thousands of information archives and to million of web-pages.

Because of these differences, the teaching and learning environment finds new frontiers and educators are finding powerful new ways to integrate digital ICT into the curricula at the higher education levels, all over the world. Of course India is not an exception.

The various information and Communication technological tools such as web resources, educational CDs, computers, multimedia etc find place in teaching, learning, research, administration and data management. These ICT tolls have changed the learning styles of the students. Learning in the higher education level is not simply knowledge acquisition but knowledge 'managing' and knowledge 'creating'. Hence the present study attempts to find out the impact of ICT tools in the learning style, and awareness about these tools among graduate and postgraduate students, their attitude towards the integration of these tools in the learning process which enables the educational planners and policy makers to update or modify the present curriculum and methodology of teaching.

The impact of Technology on teaching and learning in Higher Education has enhanced students' achievement in mastering the following skills.

Basic Skills Instruction

- Computer assisted instruction to drill
- Multi-media software–teach to a variety of learning styles.
- Videodiscs–strengthen basic skills.
- Video and audio technologies–bring material to life.
- Distance learning –at least as effective as traditional methods of instruction.
- All forms–develop new skills related to use of technology itself, necessary in workplace.

A five-year report (1987-1992) by the Sacramento School District in California found that students using multimedia and telecommunications showed improved attitudes toward reading, social studies, and science and became more active and independent in learning. Some also showed improved reading scores. Whether Computer Assisted Instruction (CAI) can improve reading achievement of students has been a crucial question addressed by studies in the past. Many research studies reveled that Computer Assisted Instruction does have a positive effect on reading achievement. Although the effects of CAI in many studies were not homogeneous there seems to be no particular study characteristic that might have caused the heterogenity.

There is general agreement that reading is essential to success in our society. The ability to read is highly valued and important for social and economic advancement. The consensus supports the belief that reading is fundamental.

Most children learn to read fairly well. However there are children whose educational concerns are at risk because they do not read well enough to ensure understanding or to meet the demands of an increasingly competitive economy and changing demographics. It is the opinion of educators that not all of the children in schools are learning to read as well as they should. Many of them are experiencing serious difficulty in learning to read and as they progress through the grades they continue to lag in reading achievement.

Computer assisted instruction (CAI) is among the range of strategies being used to improve students achievement in school subjects including reading. Programs for CAI have come a long way since they were first developed over two decades ago. These programmes tutor and drill students diagnose problems, keep records of students progress, and present material in print and other manifestations. It is believed that they reflect what good teachers do in the class room.

Students are expected to benefit from CAI. Among the benefits that have been expected are better and more comfortable learning for students since they learn at their own pace and convenience; opportunities to work with vastly superior materials and more sophisticated problems; personalized tutoring; automatic measurement of progress, and others.

Teachers as well are expected to gain from CAI. Among the benefits that have been expected are better and more comfortable learning for students since they learn at as they experience less drudgery and repetition greater ease in up dating instruction materials, more accurate appraisal and documentation of students progress and more time to work directly with students. With increasing advances in computer technology Computer Assisted Instruction (CAI) is now seen by many as a method of providing relevant instruction for large number of students.

Learning from computers encompasses approaches to CAI in which the computer is used as a means for transmitting specific subject matter, such as reading. The flow of information is basically from the computer to the student with the computer presenting learning material or activities for student responses.

The computer retains records of the student's progress Through the course of study. Based on the degree of interaction between student and computer researches have identified three levels of CAI:

Drill and Practice: The computer provides the student with exercises that reinforce the learning of specific skills taught in the class room and supplies immediate feedback on the correctness of the response. Used in this manner, CAI functions as a supplement to regular classroom instruction and may be especially useful when a teacher does not have the time to work individually with each student. Drill and practice on the computer may also motivate students more than traditional work book exercises.

Tutorial : Tutorial CAI provides some information or clarifies certain concepts in addition to providing the student with practice exercises. In this sense the computer begins to take over actual instructional functions tailored to the student's individual level of achievement.

Dialogue : With this type of computer use the student takes an active role in interacting with the computer giving instructions in the form of a computer language so as to structure the student's own curriculum. The computer provides information, exercises and feed back Dialogue CAI is believed to come closest to actually substituting for regular instruction.

The verdict for the use of computers in education seems to be in. As stated by the National Center for Education statistics (NCES) computers have become an essential tool in our society. Early exposure to computers may help students gain the computer literacy that will be crucial for future success in the workplace. Access to computers at school and at home allows students to retrieve information, manipulate data and produce results efficiently and in innovative ways. Examining the extent to which students have access to computers at school and at home may be an indicator of how well-prepared students will be to enter an increasingly technological work place.

Has computer assisted instruction CAI produced benefits that result in greater achievement for students in this case in reading?

Soon after the introduction of CAI educational researches began to develop evaluation studies produced potentially useful information on the effects of CAI their messages were shrouded in ambiguity. One reason for unclear messages was that each evaluation report was published separately making the total picture somewhat murky.

Another problem had a deeper and more serious nature. These evaluation studies were never exact replications of one another. They differed in experimental design and execution, setting and the type of computer applications investigated. To confound matters evaluation findings or results tended to differ from one investigation to another findings from different studies differed from each other with some studies producing contradictory results. As well many of the reviews are typically narrative and discursive in presentation resulting in their multiplicity of findings not capable of being absorbed by the nearer without quantitative methods of reviewing.

Conclusions : Alarms about a "literacy crisis" among young people have been sounded on a regular basis for more than a century. Yet as each generation of students matures, it is able to accomplish the reading and writing tasks necessary for society to continue. Perhaps then, rather than sounding more alarms, it is time to consider what anxieties, particularly economic anxieties, drive the perpetual literacy.

Computer-Supported Collaborative Learning (CSCL) is often presented as a promising learning method. However, it is also facing some new challenges. Apart from answering the question of whether or not working with CSCL generates satisfying learning outcomes, it is important to determine whether or not all participants profit from collaboration, with the computer as a means of communication.

Students whose language, ethnicity and race are not represented in a school's dominant culture experience varying degrees of success in reading achievement, resulting in persistent gaps in reading achievement. Culturally responsive instruction can help to close that gap. This is teaching strategy capitalizes on the knowledge and literacy strategies students learn in their homes and communities.

Experiments that assign intact groups (usually schools) to treatment conditions are increasingly common in educational research. The design of group randomized experiments requires knowledge of the intraclass correlation structure to compute statistical power and to determine the sample sizes required to achieve adequate power.

Some researchers have argued that the different domains comprising language (e.g., phonology, semantics, and grammar) may influence reading development in a differential manner and at different developmental periods. The purpose of this study was to examine proposed causal relationships among different linguistic subsystems.

Use of Software for Individuals with Special Needs—Teaching, Remediation

Effective communication for a teacher with special needs children can develop a unique sense of confidence, which helps them to have greater engagement and classroom adjustment with their peer group. It is a means by which special needs children can be motivated for effective learning.

Effective communication helps them to understand something special of interest to them and of interest to their peers In this way both teachers and special children can understand each other and both can feel free in the teaching and learning process. Thus effective communication of teachers with special children can help to improve interpersonal relationships and to establish healthy contacts between teachers and students and students of special needs and their peers.

Effective communication helps to widen the horizon of special needs children. With effective communication special needs children can be made to feel important and recognize their individual identity in the society. It enables teachers to acquire adequate information about their special needs and to develop a suitable curriculum according to their special needs.

Effective communication helps in overcoming nervousness, stage fright, shyness and thus helps to improve the self image of special needs children. During effective communication, special needs children can express their feeling in a more better and expansive manner. With the help of effective communication, teachers can create an influence on special children.

Effective communication enables special needs children to become more organized, enhance the impressiveness of their self expression and helps them to effectively exchange and interpret their desires and feelings. Communication should be such that it makes the learning environment more pleasing and satisfying for students with special needs and special modes of learning.

Thus effective communication can help special needs children in their social adjustment. It can help special needs children to form an impressive personality. Effective communication can help special needs children to develop understanding among each other and among their peers. Effective communication will help special needs children to be more pleasant, active, increase their performance level, and help them positively march towards the path of life success.

Applications of Educational Technologies for Pre-service and In-service Programmes

Current technological advances have become the impetus for a large number of reform efforts for the U.S. education system. Two fundamental questions seem to frame the discussions about these educational changes. The first question, What technological skills will workers need in an information-based society? determines the teaching content across the various disciplines, whereas the second question, Can current technologies improve the way we learn and teach? explores technology as an instructional tool. This dual function of technology as instructional content and as instructional tool, as described by Fulton (1998), provides the underlying definition for the discussion in this section of what "technological fluency" or "technological literacy" actually means in the context of FL education and, consequently, for FL teacher preparation. Fulton states, "Today's definition of technological fluency evolves from the intersection created by the *technological pull* [italics added]—that is, advances in what technology can do, and how it is used in the world beyond the classroom—as well as the *pedagogical push* [italics added]—changing views of learning reflected in the educational standards and assessments that drive instruction."

The Technological Pull

Most educational visions for the next decades recognize the need for change in education due to the driving force of information technology "generating the great transformation of economic, political, and social life in recent years. Information has become central to every domain of human life and pervasive in every venue of human existence. Human beings have always had the task of obtaining, integrating, and using information as a basis for their thoughts and actions, but at no point in human history has day-to-day life for the preponderance of the population put them in such proximity with informational resources of the culture" (Bosco, 1995). Based on the premise that "success as a nation will depend substantially on our students' ability to acquire skills and knowledge necessary for high-technology work and informed citizenship" (*Getting America's students ready for the 21 century*, 1996), the U.S. government issued the "Technology Literacy Challenge" calling for every young person to enter the workforce technologically literate in the 21 century. Consequently, students will have to develop new skills to use advanced technologies effectively in the "information-based society," while schools in turn have to provide the necessary tools and training in the area of technology to prepare students for the challenges ahead of them.

What exactly are these new "skills" that are required of students in order to learn, work, and flourish in the digital age? According to the Department of Labor report *What Work Requires of Schools*, the Secretary's Commission on Achieving Necessary Skills (1991) identified a core of basic skills, thinking skills, and personal qualities, as well as five competencies that are the "hallmarks of today's expert worker:"

1. identify, organize, plan, and allocate resources;
2. work with others;

3. acquire and use information;
4. understand complex interrelationships;
5. work with a variety of technologies.

According to this report, preliminary studies show that the educational use of newer technologies, such as computer-based information and communication tools, linked with constructivist learning models help to prepare students better to meet the demands of a skilled worker in an information based society. For example, the U.S. Department of Education claims that "access to computer-generated simulations, videodiscs, the Internet, and software on CD-ROM offers students experiences available nowhere else—experiences that students will need for the 21 century. In fact, students with extensive access to technology learn how to organize complex information, recognize patterns, draw inferences, and communicate findings. ... They exhibit superior organizational skills as compared to students in more traditional high school programmes" (*Getting America's students ready*, 1996). (See also The Secretary's Commission, 1991; Carnegie Forum, 1986, President's Commission, 1992.)

Even though, at this time, the FL profession cannot point to adequate research data indicating students' higher performance level due to the use of educational technologies than without, and even though FL educators may question the effectiveness of applying technology in acquiring a second language (e.g., Schwartz, 1995), it is indisputable that the current, mostly computer-based technologies, are changing those professional profiles that include FL components. For instance, students who want to succeed in global market situations and in multicultural settings need to be trained in combining their technological skills with their linguistic and cross-cultural knowledge. The expansion of transportation and communication, the international trade growth, new international political orders, and the rising population of people who use languages other than English provide new global contexts for intercultural communications and require changing professional profiles that involve international standards, training, and accreditation (Brecht & Walton, 1995). Consequently, in an information-based society, workers of the 21 century also have to be able to make use of electronic communication tools in order to access, interpret, and evaluate information beyond their own linguistic and cultural borders.

This need for new "global communication skills" combined with the use of newer technologies not only strengthens the arguments for foreign language learning but also challenges traditional views of foreign language teaching and learning. For instance, Brecht and Walton (1995) argue that teaching "global communication management" strategies, in particular cross-cultural skills and self-managed learning, must play a greater role in preparing students for the future, and that, therefore, colleges and universities should be structured around two basic premises.

First and most commonly accepted, learning is lifelong; and so the instructional task of the formal educational system is to provide the students not only with a basic set of facts and skills, but also to enable students to manage new and developing knowledge throughout their lives. Second and less well understood, more and more knowledge is generated, stored, transmitted, and applied across cultural lines. Accordingly, success in any aspect of 'knowledge management' requires an understanding of sociological and cultural basis of knowledge as well as the skills to manage communications across cultural lines.

Brecht and Walton's argument that in a global market the demand for cross-cultural skills will be greater than for foreign language skills seems to be confirmed by Fixman's (1990) study in which companies were asked in which way(s) foreign language competence and cross-cultural skills played a role in their hiring practices. Even though this study was conducted on a very small scale, one preliminary conclusion that can be drawn from it is that most of these companies separated cultural and linguistic proficiency and valued cross-cultural skills more than language skills.

The Pedagogical Push

The changing job profiles for an information-based society bring about a number of challenges for the educational system charged with preparing students adequately for these new roles. How can FL educators equip students with skills and cultural knowledge bases required in an information-based society? How can technology itself help to facilitate the learning and teaching process? And how can colleges and universities prepare FL teachers for effective technology integration into their curriculum and classroom activities so that they in turn can guide their students?

In an effort to find answers to these complex and intricate questions, many FL experts, such as Nina Garrett (1991a), call for more fundamental research and stronger research paradigms in the area of language learning and processing. Garrett states, "The most important requirement is that teachers and students alike should have a clear and purposeful idea of how each use of technology is expected to contribute to language learning, and that, of course, begins with a clear notion of how language learning happens." Indeed, we need to collect research data on a large scale and over a substantial period of time in order to investigate the effectiveness of computer-based technologies used to learn specific linguistic and cultural skills in specific learning environments, and even technology itself may be a valuable tool to collect and analyze research data.

In addition, more research data (as well as closer collaboration between schools, colleges, and governmental institutions) are needed to clearly identify the challenges teachers and teacher educators may still be facing today when trying to integrate technologies into FL curricula and classrooms (see Bernhardt & Hammadou, 1987; Coleman, 1991; Jarvis & Taylor, 1990; Matthews, 1994; Schrier, 1994; Tedick & Walker, 1995). However, all of these questions about the effectiveness of various technologies in FL learning cannot be answered if we do not explore the potentials of the newer technologies by actually using them in the classroom.

The Need for Technology Training

Given the obvious benefits of current technologies, for example, access to an abundance of authentic multimedia resources via the Internet and the motivational influence they have on students, it is not surprising that more and more FL teachers use computer-based classroom activities. A recent national survey (Branaman & Rhodes, 1998) of foreign language instruction in elementary and secondary schools by the Center for Applied Linguistics reveals that in 1997 computer-based instructional materials were used by 41% of elementary schools with foreign language programmes versus 14% in 1987 and by 57% of secondary schools with foreign language programmes versus 20% in 1987. While these numbers sound promising, the authors concede that they "do not have data on the effectiveness of technology in the language classroom." In other words, we do not know what kind of computer-based applications foreign language teachers use, how (if at all) they are integrated into lesson plans and curricula, and most important, how much computer-based activities improve the learning environment.

While these numbers demonstrate a more than 50% growth rate within a decade, they also reveal that one half of the teacher population either does not have access to computer technologies, does not have adequate training in evaluating, selecting, applying, and integrating technology into the FL classrooms and curricula, or does not see the potential of technologies to enhance FL instruction. Access, then, does not merely mean sufficient computers for teachers and students but also "the need to modify the curriculum and train teachers to use new technologies appropriately" (Otto & Pusack, 1996).

Similar studies in education in general as compiled in a 1996 report by the U.S. Department of Education mirror the situation in the area of FL instruction. That report states that "[o]nly 14 percent of public school teachers had more than 8 hours of training (in-service or professional development programmes) in the area of educational technology in the 1993-94 school year," and "as many as 50 percent of teachers had little or no experience at all with technology in the classroom" (*Getting America's students ready*, 1996; see also Milken Family Foundation & International Society for Technology in Education [ISTE], 1999).

Another national study about computer use in K-12 classrooms (all subject areas) by the governmental agency Office of Technology Assessment (OTA) shows that "overall, teacher education in the United States does not prepare graduates to use technology as a teaching tool" (Office of Technology Assessment, 1995). According to OTA, if teachers use computers, they generally use them for low-level tasks such as drills and word processing and that they do not sufficiently integrate them across the K-12 curriculum.

Among the reasons for this inadequate technology integration into K-12 classrooms, OTA cites that most of the money is spent on hardware and software and very little on teacher training, that teacher educators and teachers are often unaware of the resources technology can offer them, that they struggle with technology integration into the curriculum, that new teachers graduate from teacher preparation institutions with limited knowledge of the ways technology can be used in their professional practice, and that federal government has tended to focus more on inservice than preservice education (see also Northrup & Little, 1996). The results of a report by Technology: The training of staff (1997) for the National Education Association confirm the findings by OTA by claiming that at least 50% of today's school teachers have not had adequate training and technical assistance in the area of technology. Only 18 states require technology training as part of their school teacher certification processes. Thus, many teachers enter the profession with only cursory exposure to computers as a learning or teaching resource.

All of these studies, including the results of the most recent report by the International Society of Technology in Education (ISTE), clearly demonstrate the need for preservice and inservice technology training that goes beyond the use of hardware and software (see Milken & ISTE, 1999). Drawing similar conclusions, Garrett (1996) summarizes that "[t]hey [teachers] also need a new in-depth understanding of how technology use affects teaching and learning. Very few teachers have had any preservice training, or more than an occasional conference workshop session, in how to evaluate the pedagogical design of existing software, how to think about pedagogical design when they want to author software, how to integrate students' outside-of-class technology into their curriculum, or how to evaluate what technology use is accomplishing for their students." But even though there are still many questions left unanswered as to how advanced technologies can be used most effectively in the FL classroom and as to how and by whom FL teachers should receive training in the use of technology, FL programmes with teacher education programmes have to react to the changing professional profiles of the workforce in globally oriented, information-based societies.

Researching Technology Integration Models

After establishing a rationale for the need of offering technology training for students in our FL teacher education programme, the question of how the department could best integrate technology instruction into our existing programme was addressed. Gillingham and Topper's (n. d.) descriptions and critical analyses of four different technology integration models of teacher preparation in "flexible and adaptive technology use" were especially useful to us in determining which approach would fit our needs and would also be feasible at our institution:

1. Single course approach;
2. Program infusion approach;
3. Individual student performance approach;
4. Case-based approach.

These curricular models have been developed for teaching technology in education and are, therefore, generic in nature, but their constituent parts are readily adaptable and applicable to technology curricula in FL teacher preparation programmes. Research on these four approaches has revealed both benefits and drawbacks as the following condensed version of Gillingham and Topper's discussion shows.

Single Course Approach

One of the benefits of a single course approach is that it takes faculty workloads into account and is easy for students to enroll in and complete. The accomplishments are readily visible from a student transcript, and the course can be taught by expert faculty who have both knowledge in technology use in the classroom and in the subject matter. A single course approach is also easier to implement than the others because it is just an add-on to the existing curriculum. This last point has also an obvious downside because there is often times no room in the programme of study to add a course, and, if such a course is added, it is often no more than a survey course of computer systems and software which does not provide enough focus on technology integration into the curriculum and classroom activities. And finally, Gillingham and Topper argue that a single course as a separate entity in the teacher education programme gives students only a one-time exposure to technology, and its course content can be easily forgotten.

Technology Infusion Approach

In the technology infusion approach, aspects of technology are placed within each course of a teacher preparation programme. Advocates of the infusion approach claim that the use of technology in educational settings "can no longer be relegated to a single technology course, separate from isolated workshops, or one topic in a given course. Technology must be fully integrated into college programmes and its use modeled by faculty throughout the college, not just in the school/college of education" (Faison, 1996). According to Gillingham and Topper, the major benefit is students' long-term exposure to technology and technology modeling within subject matter courses. However, on the downside, the technology infusion model suffers from inconsistent implementation and administrative difficulties in calculating faculty workloads, faculty instruction time, and faculty support. Faculty may need special support systems to encourage them to use technology in their classrooms that include examples and incentives. Finally, this kind of approach is not readily apparent on students' transcripts.

Beyond the reasoning for and against the infusion approach by Gillingham and Topper, this author finds that using modeling as the only teaching strategy presupposes that all educators in the teacher training programme have the necessary pedagogic knowledge and technological skills, as well as the necessary equipment, to provide exemplary models of technology integration into the classroom. But even if well trained educators could provide pedagogically and technologically sound models, the infusion approach still would not involve teacher candidates in the planning and assessment stages of using technology in a class period or in the curriculum. Mere class observation and perhaps some hands-on experience with technology do not reveal all the methodological considerations educators have to take into account before, during, and after the actual use of technology in the classroom. For instance, teacher candidates need to learn to address issues such as selecting, implementing, and evaluating different kinds of technologies, finding adequate resources, determining whether technology helps to achieve learning goals, and integrating technology into specific classroom activities.

Individual Student Performance Approach

This approach places the final responsibility of technology knowledge on students rather than on faculty. Several times during their programme, students choose their technology-enhanced projects and performances from a number of categories. On the positive side, students do not have to relearn information they already know; they can concentrate on advancing their existing knowledge. Students have long-term exposure to technology, develop a habit of life-long learning about technology, and learn to implement and model technology within subject matter courses.

This approach involves self-directed learning and is followed by an assessment of technology proficiency. On the negative side, it is more difficult for the teacher educator to keep track of individual student performances and to assess performances at different technology competency levels. Again, students' expertise in technology applications may not be apparent from entries on standard transcripts.

Case-Based Approach

The last of the four approaches discussed by Gillingham and Topper, the case-based teacher education model, is the inclusion of a series of cases in which teachers use technology as part of a broad case-based teacher preparation programme. Prospective teachers study and reflect on the efforts of teachers who have incorporated technology into their classroom practice.

In the case studies, students examine lessons and units which have been collected from field experiences and teachers share their perspectives on how technology has shaped their classroom environments. For instance, the LETSNet project at Michigan State University provides some cases in FL instruction (http://commtechlab.msu.edu/ameritech/).

The obvious benefits to students are that these models in subject areas are used to develop and adapt similar models for their own classroom. So far, however, only a limited number of case studies in foreign languages are available that demonstrate the uses of newer technologies in the foreign language classroom.

Addressing Student Needs and Institutional Constraints

After we had researched these existing models of technology integration, we came to the same conclusion as Gillingham and Topper who point out that "(e)ach method requires various programme compromises in order to fit within the constraints of student and faculty loads and other institutional requirements." We opted for an eclectic approach that extracts pertinent facets from the single course approach and the programme infusion approach. As our eclectic approach evolves over time, we anticipate the inclusion of elements of the case-based approach as well. We launched a curricular initiative to incorporate a new—still experimental—2-3 credit hour course entitled "Technologies in Foreign Language Teacher Education" into the existing curricula for the teacher education tracks in French, German, Russian, and Spanish.

The decision to apply this hybrid model to our teacher education programme was based on factors such as

- time (the department cannot wait until everyone is ready for an infusion model because of the implication that all the teacher education faculty must have a fairly homogenous level of technology proficiency);

- faculty training (faculty in FL departments have diverse academic backgrounds that do not always include adequate pedagogic and technological expertise);
- a separate technology course entry on students' transcripts stands out as an additional qualification for teacher candidates.

Another reason why we opted for this model was that traditional courses in FL methodology do not afford enough time to discuss in-depth the details of the use of technology in the FL classroom or to give prospective FL teachers hands-on experience with technologies that can enhance FL instruction.

Of course, we also faced a number of obstacles. For example, concerns were voiced by those who question the validity of the claims that technology enhances language learning, by those who oppose increased credit hour requirements for graduation, by faculty members of the College of Education who already teach courses in educational technology (and fear for loss of territory), by those who question the need for discipline specific courses or programmes in educational technology, and by administrators who have to address issues such as additional staffing, faculty development, funding, and resource requirements.

A number of publications in professional journals summarized by Northrup and Little (1996) confirmed our arguments to select a model that allows us to gradually shift to a fully integrated approach.

Roblyer (1994) recommends that full infusion of technology into all methods and content course work should be the eventual goal. However, the infusion approach, though successful in some institutions (Todd, 1993), does not appear to be working at this time. It is recommended that a separate instructional technology course providing a combination of technical and integration skills should be included (Roblyer, 1994). The course should have a problem-oriented approach with projects and meaningful instructional activities. Handler (1993) and Wetzel (1993) recommend a similar structure for educating undergraduate teacher education majors in the application and use of instructional technology. Initially, a technology course should be taught independent of other courses, with technology modeled throughout other courses.

Our decision to house the technology component in our department rather than in the College of Education follows the recommendation by ISTE (Milken & ISTE, 1999) that "to increase the technology proficiency of new teachers in K-12 classrooms, training institutions should increase the level of technology integration in their own academic programmes," and it follows a discernable trend in the field of education towards a specialization of technology instruction relative to subject areas, for "it has become more content-specific and more theory laden" (Willis & Mehlinger, 1996; see also Hammond-Darling, Wise, & Klein, 1995).

At UNI, the combination of technical and integration skills in one course as suggested by Roblyer (as cited in Northrup & Little, 1996), is actually split into two technology courses required for all teacher candidates. Foreign language education majors can select one out of two technology courses (2-3 credit hours each) mandated for education majors and offered through the College of Education, and they are required to take the newly developed technology course (2-3 credit hours) housed in the Department of Modern Languages. While the course for all education majors emphasizes

the technical skills of students, the course for FL majors emphasizes technology integration into the subject area. In this new model, foreign language majors with a teaching emphasis in secondary education have to fulfill the following graduation requirements at our institution: General Education Courses (47 credit hours); Professional Education (32 credit hours); Major, Minor, Electives (51 credit hours). As part of the licensing requirement within the subject area for the preservice portion, students have to register for three courses in the area of foreign language pedagogy:

- The Teaching of Foreign Languages (3 credit hours)
- Practicum (2 credit hours)
- Technology in Foreign Language Teaching (2-3 credit hours).

Even though the three courses are formally separate entities, they are closely articulated and conducted as an integrated whole. The three courses are designed to avoid overlap in the course content which guarantees that students have the necessary tools to continuously progress and to build their professional portfolios.

National Technology Goals and Standards for Teachers

Our particular curricular model was not only framed by institutional conditions but also by the need to include national technology goals and standards. While most of the goals and standards as defined by governmental agencies and various professional organizations include sections on technology, only a few go beyond general references about the need for technology integration into teacher education programmes. Parts of two guidelines, however, the "ISTE Recommended Foundations in Technology for all Teachers" (1995) and the "ACTFL Provisional Program Guidelines for Foreign Language Teacher Education" (1992) were helpful in the design of our technology course.

The ISTE Recommendations provided the overarching goals under which we subsumed discipline specific objectives, and the ACTFL Guidelines acted as defining framework for establishing the outline and content areas for the new course on technology in FL teaching. Although under discussion, the state of Iowa has not yet implemented any standards for teacher education programmes, and, therefore, we could not take state standards into consideration for our curriculum changes. However, it is important to point out that more and more states across the country are adopting policies and programmes to enhance standards for teacher education programmes in order to ensure that teachers are well trained for requisite professional tasks.

Even though the ISTE Recommendations have been developed as standards for educational technology components in general education typically housed in Colleges of Education, we had two major reasons for using the ISTE guidelines as a framework for our new technology course. First, as mentioned before, teacher education programmes seem to move into the direction of providing prospective teachers with a more integrated educational experience that combines pedagogy, knowledge of the subject area, subject area pedagogy, and technology. Therefore, FL education programmes and general teacher education programmes should coordinate their standards and goals and articulate curricular components. Second, as announced in the 1998 spring issue of the *ACTFL newsletter*, ACTFL (and TESOL) have become constituent members of the National Council for the Accreditation of Teacher Education (NCATE) in an effort to advance and to strengthen standards for professional teacher preparation. NCATE is a partnership of national organizations whose goal it is to set professional standards for colleges and universities with teacher preparation programmes.

It recognizes the standards developed by the National Board of Professional Teaching Standards which in turn recognizes the ISTE Recommendations as national benchmarks for teacher technology training. In the future, if FL education programmes seek professional accreditation, it can be inferred that they will have to be in compliance with the national teaching standards recognized by NCATE. Since the technology courses offered in the College of Education at our institution addresses the hands-on use of technology as described in Goal Area A of the ISTE Recommendations, the Department of Modern Languages decided to focus on Goal Areas B and C which can easily be adopted and/or modified for integrated, subject-based technology instruction.

The ACTFL Provisional Program Guidelines for FL Teacher Education provide specifications "intended to serve a programme development function; that is, to represent forward-looking views as to what knowledge, skills and experiences are deemed by the profession as holding the most promise for the preparedness of foreign language teacher candidates" (Gunterman, 1993). At the same time, these guidelines and subsequent discussions should assist FL programmes in assessing their teacher education programmes in terms of the overall effectiveness of the programme and in making strategic decisions for the future. The Guidelines center around three areas in the preservice preparation of FL teachers: (a) Personal Development (focus on a strong liberal arts background), (b) Professional Development (focus on knowledge and experience in pedagogy), and (c) Specialist Development (focus on knowledge and skills in the area of language and culture) (Gunterman, 1993). Even though all three areas directly or indirectly address the need for adequate technology training opportunities for teacher candidates in the FL education programme, the most relevant categories for defining goals and content areas for technology courses are Area III Curricular Development and Area IV Instruction, both of which are part of the Professional Development sequence.

UNIT-X

Policies and Legislations for Special Education & Rehabilitation

International Legislations for Special Education

In addition to assurances of civil rights of students with disabilities, other legislation exists that addresses their educational rights. The first major law that guaranteed the right to a public education for all children, ages 5 to 21, was the Education for All Handicapped Children Act of 1975.

The Education for the Handicapped Act (EHA) (P.L. 94-142)

The Education for all Handicapped Children Acts is more commonly known as the EHA; it had as its purpose:

- To guarantee a Free and Appropriate Public Education (FAPE) for all children with disabilities, ages 5-21
- Special Education and related services must be free, provided by the public agency at no cost to the parents
- Appropriate education is the provision of regular and special education and related services designed to meet students' individual educational needs.
- To develop an Individualized Education Program (IEP) for each child eligible for special education and related services; plan is based on multi-disciplinary assessment and includes a statement of specific special education and related services to be provided to the child.

- To the maximum extent appropriate, all children and youth with disabilities will be educated in the least restrictive education (LRE) environment
- Parents have the right to participate in every decision related to the identification, evaluation, and placement of their child. Parents must give consent for any initial evaluation, assessment or placement decision. Due process procedures assure parents rights to appeal.

EHA Amendments

1986 Amendments (P.L. 99-457) Preschool and Infant/ Toddler Programs

In 1986, an amendment to the EHA, extended the purpose of EHA to include children ages 0-5 and included:

- To extend the guarantee to a Free and Appropriate Public Education (FAPE) to children with disabilities, ages 3-5.
- To establish Early Intervention Programs (EIP) for infants and toddlers with disabilities, ages 0-2
- To develop an Individualized Family Service Plan (IFSP) for each family with an infant/toddler with disabilities

1990 Amendments (P.L. 101-476)

In 1990, amendments were again added to EHA, considerably adding components to the law:

- To rename the EHA as the Individuals with Disabilities Education Act (IDEA). The amendment also replaced the phrase "handicapped child" with "child with a disability".
- To provide Transition Services for students by age 16
- To extend eligibility to children with autism and traumatic brain injury
- To define Assistive Technology Devices and Services for children with disabilities for inclusion in the IEP
- To extend the Least Restrictive Environment (LRE) to require the child, to the maximum extent appropriate,

be educated with children without disabilities — in the same class s/he would have been but for the disability

1997 Amendments (P.L. 105-17)

1997 amendments further strengthened the rights of students with disabilities.

- To extend LRE as an assurance that all students would have "access to the general curriculum"
- To "consider" Assistive Technology Devices and Services on the IEP's of all students. Use of school-purchased AT in a child's home or other settings is required if the child needs access to those devices to receive FAPE.
- To include orientation and mobility services to the list of related services for children who are blind or have visual impairments, as well as for other children who may also need instruction in traveling around their school, or to and from school.

National Legislation

The Status of Children with Disabilities

Around 10% of the world's population, or 650 million people, live with a disability. They are the world's largest minority. 20% of the world's poorest people are disabled, and tend to be regarded in their own communities as the most disadvantaged. 80% of persons with disabilities live in developing countries

Between 120 and 150 million disabled children and young people live in the world. Less than 10 % of these children attend school. The global literacy rate for adults with disabilities is as low as 3 % and 1% for women with disabilities. 30% of street youths are disabled. Violence against children with disabilities occurs at annual rates at least 1.7 times greater than for their non-disabled peers. For every child killed during armed conflicts, three are injured and permanently disabled. Comparative studies on disability legislation shows that only 45 countries have anti-discrimination and other disability-specific acts.

Disability is a source of stigma for the child and his/her family. They are ostracized and looked down upon by the community. Children with physical, psycho-social, intellectual or sensory impairments encounter in their daily lives a combination of social, cultural, behavioral and physical barriers. Those suffering from mental illness or mental retardation are subject to the worst stigma and severe social exclusion.

Children with impairments are particularly exposed to discrimination from individuals, community and institutions that fail in their obligation to protect them and to include them in society. They have little or no access to basic social services, especially education and health. The majority of these children (about 90%) remains out of school and is completely illiterate.

In daily life, their abilities and capacities are underestimated and their needs are given low priority. Their civic, social and political rights are violated or neglected in almost all areas of their lives and they are for example largely deprived of personal freedoms as well as of effective and full participation in family life and in society. They are also especially vulnerable to neglect, physical abuse, sexual violence, exploitation and they lack recognition of their equal humanity by their families and communities. They are less likely to obtain preventive care police intervention or legal protection. Girls with disabilities suffer still further discrimination, experiencing exclusion on account of their gender and their disability. They are more likely to be abandoned, discriminated against, and excluded from education, marriage and motherhood. They are also particularly vulnerable to all kinds of abuse.

The situation of these children is slightly improving, but there are still severe gaps both between and within countries. In many countries, local groups and NGOs have joined forces to create regional or national organisations that have lobbied for reform and changes to legislation. However many countries have not enacted protective legislation at all and physical barriers to their integration remain.

What are the Preventable Causes and Factors of Disability

The majority of factors for disabilities are genetic, biological and birth defects. They are also largely preventable when they are linked to natural disasters and war, lack of health care and poverty. It is possible to reduce the secondary impacts of disabilities in promoting early intervention.

The most significant causes of disability include:

- Communicable disease;
- Insufficient or inaccessible health care services and inadequate sanitation;
- Natal complications such as lack of oxygen to the foetal brain, haemorrhage or precipitate birth;
- Early motherhood and lack of required care of the mother during her pregnancy;
- Infection in early childhood like meningitis, encephalitis, polio or head injuries;
- Nutritional deficiencies;
- Consanguineous marriages;
- Use of toxic drugs.

Several protection issues may increase risk of disability, such as trafficking, physical abuse and corporal punishment, sexual abuse and sexual exploitation of children. Children living on streets or without any parental care are also particularly exposed to accidents causing physical disability.

Situation in India

- Facts and figures.

Disabled population within the age-group 0-19 by type of disability						
Total disabled population	21906 769	Type of disability				
In Seeing	In Speech	In hearing	Physical	Mental		
10634881	1640868	1261722	6105477	2263821		
Disabled population in 0-19 age-group	7 732 196	3605553	775561	90452	2263941	796689
Disabled children as % of total population in 0-19 age-group	1.67%	0.78%	0.17%	0.01%	0.48%	0.17%
Disabled children as % of total disabled population	35.29%	33.9%	47.26%	23.02%	37.08%	35.19%

The Indian Census 2001 reports that 21.9 million persons in the Indian total population (2.13%) are disabled, and that 1.67% of the total population within the age-group 0-19 years

(7 million) are living with disability. This data includes persons with visual, hearing, speech, physical and mental impairments.

Of all persons with disability, 35.9% are in the 0-19 age-group. One in every 10 children is born with, or acquires, a physical, mental or sensory disability. 75% of the disabilities are preventable. Only 1% of children with disability have access to education. Hardly 50% of disabled children reach adulthood, and no more than 20% survive to cross the fourth decade of life. However some other estimates state that India has some 40 to 80 million persons living with disability. Even today, data related to disability among adults and children varies from one source to another. Lack of reliable figures regarding children living with disabilities and the different types of disabilities they face has been an obstacle in planning and making adequate interventions.

This illustrates the insignificance accorded to the lives of the disabled children. There is a need for a more accurate data collection and for harmonizing definitions of disability in government surveys and the Indian census.

- *Vulnerability of Children With Disabilities:* Indian society continues to treat disability with indifference, pity or revulsion. Low literacy, school enrolment and employment rates as well as widespread social stigma are making disabled people among the most excluded in Indian society and deter them from taking an active part in the family or community. Among them, disabled from birth, disabled children and disabled women are less likely to seek health care.

There is also stark regional disparity. In general, states that lack social, welfare and health services also fail to care children with disabilities. Those suffering from mental health disorders face the worst stigma and social exclusion. Mental illness account for nearly a sixth of all health-related disorders but India spends less than 1% of its total health budget on mental health.

Despite years of public intervention, a growing disability rights movement and one of the most progressive policy frameworks for persons with disabilities, only a few disabled people have access to aids and appliances. India falls short in implementation and in accountability of public funds devoted to disability, lacks resources and strong monitoring mechanisms. Poor enforcement of the existing legislation means that disabled people in India continue to be discriminated against in terms of access to basic services and opportunities.

A large number of disabilities in India are preventable, including those arising from malnutrition, accidents and injuries as well as medical issues during pregnancy or birth. However, the health sector most of the time is too weak to react on time or proactively to disability, especially in the rural areas. There are few special services for disabled children. Paediatric units at government hospitals are incapable of dealing with children with disabilities as they lack infrastructure and resources. Very little research has been done in the areas of mental or physical disability. Children with disabilities are 4 to 5 times less likely to be enrolled in school. If they remain in school, they rarely progress beyond primary levels. The main barriers they face to access school include: lack of specialised teachers for both physically and mentally challenged children, absence of teacher training programmes, absence of disabled-friendly infrastructure, including ramps, special chairs and toilet facilities as well as the mockery of adults and other children.

People with disabilities are generally considered ineligible to marry to people without disabilities unless "adjusted" by high dowry. Disabled girls are usually married to older men, leading to a higher incidence of widowhood.

International and National Framework

International Framework: The United Nations Convention for the rights of children has special provisions for disabled children. Article 2 (link with UN CRC, pdf doc) provides all children with the enjoyment of all rights and freedoms set out in the UN CRC, including for children with disability.

A Special Rapporteur on Disability of the UN Commission for Social Development was also appointed in 1994.

In 1997 the Committee of the right of the child (internal links with the part Child Portection and Child Right/Operational mechanisms/ International level/The Committee) devoted its *Day of General Discussion* to children with disabilities. It resulted in an elaborated set of recommendations.

In October 2006, the Committee on the Rights of the Child published a *General Comment* on "The Rights of Children with Disabilities." This General Comment provides guidance and assistance to States parties in their efforts to implement the rights of children with disabilities and the provisions of the Convention for the rights of children. On 13 December 2006, the United Nations General Assembly adopted a new Convention on the rights of persons with disabilities. It adopted also the same day an Optional Protocol on the rights of persons with disabilities.

India signed the Convention on 30 th March 2007 and ratified it on 1 st October 2007. The Convention introduces a specific article on awareness-raising to promote respect for the dignity of people with disabilities and new obligations on government and non government actors to take all the necessary measures to ensure that the rights of disabled are fulfilled. It recognizes the rights of disabled people to participation in their community (Article 19), to equal participation in public, political (Article 29) and cultural life (Article 30).

The Convention also includes specific provisions for children with disabilities referring to the respect for the evolving capacities of children and to their right to preserve their identities. It provides them with the same rights and freedoms as all children, with particular reference to the rights to be protected from exploitation, violence and abuse; to express their views on all issues which affect them (Article 7) and to access to justice (Article???)

Measures must be taken to ensure that children with disabilities are registered immediately after birth as well as to provide rehabilitation services and specific legislation to ensure that violations of their rights are identified and effectively investigated. Children with disabilities should be provided with all necessary support and technical aids to access to general education as well as with equal access to participation in play, recreation, and sporting activities.

National Framework: The Persons with disabilities (Equal Opportunities, Protection of Rights and Full Participation) Act, 1995. This Act provides for both preventive and promotional aspects of rehabilitation such as education, vocational training, job reservation, research and manpower development, creation of barrier-free environment, rehabilitation of persons with disability, special insurance scheme for the disabled employees and establishment of homes for persons with severe disability, etc.

The Mental Health Act, 1987

This Act consolidates and amends the Indian Lunacy Act, 1912 relating to the treatment and care of mentally ill persons, with a clear aim to making better provision with respect to the management of their properly and affairs.

National Policy for Persons with Disabilities, 2006

The National Policy recognizes the dignity of persons with disabilities and seeks to create an environment that provides them protection of their rights and freedoms as well as full participation in society. It focuses especially on prevention of disability, rehabilitation measures, education, protection of children and women with disabilities. A list of Regional Conventions, Declarations or National Legislations adopted in different countries on Disability is available on CRIN website:

Some Initiatives Developed to Tackle Child Disabilities

A real political will and a strong social commitment are necessary to investigate and put into practice the most effective initiatives to prevent discrimination against children with disabilities as well as to act to reduce disabilities with the participation of all levels of society. Children with disabilities have special needs that society must address. Disability can be gradually addressed through a range of methods, including information, advocacy and family counselling, strengthening policy and facilitating access to medical or psychological services. This includes preventive health programmes, early detection and screen of all children at a young age. The quantity and quality of these medical infrastructures have to be developed.

Efforts to address discrimination against children with disabilities must include initiatives to ensure their full integration by overcoming stigma, promoting newer thinking and better understanding of disability. Workshops, local campaigns as well as publications or TV spots are useful tools to increase awareness and understanding of disability. These initiatives against discrimination may also have the positive effect of preventing the development of discriminatory attitudes towards those with disabilities in future generations. It is essential to develop awareness actions especially among disabled children and their families as well as among health professionals, teachers, in schools and communities.

There is a need to spread awareness of the existing laws, to ensure their implementation, to develop more disability-friendly facilities and programmes and to favour a better coordination of the existing programmes. A specialized education for children with intellectual or sensory disabilities is necessary as a specific t eacher's training programmes. Education is important for them as it contributes to their overall development. Through appropriate teaching and training they can even be taught life-supporting skills, which can provide them an opportunity to earn a decent living. It is indeed of utter importance to empower disabled young adults with employable skills and to encourage the private sector to employ people with disabilities. The question of children with disabilities living in poverty should also be addressed by allocating adequate budgetary resources as well as by ensuring their access to social protection and poverty reduction programmes.

The link between disability and protection must be recognized and adequate support services should be provided for those who are disabled in the various fields of health, nutrition, technology, education, employment, sports or culture. Various government and non-government organizations are committed in these initiatives. A primary object is to promote access to social services for children with disabilities, so that they are encouraged to become functionally independent through opportunities of medical rehabilitation, education, vocational training and socio-economic rehabilitation. It is also necessary to help children with disabilities to become active participants in their family or community.

National Policy on Education with Reference to Programme of Action 1992

Educational Management System

The National Policy on Education (NPE) is comprehensive and envisages wide-ranging action on a variety of issues and problems. Yet it seeks a convergence of such action to secure a total and coordinated impact. It also reaches beyond the education sector to link effectively with other sectors of social development to achieve quick and positive results. The task of ensuring effective implementation of the NPE rests on the education management system. Flexible and relevant management structures and organisations, processes and procedures are needed all along the line to secure the detailed planning and implementation of the Programme of Action (POA).

Education in India has been largely a budget-based system where efficiency is rated by ability to "consume" budget and to demand more. Performance at delivery point has not been an important criterion. The on-going economic reforms and structural adjustments would, therefore, demand a shift from inputs to performance and outcomes-consideration of cost effectiveness should inform all levels of educational administration and planning. Absence of effective decentralisation, failure to evolve priorities and pursue objective-oriented programmes, weak personnel management system, and ineffective intra-departmental and inter-departmental coordinating mechanisms have adversely affected the performance of the education system. Even routine tasks like the supply of text-books, conduct of examinations and operation of academic calendar are not being properly attended to. The highest priority in POA should be to ensure that these routine tasks are performed properly and that the delivery of education services improves at all levels.

Soon after adoption of POA 1986, the Central Advisory Board of Education (CABE) had constituted committees to recommend measures for toning up educational management.

These committees prepared draft reports for pursuing action with the states and other authorities concerned. However, due to frequent political changes, action could not be pursued on many of these initiatives. It is now necessary to resume action and pursue these objectives vigorously. This book covers only management issues which cover the entire field of education and those which cover more than one sub-sector of education.

Decentralisation and Involvement of People

The NPE and POA have emphasised the importance of decentralising planning and management of education at all levels and involving people in the process. Decentralization implies democratic participation by elected representatives of people in decision making at the district, sub-district and Panchayat levels. In pursuance of the POA provision the State Governments have been taking steps to set up structures for decentralised planning and management. The future course of decentralisation would be influenced to a great extent by the proposed Constitution Amendment (Seventy-second) Bill, 1991; they would have to be finalised after the Bill is enacted.

(a) The Constitution (Seventy-second) Amendment Bill, 1991

The Constitution (Seventy-second) Amendment Bill of 1991 on Panchayati Raj institutions envisages introduction of democratically elected bodies at the district, sub-district and panchayat levels. These bodies will be responsible for the preparation of plans for the economic development and social justice. The Bill provides for representation of women, scheduled castes and scheduled tribes. The proposed Eleventh Schedule of the Constitution provides, among other things, for entrusting to Panchayati Raj bodies of :

> *"Education including primary and secondary schools, technical training and vocational education, adult and non-formal education, libraries, and cultural activities".*

The subjects closely allied to education, namely, health, welfare, women and child development are also to be entrusted to the Panchayati Raj bodies.

(b) State Legislation

The Panchayati Raj Bill is an enabling legislation. The states are to frame their own legislation in their turn. The states would need to draw up appropriate legislations which, among other things, must provide for Panchayati Raj Committees for Education.

(c) District Level Body

Within this legislation a district-level body may be setup with the responsibility for implementation of all educational programmes including non-formal and adult education, and school education up to the higher secondary level. The district body will provide for representation of educationists, women, youth, representatives of parents, scheduled castes/ scheduled tribes, minorities and appropriate institutions in the district. Representation may also be provided for urban bodies and cantonments which organise educational activities.

The district body will also be vested with the responsibility for planning which would include, inter alia, area development, spatial planning, institutional planning, administrative and financial control and personnel management with respect to primary, middle, secondary and higher secondary schools and other educational programmes. Implementation of different educational programmes at the district level will be supervised at-id monitored by the body. The district educational plans will also go into the levels of participation and retention of boys and girls under different age-groups by socio-cultural and economic categories, particularly SC & ST, and plan for measures for ensuring physical infrastructure, equitable access as well as qualitative aspects of education.

In order that the district body discharges the functions allotted, it would be necessary to assign state funds for implementation of the various programmes. Provision will also be made to enable the district body to raise its own resources. Funds, which are not earmarked, will also be placed at its disposal so that these resources can be used for any purpose that may be considered essential by raising matching funds of its own.

The relationship of the State Government with the district level body in terms of administrative and financial control and personnel management will be clearly spelt out in appropriate guide lines to be issued by the State Governments. It will also be necessary to clarify the levels of recruitment and structure of cadres of teachers of different categories. There will be a Chief Education Officer for the District to look after all levels of schools, adult and non-formal education. Under him, there will be a District Education Officer looking after establishment, budgeting, planning and the educational data base. In addition, there will be district-level officials of appropriate rank engaged in specific educational programmes. The Chief Education Officer will be the principal education officer of the district body.

The district body will draw upon the expertise of the District Institute of Education and Training (DIET), and other institutions for substantive curricular and pedagogic inputs into all programmes of elementary education, non-formal education and adult education at the district level. It may also seek the support of institutions of higher education in the district. In states and areas where the Constitution (Seventy-second) Amendment Bill, 1991 will not apply, such bodies on similar lines may be set up at district level.

(d) Village Education Committee

Under the Constitution Amendment Bill, Panchayats will be formed for a village or a group of villages. The Panchayat will have elected representatives. Besides, each Panchayat may constitute a Village Education Committee (VEC) which would be responsible for ad-ministration of the delegated programmes in the field of education at the village level. The major responsibility of the VECs should be operationalisation of micro-lovel planning and school mapping in the village through systematic house to house survey and periodic dis-cussion with the parents. It should be the endeavour of the committee that every child in every family participates in the primary education. In these activities they will be provided expert guidance and support by DIET. The State Governments may consider entrusting the following functions to the VEC: Generation and sustenance of awareness among the village community ensuring participation of all segments of population; and Developing teacher/instructor and community partnership to oversee and manage the effective and regular functioning of the schools and centres.

In view of the critical role and function of VEC, it should be vested with appropriate statutory and necessary financial and administrative authority.

(e) Model Legislation

It would be necessary for the Ministry of Human Resource Development (MHRD) to prepare, model statutory provisions for the guidance of states when they formulate their legislation under the Panchayati Raj Act. As other sectors such as health, women and child development, social welfare are also involved, MHRD may also consider preparing comprehensive model legislation covering all these areas for achieving coordination. This may be done in collaboration with the concerned Central Ministries/Departments and Planning Commission. The preparation of this model Bill may commence immediately as it will be required by the States when the Constitution Amendment Bill is brought into effect.

(f) Urban Local Bodies

The Constitution Amendment Bill on Urban Local Bodies provides for constitution of Municipal Corporations, Municipal Councils and Nagar Panchayats. The proposed Twelfth Schedule to the Constitution provides for entrusting these bodies with "promotion of cultural, educational and aesthetic aspects". These bodies would be entrusted with appropriate statutory responsibilities with regard to the education sector by an appropriate state legislation.The MHRD may prepare model legislation in this area also for the consideration of the states.

Involvement of Voluntary and Non-governmental Agencies

The successful implementation of programmes like elementary education including non-formal education, early child-hood care and education, adult education, education of the disabled, etc. will require people's involvement at the grass-root level and participation of voluntary agencies and social activist groups on a much larger scale. Considering the need for ensuring relationship of genuine partnership between the government and voluntary agencies, the government will take positive steps to promote their wider involvement. Consultations will be held with them from time to time about programmes and procedures for selection of voluntary and nongovernmental agencies. The procedures for financial assistance will be streamlined to enable them to play optimal role.

It would be desirable for the state governments to develop specific action plan for entrusting selected programmes of educational development to voluntary agencies and nongovernmental organisations. They could be used to supplement effectively the on-going programmes to enhance their quality and impact. They should be allowed to function in a congenial and supportive atmosphere. It is expected that appropriate indices of accountability in terms of performance would be evolved in consultation with the voluntary organisations and NGOs.

Accountability and Efficiency

Norms of performance by the different categories of educational personnel and institutions must be prepared by the states. The MHRD may assist them in the preparation of such norms. These should be finalised after due consultation and discussions with the representative groups. Norms which are finalised must be given publicity and the performance should be duly notified. Non-observance of norms must result in disincentives while good performance must receive recognition, incentives and due publicity. Monitoring of all educational programmes for implementation at the district will take place at the state level and relevant indicators for inter-district comparison will need to be worked out. Suitable incentives may be provided to the districts linked to their achievements. Similar arrangements may be developed for the Block and Panchayat level institutions. In view of the constraint of resources, cost effectiveness has to be promoted in educational planning and administration at all levels. Financial and administrative norms relating to the educational programmes will need to be evolved and enforced with greater diligence.

Mere budgetary concern must be replaced by assessment of efficiency on the basis of carefully developed indices of educational and institutional achievements. Location and establishment of institutions should be planned rationally with due regard to the catchment areas of existing institutions, identification of unserved and underserved areas, and the possibility of expanding facilities in existing institutions. As far as possible facilities should be shared among institutions and extrashifts resorted to in urban areas to provide better utilisation of resources.

The chapters on higher Education and Technical Education (chapters 11 and 15) have spelt out some measures in this regard. All procedures and processes which hamper the functioning of institutions and hold up programme implementation must be reviewed and simplified. For example, migration, conduct and identification certificates and similar other plethora of outmoded practices only hinder programmes of education. Simplified manual of instructions and codes must be evolved to facilitate the proposed reforms in education. Modernization of educational offices will enhance their efficiency.

Strengthening of Educational Planning and Administration

(a) School and Educational Complexes

School complexes will be promoted as a network of institutions on a flexible pattern to provide synergic alliances to encourage professionalism among teachers, to ensure observance of norms and conduct and to enable the sharing of experiences and facilities. The school complex will serve as the lowest viable unit of area planning and will form a cluster of 8-10 institutions in which different institutions can reinforce each other by exchanging resources, personnel, materials, teaching aids, etc. and using them on a sharing basis.

It is expected that in course of time, school complexes when fully developed, will take over much of the inspection functions including educational mapping, grading of institutions and identifying strength and weakness of individual schools.

Inspection to be con-ducted will invoke a culture of participation and providing correctives rather than the existing practice of finding faults. These inspections will be in addition to the normal routine inspection functions of district/block level inspecting authorities. Guidelines for functioning of school complexes have been prepared and communicated to the State governments.

Although a number of states have experimented with the scheme of school complexes, the programme is yet to emerge as a comprehensive and systematically administered one. As the institutional resource endowment varies from place to place, there can be no single model for creation of school complexes. Every state has to evolve its own operational model based on its experiences or by drawing upon experiences of other states. The states may prescribe necessary guidelines for creation and functioning of school complexes and define the nature, mode, type of planning and inspection work to be performed by them. Considering that some of the schools forming part of the complex will be non-government institutions, the State governments may give them necessary assistance to facilitate their participation. It would be desirable that the recommendations regarding the school complex programme are implemented on a state-wise basis during the Eighth Plan period.

At the same time it is desirable to attempt larger networking of institutions in a district in the shape of educational complexes on an experimental basis during the Eighth Plan period. In the educational complex, the networking could be done from the primary to college and university level. The Central Government may develop in the next two years guidelines for organising this on an experimental basis in situations where the atmosphere is congenial for launching such complexes. While developing the educational complexs, support from institutions like DIET, Teacher Education Colleges, ITIs, Polytechnics, particularly Community Polytechnics may also be sought.

(b) Block Level Administration

It is observed that the block-level setup of educational administration is very weak almost all over the country. The supervisors often have little contact with the schools. The routine administrative duties such as collecting statistics, disbursement of salaries, posting and transfers of the staff take up most of their time. The following steps may be taken to improve the functioning of block-level education set up:

(i) Norms, not only on the basis of number of schools but also number of teachers should be evolved through systematic studies so that the block-level education officer may effectively cope with his administrative responsibilities and supervisory functions.

(ii) Most of the time of block-level education officers is spent on routine administrative work. Their duties may be laid down in detail so that their support for the academic programmes gets due importance.

(c) District Educational Administration

The jurisdiction of a district for the educational purpose may be co-terminus with its revenue jurisdiction. The big districts could be divided into sub-educational districts but these will be coordinated and controlled by a Chief Education Officer (CEO) for the whole district. He will look after all levels of education — primary, middle secondary and higher secondary, non-formal and adult education. The planning and statistics branch of CEO will be provided with computer facilities for Educational Management Information System (EMIS).

Government Schemes and Provisions—Employment Agencies and Service

Government of India has taken number of steps to strengthen the educational base of Scheduled Castes and Scheduled Tribes. The following special provisions have been incorporated for SCs and STs in the existing schemes of Department of Higher Education:-

Central Institute of Indian Languages (CIIL): The Central Institute of Indian Languages, Mysore has a scheme of development of Indian Languages through research, developing manpower and production of materials in modern Indian Languages including tribal languages. The Institute has worked in more than 90 tribal and border languages.

National Merit Scholarship Scheme (NMSS): The National Scholarship Scheme and Scheme of Scholarship at the Secondary Stage for Talented Children from Rural Areas are in existence since 1961-62 and 1971-72 respectively. These have been merged and a new scheme entitled 'National Merit Scholarship Scheme' has been framed for implementation with revised provisions from 2005-06.

The objective of the National Merit Scholarship Scheme is to support talented students and encourage them to excel academically in studies by giving recognition and financial assistance at post-metric level on state wise merit basis and also separately to talented and meritorious students in rural areas for Classes IX to X for all categories.

The revised rate of scholarship varies from Rs. 250/-to Rs. 750/-p.m. depending on the level of education and course of study. The Scheme has been discontinued with effect from April, 2007. However, a New Central Scheme of Scholarship for College and University Students is proposed to be implemented.

National University of Educational Planning & Administration (NUEPA): Educational development of Scheduled Castes and Scheduled Tribes is an area of major concern of NUEPA. It carries out studies, seminars, symposiums, etc. and evaluates ongoing programmees/existing educational programmes. It covers programmes and schemes for scheduled castes and scheduled Tribes. It also generates material for educational institutions.

University Grants Commission: University Grants Commission runs the Remedial Coaching Scheme with a view to improve the academic skills and linguistic proficiency of the Scheduled Caste and Scheduled Tribe students to prepare them for the National Eligibility Test (NET) conducted by UGC/ CSIR.

— UGC has earmarked 15% and 7.50% reservation for SCs and STs respectively in appointments, both in teaching and non-teaching posts, admissions, hostel accommodation, etc. in universities/colleges. State universities follow reservation policy of the respective state governments. The Commission issues guidelines/ directives/instructions from time to time for implementation of reservation policy of the Government of India.

— There is relaxation in the minimum qualifying marks for admission for SC/ST candidates.

— UGC implements the Career Orientation programme for the graduates for gainful employment in the wage sector in general, and self-employment in particular for all including SCs/STs.

— Commission provides financial assistance for extension activities to SCs/STs.

— Commission has created a Central Pool Database of eligible SC/ST candidates and recommends their candidature for teaching positions in universities and colleges.

SC/ST Cells: University Grants Commission provides assistance to universities/deemed universities for establishment of Special SC/ST Cells, to ensure effective implementation of reservation policy for SCs/STs in admissions, recruitment both in teaching and non-teaching posts, staff quarters/hostels, fellowships etc. Till now, 123 SC/ST Cells have been established in universities including deemed Universities.

— In order to oversee the implementation of the reservation policy in Central/Deemed Universities, the Commission has constituted Monitoring Committee under the chairmanship of Secretary, UGC.

— There is a Standing Committee on SCs and STs to review the performance of the implementations of reservation policy and advise the Commission on the matters.

Engineering Colleges: The higher educational institutions administered by the Central Government including IITs, IIMs, Regional Engineering Colleges, etc. provide reservation to the extent of 15% and 7.5% for SCs and STs students respectively in admissions.

Apart from reservation, there is relaxation in minimum qualifying marks for admission and seats are reserved in hostels for SC/ST students. Reservation percentages vary in institutions run by the State Governments as per State Government's policy.

Following facilities are provided to SCs and STs in Joint Entrance Examination conducted by IITs:

— 15% and 7.5% reservation for SCs and STs respectively. 50 seats for SCs and 22 seats for STs are available at IIT, Delhi.

— Relaxation in qualifying norms.

— Reduced cost of application form.

— SC/ST candidates called for Counseling are paid single second class rail fare.

— All SC/ST candidates admitted to IIT-BHU and IT-BHU are exempted from payment of tuition fees. In addition, all SC/ST students are granted free mess and a pocket allowance of Rs. 70/-per month subject to the fulfilment of norms of parental income.

— Special facilities of Book Banks are provided. Some IITs have special Book Banks for exclusive use of SC/ST students.

Community Polytechnics: The scheme of Community Polytechnics has been in operation in selected diploma level institutions since 1978-79. It provides platforms for transfer of appropriate technologies to rural masses/local communities. Preference is given in training to rural youths, SCs, STs, women, school dropouts and other disadvantaged groups and helps them to obtain need based gainful employment. It applies Science and technology through skill oriented non-formal training, technology transfer and technical support services.

Bibliography

Alexander P.K. : *The Effects of Brain Damage on the Visual Functioning of Children,* Journal of Visual Impairment and Blindness, 1990.

Allen, K. E. and Marotz, L. : *Developmental Profiles: Pre-birth through Eight Second Edition.* New York, USA, Delmar, 1994.

Batshaw, M. and Perret, Y. : *Children with Disabilities : A Medical Primer Third Edition,* Baltimore, Paul H. Brookes, 1992.

Batshaw, Mark L. : *Children with Disabilities,* Baltimore, Brookes, 1997.

Buultjens, M., Mason, H., & Odor, P. : *Video for Visually Impaired Learners,* Edinburgh, Scottish sensory Centre, 1997.

Dykens, Elisabeth M. : *Genetics and Mental Retardation Syndromes,* Baltimore, Brookes, 2000.

Fraiberg, S. : *Insights from the Blind,* Londres, Souvenir Pres, Madrid, INSERSO, 1990.

Ingsholt, A. : *How Does a Blind Child Develop an Identity?* Proceeding of the International Symposium of Visually Handicapped Infants and Young Children. Edinburgh, 1988.

Jervis, F.M. : *A Comparison of Self-concepts of Blind and Sighted Children, Guidance Programs for Blind Children,* Watertown, MA, Perkins, 1959.

Lord, Catherine, and Risi, Susan : *"Diagnosis of Autism Spectrum Disorders in Young Children,"* Prizant, Baltimore, Brookes, 2000.

Moore, J.C. : *The Visual System,* Paper Presented at the Conference of the Australian and New Zealand Association of the Visually Handicapped, Perth, 1995.

Morse, M.T. (1999). Cortical vision impairment: Some words of caution. *Review*, 31 (1):21-26.

Orelove, Fred P., and Sobsey, Dick. : *Educating Children with Multiple Disabilities: A Trans-disciplinary Approach,* Baltimore, Brookes, 1996.

Perinat, A. : *Psicologia del Desarrollo, Un Enfoque Sistemico,* Barcelona, EUOC, 1998.

Peterson, Candida : *Looking Forward Through the Life Span,* Sydney, Prentice Hall, 1989.

Puig Rovira, J.M. : *Educacion en Valores y Fracaso Escolar, Comunicacion Presentada en la Conferencia* "Valores sociales y fracaso escolar, Madrid, 2001.

Smith, Romayne : *Children with Mental Retardation: A Parents' Guide Edited by Romayne Smith,* Bethesda, USA, Woodbine House, 1993.

Steendam, M. : *Cortical Visual Impairment in Children,* Sydney, Royal Blind Society of New South Wales, 1995.

Tort Bardolet, A. : *Identitat Afectivitat en l'aprenentatge dels Sabers Escolars,* Escola Catalana, 2000.

Trent, James W., Jr. : *Inventing the Feeble Mind: A History of Mental Retardation in the United States,* Berkeley, University of California Press, 1994.

Umansky, W. and Hooper, S. : *Young Children with Special Needs Third Edition,* New Jersey, USA, Prentice-Hall, 1998.

Warren, D.H. : *Blindness and Children, an Individual Differences Approach*, Cambridge, Cambridge University Press, 1994.

Zeki, S. : *The Visual Image in Mind and Brain,* Scientific American, 1992.

Index

A

C

D

E

F

G

H

I

L

□□□